DOCTRINE FOR DIFFICULT DAYS

DOCTRINE FOR DIFFICULT DAYS

J. VERNON McGEE
FOREWORD BY JOHN WALVOORD

THOMAS NELSON PUBLISHERS
Nashville • Atlanta • London • Vancouver

Published in Nashville, Tennessee, by Thomas Nelson, Inc., Publishers, and distributed in Canada by Word Communications, Ltd., Richmond, British Columbia, and in the United Kingdom by Word (UK), Ltd., Milton Keynes, England.

Library of Congress Cataloging-in-Publication Data

McGee, J. Vernon (John Vernon), 1904–1988
    Doctrine for difficult days / by J. Vernon McGee.
        p.   cm.
    Includes bibliographical references.
    ISBN 0-7852-7353-0 (hc)
    1. Theology, Doctrinal—Popular works. I. Title.
BT77. M367 1996
230′.044—dc20

96–34621
CIP

Printed in the United States of America

1 2 3 4 5 6 7 8 - 01 00 99 98 97 96

CONTENTS

FOREWORD

Dr. J. Vernon McGee's extraordinary spiritual gifts have manifested themselves in a worldwide ministry of exposition of Scripture probably equaled by no one else in our generation. As far as I know, no one else has ever reached as many languages and as many millions of people with an exposition of the Bible extending over a five-year program as Dr. McGee does in Thru the Bible Radio.

My first acquaintance with Dr. McGee was as a graduate student in Dallas Theological Seminary, where he earned his doctoral degree. Subsequently I enjoyed fellowship with him in each of his churches and especially in the Church of the Open Door, where I spoke many times. In addition, Dr. McGee was often scheduled in Bible and Prophecy Conferences in which I also was included, and we had wonderful fellowship over a long period of time.

Anyone who knew Dr. McGee knows that he was a rare individual with unusual gifts and a God-given ability to take difficult doctrine and expound it in language that anyone could understand. This volume, containing the transcriptions of some of his public ministries in the Church of the Open Door, will be welcomed by thousands of his faithful listeners who still follow each broadcast with avid attention.

His exposition of the Word of God was, first of all, analytical, in that it expounded what the Bible actually said. It also was very practical. Dr. McGee had an unusual ability to take doctrine and apply it to life. When listening to his broadcast, one had the impression of a man who was sitting in a comfortable chair, talking to someone in his own living room, and discussing the things of God. People from all walks of life were challenged by his ministry and the truth that he presented.

In this volume the major doctrines of Scripture are unfolded, including the doctrine of the Bible, its inspiration and origin; the doctrine of man concerning his origin and history; the doctrine of angels and their relationship to God's program; the doctrine of Satan, tracing his beginning as well as his program of opposition to God; the doctrine of salvation and its wonderful aspects of redemption, propitiation, and reconciliation, including the great doctrines of regeneration, justification, and faith. God's program for sanctification is also faithfully expounded, along with the prophetic prediction of the Bible concerning heaven and hell. No important area of the biblical doctrine is avoided. And as all who follow Dr. McGee know, he never wavered into any of the bypasses of modern liberalism, but remained close to the Bible, accepting its inerrancy and its absolute truth for all to believe.

It would be possible through the study of this book, as well as Dr. McGee's other writings, for a person to be well-taught in biblical doctrine, even to the point where he could transmit it to others as a preacher or teacher. We trust this volume will fulfill its destiny in the hearts and lives of those who read it.

Dr. John F. Walvoord
Dallas Theological Seminary

CHAPTER 1

WHAT IS DOCTRINE?

As we begin this study of doctrine, we want first of all to answer two primary questions: What is doctrine, and does the Bible have much to say about it?

In the Book of Deuteronomy we have the song of Moses that he gave the children of Israel before his death, and he began it like this:

> *Give ear, O heavens, and I will speak;*
> *And hear, O earth, the words of my mouth.*
> *Let my teaching [doctrine] drop as the rain,*
> *My speech distill as the dew,*
> *As raindrops on the tender herb,*
> *And as showers on the grass.*
> (Deuteronomy 32:1-2)

Moses was speaking here about his teaching, his doctrine, which he was going to give to the children of Israel.

In the Book of Proverbs, Solomon wrote:

> *Hear, my children, the instruction of a father,*
> *And give attention to know understanding;*
> *For I give you good doctrine.*
> (Proverbs 4:1-2)

When we turn to the New Testament, we read where Paul wrote to a young preacher named Titus about setting things right in the church, and he mentioned three areas in which the church should function. The first was that it should be an orderly church; second, it should be doctrinally right; and third, it should be a practical church, that is, doing things. Then Paul wrote to Titus:

> *But as for you, speak the things which are proper for sound doctrine.*
> (Titus 2:1)

I think I know what Paul would say to a preacher who does not believe the Bible. He would say to him, as he said to this young preacher Titus, "Speak the things which are proper for sound doctrine." That is, if you're going to be a minister and stand in the pulpit, then your authority ought to be the Word of God, the Bible. That should be the basis of what you have to say.

Now don't misunderstand me. You have a perfect right not to believe the Bible, but you have no right to stand in the pulpit and not believe the Bible. Your liberty is to get out of the pulpit, out of the ministry, and to turn your collar back around the way it should be. When people say, "You are putting a bridle on the preacher," I say, "Oh, no. A preacher has a perfect right to leave the ministry if he doesn't believe the Word of God. But when any man stands in the pulpit, it is assumed he believes the Word of God."

I would hate to go to a doctor who did not believe in the medicines or instruments that he was using. I went to the doctor today about my eyes, regarding a pair of glasses. Boy, is he sold on his glasses and the benefit they give! I liked that. In fact, he sold me so completely that I'll be back in his office in a few days. He convinced me because he believes in his own product. If he had said to me, "Well now, you can't be sure about these glasses. I don't think you can count on them to improve your vision. I have no confidence in them," I'm sure that I would not go back! Oh, my friend, why do we have to have men who are doubting the Word of God and yet are preparing for the ministry? Well, I say they ought to go into another profession. They ought not to be entering God's service. Any man who is in the pulpit should *believe* the Word of God.

The Meaning of Doctrine

Paul said, "Speak the things which are proper for sound doctrine." This word *doctrine*—what does it really mean? The Greek word is *didaskalia,* which simply means "teaching." It is interesting to note that the words *doctrine* and *doctor* come from the same stem, if you please. Actually a doctor, primarily and originally, had nothing to do with healing the human body. He was a teacher. So I think a minister may have a better claim to the title *doctor* than the physician who originally was a teacher and attempted to improve the brain, not the body. And so this word *doctrine* means teaching. That's all in the world it means.

Now there is a great importance attached to doctrine or teaching in the Bible. I turned up an abundance of Scriptures here, but I would like to mention just one, 2 John, verse 9:

> *Whoever transgresses and does not abide in the doctrine of Christ does not have God. He who abides in the doctrine of Christ has both the Father and the Son.*

Doctrine is teaching, you see. Now John wrote his epistles even after he wrote the Book of Revelation. When he wrote this epistle, it was about A.D. 100. John was about a hundred years old at this time, and he was very adamant here, very dogmatic that if you do not have the doctrine of Christ, you are not one of His; and if you have the doctrine of Christ, you have both the Father and the Son.

At the very beginning of the church, on the Day of Pentecost when three thousand were baptized and brought into the church, we are told:

> *And they continued steadfastly in the apostles' doctrine and*
> *fellowship, in the breaking of bread, and in prayers.*
> (Acts 2:42)

Those were the four things that they continued in, so that one mark of the early church was the apostles' doctrine, their teaching. It was something that was very, very important.

————

The Importance of Doctrine

Now doctrine will lead to action, always. You remember the Lord Jesus said this:

> *If anyone wills to do His will, he shall know concerning the*
> *doctrine* [the teaching], *whether it is from God or whether I*
> *speak on My own authority.*
> (John 7:17)

The difficulty today is that it's so easy to deny and to criticize and to find fault with the Bible, saying, "I don't believe that." But God has put down a challenge to you. He says that the only way you can know the Bible is true is by testing it. In other words, God says, "You pour it into the test tube of your life, and you'll know whether this doctrine that I'm giving you is true or not." That, my friend, is the real test of Christianity. It's the real test of anything, for that matter. I'm told that there are patents in Washington for millions of inventions that have not yet appeared on the market. Why? Well, some inventions are marvelous ideas—but they didn't work. And the thing about the Christian faith is that God approaches you from the opposite viewpoint. He says, "If you will make the Word of God the authority of your life, you will find out whether it is true or not."

Now, that is the challenge God gives us. Someone has put it like this:

Doctrine without duty is a tree without fruit.
Duty without doctrine is a tree without root.

You must have right doctrine before you can have right actions. You have to think right before you can act right. This business today of saying, "It doesn't make any difference what you believe, just so you act right" is dead wrong. If you start thinking about turning off the highway to the right and you signal you're going to turn right, and then all of a sudden you turn left, may I say to you, friend, you'll find out that you have to act like you think or you're in for trouble. You can't think one thing and do another. You've got to think right if you're going to act right. Doctrine is very important. The teaching is very important.

Paul gave instructions to Titus for the church in Crete, "that they may adorn the doctrine of God our Savior in all things" (Titus 2:10). The Greek word for *adorn*, *kosmeo*, is the same word from which we get our English word *cosmetics*. In other words, ladies, if you are sound in the faith, you should be wearing the appropriate cosmetics. I would like to see more of the lipstick of a kind tongue. Speaking kindly is a mighty fine lipstick. And then there's the face powder of sincerity and reality. My, there are all kinds of cosmetics that you should use today as a Christian.

The Application of Doctrine

We're ready now for a definition of the word *doctrine*. It is *a systematic and scientific arrangement of biblical truth.* If you look it up in Webster's dictionary, you'll find that *doctrine* means principles in any branch of knowledge. And as far as the Word of God is concerned, it's the systematic and scientific arrangement of biblical truths under their different subjects. Its purpose is to see what the Word of God has to say in a systematic way on any subject.

Now we find Paul writing to the young man Timothy:

> *All Scripture is given by inspiration of God, and is profitable*
> *for doctrine.*
> (2 Timothy 3:16)

That's the first thing he mentions. Because there has been so much said about 2 Timothy 3:16, I'd like to give you the Amplified Bible translation because it is the best I've come across:

> *Every Scripture is God-breathed—given by His inspiration—*
> *and profitable for instruction, for reproof and conviction of sin,*
> *for correction of error and discipline in obedience, and for*
> *training in righteousness* [that is, in holy living, in conformity
> to God's will in thought, purpose and action].

In my opinion this exhausts the meaning of the verse. It tells us that the Word of God is profitable for doctrine, for us to organize these great subjects that we have. Therefore doctrine is the arrangement of biblical truths.

That is where doctrine differs from theology. Theology can deal with philosophy, or deal with many other things, but doctrine must rest upon Bible truths. It must rest upon what the Word of God has to say.

CHAPTER 2

THE
BIBLE

This brings us to our all-important subject. So far we have dealt with merely the preliminaries; we come now to the Bible itself. The first thing I'd like for you to notice is that the Greek words for *The Bible* are *Ho Biblos*, which mean "The Book." *Biblos* means "book," but the early church always put on the scroll *Ho Biblos*, The Book. *The* separated it from all other books. There could be any number of books, but this is *The* Book.

When Sir Walter Scott was dying, he asked Lockhart to read to him from "the book." Puzzled, Lockhart scanned the shelf holding all the writings of Scott, and he asked, "Which one?" Scott shook his head and said, "Why do you ask that question? When a man is dying, there is only one book. Bring the Bible."

The early church separated the Word of God from all other writings. They called it The Book. Actually The Book is a collection of 66 books. There are 39 in the Old Testament and 27 in the New Testament.

I didn't learn the arrangement of the books of the Bible until I was in seminary. I was embarrassed. One night when I was in my first year in seminary, one of the fellows at the table, kidding another one, said, "I bet you've never read the fifteenth chapter of Hezekiah." And everybody laughed—I did too, although I didn't know what they were laughing at. And the fellow being kidded answered, "You can't fool me, the book of Hezekiah doesn't have fifteen chapters." And everybody laughed again—and I laughed again. When I got back to my room, I got out my Bible to find how many chapters the book of Hezekiah had. Well, I never have found how many chapters it has (since it doesn't exist), but I did find that I needed to memorize the books of the Bible. And I worked out a system of doing it.

Now these 66 books of the Bible were written over a period of about 1,500 years by about 45 different authors. We marvel at the unity of their writings. Some of these men never even heard of the others, and there could have been no collusion among 40 of them. Two or three of them could have gotten together, but the others could not have known each other. And yet they have presented a Book that has the most marvelous continuity of any book that has ever been written. Also, it is without error. Each author expressed his own feelings in his own generation. Each had his limitations and made his mistakes— poor old Moses made mistakes, but when he was writing the Penta-teuch no mistakes got in there.

It is a very human Book, written by men from all walks of life, prince and pauper, the highly intellectual and the very simple. For example, Dr. Luke writes almost classical Greek in a period when the Koine Greek was popular. His Greek is marvelous! But Simon Peter, the fisherman, wrote some Greek also. His was not so good, but God the Holy Spirit used both of these men. He let them express exactly their thoughts, their feelings, and yet through that method the Spirit of God was able to overrule in such a way that God said exactly what He wanted to say. That's the wonder of The Book, the Bible.

The Canon of Scripture

How did these 66 books become the Bible? That's always been a big question. The Bible is also called the Canon of Scriptures; *canon* is a Latin word meaning rule or measurement. Therefore, each book was measured by certain standards before being put in the Bible.

The Bible is comprised of those books universally accepted as holy writ according to standards of the church in the apostolic period. The Old Testament is composed of those divine writings compiled by the Israelites during their history before the advent of Christ, and they were authenticated by Jesus Christ Himself. What actually happened is this: Moses wrote the first five books in the Bible. That can be sustained easily today.

Incidentally, I wish that when critics of the Bible come out with things like "the Garden of Eden is a myth" or "the virgin birth of Christ is not true," that they would try to be more original. The arguments they present are the Graf-Wellhausen and Teubingen hypotheses, which are both well over one hundred years old. These hypotheses are referred to as higher criticism. The higher critical movement is a system of criticism whose main object was to impugn the authority of God's Holy Word. These philosophers for the most part were not Christians and had no faith in God's divine revelation but set about to discredit and throw doubt upon its authority. It was all answered long ago. Apparently the current critics have never read but one side of the question, yet they are the ones who talk about being broad-minded! These questions raised by the German high critical scholars a couple of hundred years ago—and added to for a hundred years—caused conservative scholars to do a great deal of research and study, so that now we do have solid answers to all of their suppositions.

Moses wrote the first five books in the Bible. Then Joshua wrote, and these books were added to the scroll. And when you come to the time of Samuel, you find that he did a great deal of writing and collecting. And then Ezra, during the time of the Captivity, gathered together the books of the Bible. By the time of Ezra's death, the Old Testament was complete. As you can see, the church had nothing in the world to do with that.

May I say to you that I have never tried to sustain the thesis that the arrangement of the books of the Bible was inspired. But I do insist that the inclusion of certain books in the Bible, as well as the exclusion of other books, was inspired by the Holy Spirit.

As for the New Testament: By the end of the first century, all the books of the New Testament had been written and were circulating in the church. May I say that the gradual assembling of these books was superintended by the Holy Spirit.

By the fourth century the New Testament was intact, and by that time certain books were already excluded, although they are still found in Roman Catholicism today. For instance, you will never find anything about purgatory in the New Testament. If you ask Roman Catholics where they get their doctrine of purgatory, they will cite one of the books that had been excluded early on—one of the apocryphal books, you see. Purgatory is not mentioned in the 27 books of the New Testament at all.

For several hundred years the church was neither Protestant nor Roman Catholic, nor did it bear resemblance to any church today. It was in that congregation of believers which we call the early church, under the guidance of the Holy Spirit, that the New Testament came together. May I say that when you read the apocryphal books and you read the books of the Word of God, you can see the difference immediately!

Therefore when we come to the fourth century, we find the complete canon of Scripture as we have it today, 66 wonderful books in which we can have absolute confidence.

———

The Character of Scripture

Now I want you to notice the following four words:

Revelation
Inspiration

Illumination

Preservation

We need to understand the meanings of these words. And we need to know the differences between them, because this is where there's so much confusion. The critic today is far too effective because people so often don't know how to make the distinction between revelation, inspiration, illumination, and preservation.

Now let me give a brief word or two concerning the meaning of each of these.

Revelation (don't confuse this with the Book of the Revelation—we're not discussing that here) means "God has spoken," and that's all it means. *Inspiration* guarantees what God has said—that it is reliable, it is accurate, and it is without error. *Illumination* means that if you are to understand God's revelation you must have the Holy Spirit to teach you. He alone can illuminate our minds so that we can understand His Word.

For example, when a prominent churchman says that the Book of Genesis contains myths, he is admitting that he is an unbeliever, and I don't expect him to say anything else. But if he said he believed the creation story but he denied the virgin birth of Christ, I would have been confused because the churchman would first be affirming and then contradicting the Bible. You see, the Word of God says that the unbelieving man will not accept the things of the Spirit of God. They are foolishness to him—he cannot understand the Word of God until the Holy Spirit opens his heart. An unbeliever can learn the history of the Bible, he can learn a great deal about the facts that are in the Bible, and he can appreciate the poetry of the Bible, but he cannot understand its spiritual truths. The only way any of us can comprehend the spiritual truths of the Bible is by illumination of the Holy Spirit.

Preservation refers to God so watching over His Word that He has preserved it, and through the centuries it has come down to us intact.

We today can know that it is the Word of God. That is what preservation means.

Now we will discuss revelation, inspiration, illumination, and preservation in more detail.

REVELATION

Revelation means that God has spoken. It means God has revealed Himself.

First of all, let me call your attention to the fact that intelligent creatures communicate with each other. That has always been true. They have some way of expressing themselves. Even the animal world does that, although it's not an intelligent method of communication. But the human family finds some intelligent way to communicate. Since God has given mankind a certain amount of intelligence (probably very little) it would be strange indeed if the Creator, the God of this universe, had not revealed Himself to man in some way. Turn that over in your mind for a while. You would never, never expect the Creator not to attempt to communicate with His creatures. My friend, this is such an axiom that if today you and I had no revelation from God, I think we could sit right here until God broke through and let us know something. But God will not break through to reveal anything more to us because He has already spoken.

God has spoken in two different ways. He has spoken in a natural way, in the cosmos, His natural creation which is around us. And He has also spoken in a supernatural way, and that is through the Bible. It is well for us to notice these two ways in which God has revealed Himself to us.

He has spoken in a natural way. That is, He has spoken through creation. The psalmist says in Psalm 19:1-3,

> **The heavens declare the glory of God;**
> **And the firmament shows His handiwork.**

Day unto day utters speech,
And night unto night reveals knowledge.
There is no speech nor language
Where their voice is not heard.

Creation doesn't say a word. It doesn't speak Greek or Hebrew or English. It doesn't have an accent. But it is speaking to every creature on topside of God's earth. The heavens declare the glory of God. This is so important that when God, speaking through Paul, begins to show that man is a sinner (Paul never attempted to prove it, he just stated the fact), there will be no excuse for someone to say, "Well, after all, man started out with no knowledge of God. And the story of man is his stumbling around in the dark seeking after God." The Bible says that is not true. From the beginning man had revelation from God so that he is absolutely without an excuse. Really, creation ought to keep man on the track. He ought never to go into idolatry. He ought never to go aside either to worship a creature or become an atheist, as many scientists have become. Why? Well, because of the fact that creation itself is speaking to us.

Now notice this:

Because what may be known of God is manifest in them, for God has shown it to them. For since the creation of the world His invisible attributes are clearly seen.
(Romans 1:19-20)

What is it that is so clear in creation? I think that today this universe is yelling its head off, telling man something. What is it saying? Just two things about God:

For since the creation of the world His invisible attributes are clearly seen, being understood by the things that are made, even His eternal power and Godhead, so that they are without excuse.
(Romans 1:20)

This verse says, first of all, that back of creation there is a Person. Behind the thing is the Thinker. All nature is crying out that back of the creation there is a Creator. The human family is without excuse.

The second thing it says is that the God of this universe is a God of tremendous power. His Godhead (His person) and His power are the only two things you'll find in nature. You don't find the love of God in nature. Say you go to the beautiful Yosemite Valley, walk up from the floor of the valley to the top of El Capitan, admire the view, then step off. Do you think a God of love will stop you? No? Why? Because you won't find the love of God in nature!

Incidentally, I think that this age, which untied the atom and found that in the smallest thing that exists there is tremendous power, will be responsible to God more than any other age. We found out that there is power in creation, a power we had not imagined before. And if you want my opinion, I believe there's power resident in this little atom that they haven't even touched today. God has a whole lot that He hasn't revealed yet, a great deal that He has not permitted into the hands of men.

This tremendous universe—how big is it? And how far does it extend in this direction and that direction? Well, we have been told that radio telescopes reveal no end to it. As far as man is concerned, there is no end. We can't even imagine it. What does this universe tell you? That back of this universe there is a Creator of infinite power.

Because, although they knew God, they did not glorify Him as God, nor were thankful, but became futile in their thoughts, and their foolish hearts were darkened. Professing to be wise, they became fools.
(Romans 1:21-22)

Do you know what God thinks today of the scientist who is an atheist? The atheist makes the statement, "I don't believe there is a God." God says, "You are a fool." I'm not giving you my opinion. God said it. God said that he is a fool. The scientist is handling the things of this vast universe, and yet he says there is no God? God says he's a fool. Our universities don't give degrees like that today, but they ought to, because there are a lot of men who have earned it. God has conferred upon them that degree.

> *Professing to be wise, they became fools, and changed the glory of the incorruptible God into an image made like corruptible man—and birds and four-footed animals and creeping things.*
> (Romans 1:22-23)

They went down and down. That's the picture of the human family. And the average man's view of God today—you don't have to go out to the jungles of Africa, just go out into your own community and ask them—people don't think much of God. Have you ever seen a beautiful image of God that the heathen made? They have never thought of God as being attractive. The average person's view of God today is that He is very unattractive.

Oh, my friend, if you are a child of God, you ought to be very careful to whom you criticize Him and whine and cry and complain and find fault, because the unbeliever is listening. Do you know what the Word of God says?

> *Oh, give thanks to the LORD, for He is good!*
> *For His mercy endures forever.*
> *Let the redeemed of the LORD say so.*
> (Psalm 107:1-2)

And if the redeemed of the Lord don't say so, nobody else is going to say so. The redeemed are the ones who have to say so! God is good.

God has also spoken in the supernatural. What about the Bible? Well, may I say to you that "what saith the Scriptures" is the important thing. The Lord Jesus, praying to His Father, said, "I have given them Your word" (John 17:14).

Notice the testimony of the Word of God to itself, and notice our key verse again, 2 Timothy 3:16, which declares every Scripture is God-breathed—*theopneustos*. *Theos* means "God." *Pneo* means "breathe." All Scripture is God-breathed, given by inspiration, and it is profitable for instruction or doctrine, for reproof, for correction, and conviction of sin, and so forth. But it is *God-breathed*. All Scripture is God-breathed.

Unfortunately, some newer Bible versions give a wrong translation: "Every scripture inspired of God is also profitable." That is not an accurate translation from the original Greek text, nor can you get that from the original at all. Notice another Scripture:

> ***Knowing this first, that no prophecy of Scripture is of any private interpretation*** [that is, no portion of the Scripture is to be interpreted apart from other references to the same subject], *for prophecy never came by the will of man, but holy men of God spoke as they were moved by the Holy Spirit.*
> (2 Peter 1:20-21)

This tells us that the Holy Spirit was the One who moved upon these men, carried them along the way a sailing ship is carried along.

Now the Bible is the Book that claims to be a revelation of God. In the Old Testament 2,500 times you find this or a similar statement, "Thus saith the Lord." It assures us 2,500 times that what we are reading are the words of the Lord!

INSPIRATION

You'll find also that the Bible is very specific. It says, for instance, in Numbers 1:1, "Now the LORD spoke to Moses." And then in Deuteronomy 31:9, "So Moses wrote this law." And I'd like to spend just a moment with Jeremiah. This man was actually unwilling when he was called to the prophetic office. He was called when he was very young, and then when he got a little older he wanted to resign. He even handed in his resignation to the Lord. Finally he had to come back and say, "Your word was a fire within my bones, and when I tried to keep silent I could not keep silent" (see Jeremiah 20:9). But now notice what God had said at Jeremiah's original call:

> **Then the LORD put forth His hand and touched my mouth, and the LORD said to me: "Behold, I have put My words in your mouth."**
> (Jeremiah 1:9)

Did you notice that God said, "I have put My *words* in your mouth"? We believe in what is known as the plenary, verbal inspiration of the Bible. We believe that the *words* are inspired, and *fully* inspired.

That is important, because you and I are living in a day when there are some very tricky interpretations. Neoorthodoxy has a very tricky interpretation of inspiration. Its proponents have said the same thing we say, "We believe that the words are inspired." But the thing they did was to go in and emasculate all of the words. They took the meaning out of the words and made the words mean something else. A retired Methodist preacher told me about speaking to an outstanding Methodist preacher some years ago. He said to this preacher, "I have heard that you have been called a liberal, but when I listened to you, you were using the same language that John Wesley used." And this was the answer of the man: "I'm using the same language that John Wesley used, but I don't mean what John Wesley meant." That's tricky, isn't it? And it's deceptive.

Also, a lady said to me concerning a certain preacher, "Dr. McGee, you said that man was a liberal, and you said he was neoorthodox, and I don't know what that means, but I do know that he preached a marvelous Easter sermon. He talked about the resurrection of Jesus." And this dear lady was very angry with me.

I said, "Did you go to him and ask him what he meant by the resurrection?"

"Well," she said, "what *could* he mean? He just said he believes in the resurrection. He talked about the resurrection of Jesus."

I said, "You should go and ask him."

Well, she didn't, until the next Easter. In fact, in the afternoon of that Easter Sunday, she called me up, weeping. She said, "Today he preached another sermon on the resurrection and I remembered what you had said, so I went to him and asked, 'Do you believe in the *bodily* resurrection of Christ?'"

He laughed and said, "Of course not."

"Then what did you mean by the resurrection of Jesus?"

"Oh, that's a spiritual resurrection."

You see, friend, how today the words are being robbed of their meaning. And that's the reason I always track a fellow down. He doesn't impress me with his words. I want to know what he means by these words. I want him to define them.

Now we believe that the words in this Bible are inspired. And when we say "the words" we mean the original words. Somebody may say, "You're beating around the bush—we don't have the original words." We will see the answer to that when we look into the preservation of this Book. But let me just say now that I hold in my hand a translation, but this translation is a reputable one in which I can have full confidence. I can believe it regarding my salvation, and there is no question about any of the great doctrines of the Scriptures. The Word of God as we have it today is clear.

As I said before, we believe in the plenary, verbal inspiration of the Scriptures. When you come to the New Testament, you find that the Lord Jesus Christ put His seal upon the Old Testament in one of the most remarkable ways. In the last chapter of the Gospel of Luke, the Lord Jesus, after He had been resurrected, walked together with two little-known disciples on the Emmaus Road.

> *And He said to them, "What kind of conversation is this that you have with one another as you walk and are sad?" Then the one whose name was Cleopas answered and said to Him, "Are You the only stranger in Jerusalem, and have You not known the things which happened there in these days?" And He said to*

them, "What things?" So they said to Him, "The things con-
cerning Jesus of Nazareth, who was a Prophet mighty in deed
and word before God and all the people, and how the chief priests
and our rulers delivered Him to be condemned to death, and
crucified Him. . . . Today is the third day since these things
happened. Yes, and certain women of our company, who arrived
at the tomb early, astonished us. When they did not find His
body, they came saying that they had also seen a vision of angels
who said He was alive. And certain of those who were with us
went to the tomb and found it just as the women had said; but
Him they did not see." Then He said to them, "O foolish ones,
and slow of heart to believe in all that the prophets have spoken!
Ought not the Christ to have suffered these things and to enter
into His glory?"
(Luke 24:17-26)

The thing Jesus rebuked His own disciples for was the fact that they
did not believe the Old Testament concerning His resurrection.

And beginning at Moses and all the Prophets, He expounded
to them in all the Scriptures the things concerning Himself.
(Luke 24:27)

ILLUMINATION

Now you will notice, He didn't end with that. There were other
appearances to His disciples after His resurrection. Remember that His
disciples were in an upstairs room, locked in for safety, if you please. And
when He appeared to them, He held out His hands to them, saying,
"Behold My hands," so they could see the nail wounds. He asked them
to feel His side, to make sure it was a real body. And He even ate some
fish with them. And after He did that He said to them:

"These are the words which I spoke to you while I was still
with you, that all things must be fulfilled which were written in

> *the Law of Moses and the Prophets and the Psalms concerning*
> *Me." And He opened their understanding, that they might*
> *comprehend the Scriptures.*
> (Luke 24:44-45)

In these verses you have three of the four things we have been dealing with. You have revelation, you have inspiration, and you have illumination—Jesus opened their eyes that they might understand. He rebuked them because they didn't know the Scriptures, so He went back and began with the first five books of the Bible, called the Pentateuch, and explained to them the things concerning Himself in all the Scriptures.

Wouldn't you have loved to have been there that day and heard Jesus go through the Pentateuch, then come on through the poetical books, the Psalms, and then move on through the historical books, and then the prophets, and to have Him turn to the Scriptures that referred to His resurrection! And I think He included His death, His burial, and His resurrection, and He took them through all the Scriptures that spoke of Him.

Now if you should ask me, "McGee, how do you know for sure this is the Word of God? I need something I can get my teeth in, something that I can stand on as firm ground, and *know* it's God's Word." Well, I can give you several proofs, but the greatest is *fulfilled* prophecy. Hundreds of prophecies were fulfilled concerning Jesus at His first coming, *literally fulfilled!* Twenty-eight of them were fulfilled while He was hanging on the cross. When He was ready to die, as you remember, He said, "I thirst." They gave Him vinegar to drink, which fulfilled the last prophecy, and then He expired.

I challenge you to show me any person who can accurately predict the future every time by reading stars, tea leaves, or anything else. Oh, they can make lucky guesses, but there has never been a person who could predict the future—not even our weatherman!

Years ago I happened to be in the state building where one of our local weathermen had his office, and he came up on top of the building where I was. So I watched him—in fact, I went over and talked with him. He took a balloon and let that balloon go up, and he stood there and watched it. The fellow with him had some instruments and measured something, I don't know what, and they went up to a higher level and looked out over something else, and I asked, "What are you doing?"

He said, "We're gathering information to make a weather prediction."

"Well, you've done quite a few things here. Are you prepared to give us a prediction?"

"Not yet."

"What else do you have to do?"

"We've got twice as many instruments down in the room below, and we have to go down and read all of those."

"Well, when will I find out?"

"You'll see it in the paper this afternoon—the prediction is for tomorrow."

"Can I depend on it?"

He laughed. "How many times do you think I get it right?"

"Well, according to my daily paper you don't hit it very often."

Now that was many years ago, and today with all his sophisticated equipment and even with the help of a satellite, he still misses it.

When we were in Minneapolis, I read the weather report and it predicted clear weather. Clear! I have never been through such a rainstorm as that which came in Minneapolis. I couldn't even see the highway. The whole area was like a lake. They said that about three inches came down within an hour. May I say to you, even the weatherman can't predict the future.

However, here is a Book filled with *fulfilled* prophecy. You can't match that, brother. Men are not in any way able to predict the future. There are other solid bases for having confidence in the Bible, but to me, fulfilled prophecy is final. And it's unanswerable. Nobody can disprove that. I believe the Bible is the Word of God. I believe it because of fulfilled prophecy, if for no other reason. But there are other reasons as well, as we shall see.

PRESERVATION

One of the objective proofs, one of the external proofs, has been the marvelous preservation of the Bible. The prophet Jeremiah tells about a king of old who, when the Word was sent to him, took a penknife and cut it to pieces (see Jeremiah 36:20-26). But it was rewritten, and we have that Word today.

Down through the centuries there have been a great many Bible burnings. Even now there's a great deal of antagonism toward the Bible. In our country today it is not being burned because we think that we are too civilized for such behavior. The way enemies of God's Word try to get rid of it now is just to outlaw it in our schools and in many other places. (Yet we talk about our freedom of religion and freedom of speech.)

In spite of all the attacks that have been made upon the Bible, it still today exists—and, of course, it's one of the best-sellers. For many years it was *the* best-seller, but it's not today. I regret to have to say that, but it is true. And that is certainly a commentary on our contemporary society. It reveals that the Bible is not really occupying the place that it once did in the history and in the life of this nation. Yet I think the amazing preservation of the Word of God is worthy of consideration.

CHAPTER 3

INSPIRATION

All Scripture is given by inspiration of God, and is profitable for doctrine, for reproof, for correction, for instruction in right-eousness.
(2 Timothy 3:16)

There are four words that we have emphasized in the chapter on Bible Doctrine that require more explanation to understand their meanings. We need to distinguish among them and not be confused by them. They are: revelation, inspiration, illumination, and preservation. These four words are all-important. We will focus on *inspiration* in this chapter, but first we'll review all four.

Revelation means that God has spoken. We've already talked about that. And we have actually two sources of revelation, the natural and supernatural. The supernatural is sometimes called *natural* and *special* revelation.

In *natural* revelation, God has spoken in the heavens and on the earth:

> **The heavens declare the glory of God;**
> **And the firmament shows His handiwork.**
> (Psalm 19:1)

23

It is a limited knowledge of God that is given in creation, of course. God has revealed His person and He has revealed His power in creation, but nothing else. You will never find the love of God revealed in creation.

Then you have the supernatural or special revelation, which is the Bible. The Bible is God's Word to man. Over 2,500 times the Old Testament says, "Thus saith the LORD," or a cognate expression such as "God says" or "God has spoken." And the New Testament confirms this. The New Testament speaks of the Old Testament as being God's Word.

The second word, *inspiration*, guarantees the revelation of God, guarantees that we do have the Word of God. *Illumination* means that the Holy Spirit takes the Word of God and makes it real to the believer, and only to the believer. Then the fourth is *preservation*. That is actually the history of the Bible from the very beginning down to the present hour.

What Inspiration Means

The Bible claims to be the Word of God, and we want to look at the validity of that claim. First of all, let's look at our key verse, 2 Timothy 3:16, in the Amplified New Testament.

> *Every Scripture is God-breathed—given by His inspiration— and profitable for instruction, for reproof and conviction of sin, for correction of error and discipline in obedience, and for training in righteousness [that is, in holy living in conformity to God's will in thought, purpose and action].*

"Every Scripture is God-breathed." The word there is *theopneustos*. *Theos* means "God." *Pneuo* means "breathe" (we get our word "pneumonia" from that word). Every Scripture is God-breathed. The New King James translation reads, "All Scripture is given by inspiration of

God." This means that God breathed in the sense that these men, as Peter says, "were carried along by the Holy Spirit" (2 Peter 1:21 NIV). He pictures it as a sailing vessel that is carried out to sea by the wind blowing into the sails, pushing it along. And these men who were chosen to write the Scriptures were carried along by the Holy Spirit.

That does not mean that these men were perfect in everything they said. Actually, they were very imperfect men. The five books of the Bible written by Moses we believe to be inspired, and we have them today as the Word of God. Doesn't this mean that Moses was holy in the sense that he never made a mistake? Oh, no, for this very record tells us of several mistakes that he himself made. But when it came to writing the Word that God had given him, he made no error there because the Holy Spirit was the One who was using him, moving him along as he wrote. That is the claim of the Word of God.

Theories of Inspiration

First of all, we'll look at some of the theories of inspiration, and there are all sorts. We're living in a day which is so complicated that when someone says that he believes the Bible is inspired, you cannot let it rest there. You have to find out what he means, because there are so many theories abroad.

The first theory that we will look at is, in my opinion, the weakest. It is the one that has no life in it whatsoever. It is called the *natural theory of inspiration*. That simply means that the Bible is inspired like Shakespeare was inspired to write *Romeo and Juliet* and that there's no more inspiration in the Bible than there is in *Romeo and Juliet*. As they see it, Shakespeare was sort of a genius in what he wrote, and these men who wrote the Bible were religious geniuses. Or they may say that Karl Marx was inspired to write *Das Kapital*, the bible of Communism today. That theory is called natural inspiration, and that is what some people understand inspiration to be—yet it is the weakest argument of all.

The second theory is *universal inspiration*, which means that anyone who professes to be a Christian is inspired. In other words, you could write something that would be just as worthy and worthwhile and be of as great a value as anything Paul wrote or David wrote. In fact, some proponents of this theory think you can do better than they did! A professor at Columbia University said some years ago that he thought he could. One of his students, apparently a pretty smart egghead in the class, suggested to the professor that if he would turn out something that would survive like Psalm 23, he would accept that theory. But so far neither that professor nor anyone else has written anything that's been the blessing that the Twenty-third Psalm has been.

Among these folks who believe in the natural theory of inspiration or that of universal inspiration, of course, are the ones who believe that Mary Baker Eddy's book, *Science and Health*, was inspired. Her book has been corrected a great deal, by the way. In the original copy, she said that when a lobster lost its claw it would grow another. Well, since it doesn't, they've deleted that from her book. And they have relieved it of several other embarrassing statements that were made in the original copies. Nevertheless, they believe that *Science and Health* is inspired.

The Mormons believe in what Joseph Smith supposedly wrote, which he didn't write, by the way. Joseph Smith was an ignorant man, totally incapable of writing anything that would compare with *The Book of Mormon*. It is well authenticated today that *The Book of Mormon* was written by a Presbyterian preacher, a fellow who did a great deal of traveling on horseback through Ohio, and he compared the hills of Ohio to the hills of Judah. If you read *The Book of Mormon*, bear that in mind, and the comparison is beautiful from that viewpoint. But Joe Smith happened to go into a print shop where this manuscript was, and after he was gone, the manuscript was missing. The strange thing is that, when Joseph Smith published the manuscript, he claimed to have gotten it from the angel Maroni on top of a mountain. He had quite a story about how the devil tried to take the golden plates away from him.[1] It is interesting that many intelligent people accept that as truth today, because they believe in universal inspiration. They think anyone could write something that would compare to the Bible.

Now there's another theory of inspiration which holds that *the thoughts and the concepts of the Bible are inspired.* For instance, these people accept the Sermon on the Mount as being inspired, but they don't like to say that all of it is inspired. They do not believe the *words* are inspired. They don't mind a new translation that uses the idiom of the day. Well, when you take the Word of God and rewrite it like that, it simply means that you believe its concepts are inspired, but you do not attach too much value to the actual words that are in the Bible.

Oh, my friend, the words are all-important. You cannot have thoughts and concepts without words. You cannot have confidence in a thought-and-concept version of Scripture, because there are shades of meaning that can be distorted. Let me illustrate with a story about a young lady who had taken singing lessons. Because her father had plenty of money, she had taken voice lessons from the best teacher. And the best teacher had taught her because the father paid well. The time came for her to give a concert. After the concert she was all excited, and when her friend came in she said, "You sat next to my teacher, what did he say?"

"Well. . . ." The friend hesitated a moment, then said, "He said that you sang in a heavenly manner."

"He did? That is wonderful!" Then she got to thinking about it—the teacher had never said anything like that before. So she insisted, "Now is that *exactly* what he said?"

"Well," this friend said, "that's what he meant."

"But I want to know the exact words he used. What did he say?"

"Well if you must know, he said, 'That was an unearthly noise.'"

May I say, thoughts and concepts are not what we base inspiration on. That's as farfetched as anything can possibly be.

Another theory of inspiration is known as *the theory of partial inspiration*. That means that the Bible *contains* the Word of God. You have to watch some of these fellows today, especially some of these preachers. They'll say, "I believe the Bible contains the Word of God." When you pin them down, this is what they'll say: "I believe that the Golden Rule is inspired. It just thrills me when I read it. But I want you to know, where it says God told the people of Israel to destroy all the Amalekites, I don't like it. That's not inspired." They say the Bible *contains* the Word of God and then pick out what they consider to be the Word of God. Well, that's putting yourself in the position of God the Holy Spirit, as if you were able to tell what is the Word of God and what is not the Word of God.

I used to sit in a ministerial meeting with a preacher like that. I had my New Testament with me one day, and I asked him if he would mind underlining what he thought was the Word of God in the Epistle to the Romans, but he wouldn't do it. I said, "Go ahead. You keep saying that the Bible contains the Word of God, and I'm in doubt about that because it's hard for me to tell which is and which is not. If I could have the benefit of knowing what is the Word of God, you could help me a great deal." It's mighty hard to pin them down, but they will always say that Psalm 23 is inspired, and then go on from there.

The theory that passes as "Bartonism" in this country holds that the Bible is the Word of God—if it is the Word of God to you. Now if you read Psalm 23 and it's the Word of God to you, then it's the inspired Word of God. But if you read another psalm that you don't like, then it is not the Word of God to you, you see. There are many Americans and especially many American preachers (quite a few of them are young preachers) who take that viewpoint. It all comes back to this theory of partial inspiration. The partial inspiration theory means that not all of the Bible is the Word of God.

Now may I take up another theory that, instead of being liberal, is based on extreme fundamentalism. It is known as *the mechanical* or *dictation theory of inspiration*. These men hold that the Holy

Spirit took up the penmen of the Scriptures, like you would pick up your pen, and He wrote with them. The Holy Spirit wrote with Moses at first, then He wrote with Joshua. And so on down through David and all the way to Paul and John. They believe that these men were nothing in the world but pens in the hand of the Holy Spirit.

May I say, that theory is wrong, and it can be proven so from this viewpoint: If it had been true, we would have the same style of writing all the way through the Bible. But we do not have the same style. Actually, Dr. Luke writes classical Greek. He is the only one who uses what is known as a periodic sentence, which is the hardest sentence in the Greek to translate. Paul does come through with a periodic sentence every now and then, but it's Dr. Luke who uses it consistently. In contrast, Simon Peter butchered the Greek language in his two epistles. But don't call him ignorant! I heard a Greek professor do that once. It was during a meeting of teachers who taught Greek. I went to him afterward and said, "Doctor, let's be very frank one with another. I'm teaching first-year Greek, but the Greek that I write is atrocious. How is yours?" He had a Ph.D. in Greek, but he was very honest about it. He said, "If you really want to know the truth, I wouldn't do any better than Simon Peter did." I said, "Then do you want somebody to call you ignorant? You ought not to call Simon Peter ignorant. He's not writing in his own language."

Actually, I think Peter did pretty well, considering his native language was Aramaic. But, you see, the differences in writing style prove that God did not use the dictation method. God is no dictator. He did not destroy the personality of these men whom He chose to write Scripture! When Paul wrote, he expressed his heart. When Peter wrote, he expressed his heart and wrote in his natural style. The thing that makes it God's Book is that through these various writers God communicated to mankind exactly what He wanted to say, and He wouldn't change a sentence of it today! Neither has He anything to add to it. He hasn't come out with a new volume of things He didn't know two thousand years ago. He gave it all at that particular time.

Now this leads me to the viewpoint which we who are Bible teachers hold today: *plenary, verbal inspiration. Verbal* means "the words." *Plenary* means "full." When you eat too much, you are plenary, meaning full. Plenary, verbal inspiration means that the words are inspired and that God spoke all these words. Some folks speak about our verse-by-verse study of the Scriptures. And I tell them, "I'm not conducting a verse-by-verse study of the New Testament. The verses are manmade. They were added years later by men. I'm conducting a word-by-word study of the Word of God." Since the *words* are inspired, and God spoke all these words, I think every word should be examined, every word should be considered.

Let me clarify an important point: I am talking about the autographs, the original manuscripts of the Greek text. Those are what the Bible claims to be the inspired Word of God. I want you to notice several passages, because it is important to see that the Bible makes this claim. We'll start near the beginning of the Old Testament:

> *Then Moses said to the LORD, "O my Lord, I am not eloquent, neither before nor since You have spoken to Your servant; but I am slow of speech and slow of tongue."*
> (Exodus 4:10)

It may be that Moses had some sort of impediment of speech. But when you hear him talking to the nation Israel, you don't get that impression, do you? He was able to talk to them. Now will you notice this:

> *So the LORD said to him, "Who has made man's mouth? Or who makes the mute, the deaf, the seeing, or the blind? Have not I, the LORD? Now therefore, go, and I will be with your mouth and teach you what you shall say." But he said, "O my Lord, please send by the hand of whomever else You may send." So the anger*

of the LORD was kindled against Moses, and He said: "Is not Aaron the Levite your brother? I know that he can speak well. And look, he is also coming out to meet you. When he sees you, he will be glad in his heart. Now you shall speak to him and put the words in his mouth. And I will be with your mouth and with his mouth, and I will teach you what you shall do."
(Exodus 4:11-15)

Notice that He said "words" and "your mouth"—not concepts. God did not leave it to these men. He didn't give them a thought and then let them put it into words. God gave them the words. That's all-important. This business today of saying, "Well, I believe the Bible contains the Word of God," or, "I believe that the concepts and the thoughts are inspired," is nonsense, my friend. Let's boil this down. How are you going to communicate a thought or a concept? You have to use words to do it. And if you don't use the right words, you'll be misunderstood.

The words are inspired. That's the reason I keep saying, "Let's get back to the actual words of Scripture and find out what really was said. What did John really say in the Book of Revelation? What did Paul really say in the Epistle to the Romans? What is the actual word he used?" I attach a great deal of importance to the words.

Let's keep reading God's instructions to Moses:

You shall not add to the word which I command you, nor take from it, that you may keep the commandments of the LORD your God which I command you.
(Deuteronomy 4:2)

Prophets' Dilemma

Now let's go to the New Testament. Oh, my friend, we can multiply these examples by the hundreds! Peter says that the Old Testament prophets wrote of things they did not understand.

> *Of this salvation the prophets have inquired and searched*
> *carefully, who prophesied of the grace that would come to you,*
> *searching what, or what manner of time, the Spirit of Christ*
> *who was in them was indicating when He testified beforehand*
> *the sufferings of Christ and the glories that would follow.*
> (1 Peter 1:10-11)

As we see in this passage, all the prophets prophesied diligently concerning this grace, this salvation that was coming. They spoke of the sufferings of Christ and the grace of God. We find this in Isaiah 53 and in Psalm 22 as well as in many other Scriptures.

"And the glories that would follow" can be found, for example, in Isaiah 11 and Psalm 45. The prophets all spoke of Christ's suffering and His sovereignty and of the glory that is to come when Christ returns as King to the earth to establish His Kingdom.

"The Spirit of Christ who was in them was indicating" tells us specifically that the prophets of the Old Testament wrote by the Spirit of Christ. This is one of the many statements contained in the Word of God declaring that the Old Testament was inspired of God. These men wrote by the "Spirit of Christ."

The prophets wrote some things which they themselves did not grasp. They searched for the meaning diligently, "searching what, or what manner of time, the Spirit of Christ who was in them was indicating when He testified beforehand the sufferings of Christ and the glories that would follow." There are many places in the Old Testament that speak of the suffering of Christ, and there are many other places that speak of the sovereignty of Christ, of the Kingdom Age. Grace and glory are combined, and it was difficult for them to understand this. For example, Isaiah wrote in the fifty-third chapter of the sufferings of Christ; then in the eleventh chapter he wrote of the Messiah coming in power and glory to the earth to establish His Kingdom. This seeming contradiction was very puzzling to the prophets, and they tried to find out how both could be true.

You and I are in the unique position of living in that interval of time between the suffering of Christ, which is in the past, and the glory of Christ, which is yet in the future.

It will help you to understand the prophecies of the suffering and sovereignty of Christ if you picture the two events as great mountain peaks. Here in Pasadena we have a backdrop of the San Gabriel Mountains. As the crow flies they are about five miles away, but driving the winding road to get there makes them about twenty-five miles away. Mount Wilson is in the foreground and is approximately six thousand feet high. Behind that peak we can see another peak, Mount Waterman, which looks as if it is the same height as Mount Wilson. Actually, Mount Waterman is over eight thousand feet high. However, it looks as if they are the same height and that they are right together. In actual fact, they are not together at all. A tremendous valley between twenty-five and thirty-five miles across separates them. And I estimate that it is probably fifty miles from one mountain peak to the other. Yet, seeing them from a distance, you would think they were right together.

In just such a way, the prophets looking into the future saw the suffering of Christ and the glory of Christ as two mountain peaks which appeared to be right together. I believe that there were skeptics and higher critics in those days who argued, "This is a conflict; the Scriptures are in contradiction. You cannot have it both ways. Either He comes to suffer or He comes to reign." Of course, we know now that both are true. And the valley between them is the church age, which already is around two thousand years in length.

They saw the Cross of Christ; they saw the Crown. They saw them as two mountain peaks, but they did not see the valley between where you and I are. And Peter says that they wanted to look into these things.

Now let's see the accuracy of the Old Testament in Paul's experience when he was in Rome, awaiting trial by Caesar. Though he was in chains, he was permitted to speak to his fellow Jews as they came with questions about Christ. Some believed, though others refused to believe:

> *So when they did not agree among themselves, they departed after Paul had said one word: "The Holy Spirit spoke rightly through Isaiah the prophet to our fathers."*
> (Acts 28:25)

In other words, Paul said to these Jews, "The Holy Spirit was speaking through Isaiah, and here is *exactly* what he said."

> *Go to this people and say:*
> *"Hearing you will hear, and shall not understand;*
> *And seeing you will see, and not perceive;*
> *For the hearts of this people have grown dull.*
> *Their ears are hard of hearing,*
> *And their eyes they have closed,*
> *Lest they should see with their eyes and hear with their ears."*
> (Acts 28:26-27)

That's a tremendous thing!

Notice our Lord's assurance to His apostles when they faced persecution:

> *For it is not you who speak, but the Spirit of your Father who speaks in you.*
> (Matthew 10:20)

Now let's look at God's directions to David in the building of the temple:

> *All this, said David, have I been made to understand in writing from the hand of Jehovah, even all the works of this pattern.*
> (1 Chronicles 28:19 ASV)

And when God was giving a message to the pagan king of Babylon, He wrote it in words: "The fingers of a man's hand appeared and wrote" (Daniel 5:5). All the way through, the Word of God makes it clear that it is the *words* that are inspired. And that, my friend, is one of the most important truths to keep before us.

Testing the Word

Somebody says to me, "How do you know, then, that the Bible is the Word of God? Have you any tests that you can make?" Yes, we can make tests. I have already mentioned *fulfilled prophecy*, which is one of the greatest proofs. Remember the great, fearsome image seen by Nebuchadnezzar in a vision representing three kingdoms which would seize world domination in the future—Babylon, Media-Persia, and Greco-Macedonia. The prophecies of the three kingdoms as seen by this man and interpreted by Daniel the prophet have been literally fulfilled. And God gave to Daniel (as recorded in chapter 8) all the details concerning the transfer of power from the East to the West. So clear is it that the critics launched an onslaught against the sixth century B.C. dating of the Book of Daniel. Porphyry, a heretic in the third century A.D., declared that the Book of Daniel was a forgery, written during the time of Antiochus Epiphanes and the Maccabees (170 B.C.), almost four hundred years after Daniel had lived. However, the Septuagint, the Greek version of the Old Testament, was written prior to that time, and it contains the Book of Daniel. And, of course, the greatest proof that the man Daniel was not a deceiver and his book was not a forgery is the endorsement by the Lord Jesus Christ who called Daniel "the prophet" and cited a prophetic truth from his book (Matthew 24:15). And believe me, friend, it's amazing. If that were the only prophecy, we might seriously question it, but we can't when there are literally hundreds of fulfilled prophecies.

This is another example: Tyre was the capital of the great Phoenician nation which was famous for its seagoing traders. They plied the

Mediterranean and even went beyond that. We know today that they went around the Pillars of Hercules and the Rock of Gibraltar and into Great Britain, where they obtained tin. They established a colony in North Africa. Tarshish in Spain was founded by these people. They were great colonizers and went a lot farther in their explorations than we used to think they did.

Tyre was a great and proud city. Hiram, king of Tyre, had been a good friend of David and supplied him with building materials. Solomon and Hiram did not get along as well as David and Hiram had. Apparently Hiram was a great king, but the center of Baal worship was there in Tyre and Sidon. A few generations later, Jezebel, the daughter of a king and former priest, married Ahab king of Israel and introduced Baal worship into the northern kingdom. Tyre was destroyed by the Babylonians at the same time Jerusalem was destroyed. Nebuchadnezzar took Tyre.

> *Therefore thus says the Lord GOD: "Behold, I am against you, O Tyre, and will cause many nations to come up against you, as the sea causes its waves to come up."*
> (Ezekiel 26:3)

When God says, "Behold, I am against you," you can be sure He is against that place. Just as the waves break on the shore, God said, nations would come against Tyre, that great commercial center that had been invincible. The ruins of Tyre stand today as a witness to the accuracy of the Word of God. And if you want to disprove the Word of God, the thing to do is go over there and build a city on that site. God says you won't.

Also, there is the red-rock city of Petra, a ready-made city. You can get an apartment down there with running water out in front of the apartment. All you have to do is go get it, and you can have that apartment rent-free! Petra is a city which God said would be without inhabitants, and it's been vacant all these years!

Let me give another example of fulfilled Scriptures, a very important one, by the way. One evening one of our friends was showing us pictures of his trip around the world. He showed pictures of Israel, and I was interested in a statement he made. When he showed the country around Jericho and Jerusalem, he said, "They call that the land of milk and honey, but I don't see how they can call it that!" Well, here is something interesting. God said that judgment would come on the land and, friend, that judgment is still on it today. But that wouldn't end it all.

> *So that the coming generation of your children who rise up after you, and the foreigner who comes from a far land, would say, when they see the plagues of that land and the sicknesses which the LORD has laid on it: "The whole land is brimstone, salt, and burning; it is not sown, nor does it bear, nor does any grass grow there, like the overthrow of Sodom and Gomorrah, Admah, and Zeboiim, which the LORD overthrew in His anger and His wrath." All nations would say, "Why has the LORD done so to this land? What does the heat of this great anger mean?"*
> (Deuteronomy 29:22-24)

How did the land flowing with milk and honey get that way? This is amazing to us! It was foretold! That's what the stranger says when he goes to that land.

> *Then people would say [and I'm going to say it too!]: "Because they have forsaken the covenant of the LORD God of their fathers, which He made with them when He brought them out of the land of Egypt; for they went and served other gods."*
> (Deuteronomy 29:25-26)

You probably have seen the pictures of the Isaiah scrolls, and the only value I can see in these Dead Sea scrolls is that they have called attention to the terrain around those caves—oh, it is desolate! If you think Death Valley is bad, you ought to have just a glimpse of the Dead Sea area. My beloved, God says, "Look at it!" And when you see it you will say, "This is not a land of milk and honey!" Of course it's not. God has judged it. And He judged it because of the idolatry of these people. He said you would ask that question. The Bible tells you the reason: It's because they disobeyed God, and it is His judgment upon the land. May I say to you, we observe today many prophecies like that which have been fulfilled. To me that is unanswerable proof.

There is also a *pragmatic test* proving that the Bible is the Word of God, and I think this is a good one. The Scripture itself extends an invitation:

> **Oh, taste and see that the LORD is good.**
> (Psalm 34:8)

God invites you to come, to taste and see. The Lord Jesus Christ said to the critics in His day:

> **If anyone wills to do His will, he shall know concerning the doctrine, whether it is from God or whether I speak on My own authority.**
> (John 7:17)

Now, my friend, you cannot be a theoretician sitting on the sidelines and know this Book is true. You've got to test it. God says so. The proof of the pudding is in the eating. In other words, God says, "I've given you a Book. If you want to know whether it's true or not, then you test it for yourself. It will stand the test."

The trouble with these soapbox artists and these agnostic professors today is that most of them have never even read the Bible, and yet they reject it outright. Oh, my friend, how unfair that is! Why not accept God's invitation?

There have been a number of prominent men who have repudiated the Bible. Do you know why Lew Wallace wrote *Ben Hur*? He was an agnostic riding on a train one day with a friend, and he was spouting off about how he disbelieved the Bible. His friend said to him, "Lew, you're a writer. Why don't you write a book to disprove the Bible since you so sincerely hate it?"

Lew answered, "That's what I'm going to do," and he began to study the Old Testament. He said, "I'll find it full of flaws and contradictions." He tested it. Do you know what happened? Lew Wallace came to faith in Christ—he became a Christian. And he did write a book, not to disprove the Bible, but to try to get other people interested in it. The book he wrote was *Ben Hur*. But, my friend, if you want to test the Bible as he did, you don't need to read *Ben Hur*. Read the Book Lew Wallace read. The Bible is the Book he read. God says, "Taste of the Lord, and see."

Why don't you be honest? Why don't you try Him out? Why don't you see whether this Book will work or not?

Another way in which we can know the Bible is the Word of God is through *archaeology*. At one time I was very much interested in archaeology; however, I've given to my daughter most of my books on it. And although I actually wanted to specialize in that field, I no longer preach apologetic sermons. Many young preachers and theological professors stay in that field, and as long as they are immature they will stay there. But we ought to grow up sometime and get away from apologetic sermons—that is, an argumentative defense, trying to prove the Bible is true.

I hadn't kept up with it too much until I read a certain article, and I'm very much interested in several statements that are here. For instance, it states that back in the Pentateuch, in three different places, it says, "You shall not boil a young goat in its mother's milk" (see Exodus 23:19; 34:26; and Deuteronomy 14:21). Have you ever wondered about that statement? Archaeology has thrown a lot of light on it. The Ras Shamra letters and tablets that were found have shown that it was a pagan practice to offer to a heathen god an animal in the milk of its mother. Now we know why God said to His people, "Don't you do that." It was a pagan practice. And I have heard unbelievers argue about that—"What's wrong with cooking an animal in its mother's milk?" There is nothing wrong in it, unless it's an act of pagan worship, which is the reason it's prohibited in the Word of God.

Now you find many other things in the Bible that the critics questioned but archaeologists have confirmed. For instance, a few years ago Sargon (mentioned in Isaiah 20) was not known in secular history as a king, but archaeologists found that he was a king. Sargon's son Sennacherib made his attack on Jerusalem in 701 B.C., and for years the doubters said, "Look, there's no mention of that in profane history, so it must not be true." Now they have found a well-preserved prism in Assyrian script that confirms the Word of God. Sennacherib, in describing the siege of Jerusalem says, "Hezekiah himself I shut up like a caged bird in Jerusalem." Like most kings, he boasted of every other thing he did, but for some reason he did not boast of the outcome of the siege. He just said, "I shut him up in Jerusalem." But the Bible records the outcome three times. It's recorded in Isaiah 36 and 37, it's recorded in 2 Chronicles 32, and it's recorded in 2 Kings 18 and 19. For years a great many rejected the Bible because they said this event is not in profane history. Well, now it's also in profane history but, my friend, it was accurate before it was found in profane history. What the Word of God says three times just happens to be accurate.

I have come to the place where I no longer require confirmation by archaeology. I'm not depending on a spadeful of dirt being turned up to satisfy my faith. However, I rejoice in the many spadefuls of dirt. I had the privilege of studying under Dr. Melvin Grove Kyle, who was the greatest Egyptologist at the time of his death. I heard him say once in a lecture in class, "There has never been turned up one spadeful of dirt that has disproved one fact in the Bible." That's remarkable, isn't it? You can't say that of any other book. That ought to make some people begin to think.

I have another reason for knowing that the Bible is the Word of God, and for me it is the final authority. That is the *endorsement of the Lord Jesus Christ Himself*. Now the Pharisees believed that the Old Testament was the Word of God. When our Lord was here, He upbraided the Pharisees on everything under the sun except one thing—He never upbraided them for believing the Bible was the Word of God. Isn't that interesting? Don't you know that since He went after the Pharisees regarding so many things that were wrong, if they'd been wrong on the Bible, He would have corrected them? But He didn't. He agreed with them. This is the one place He was in agreement with the Pharisees, and by not correcting them on it He confirmed the Scriptures.

When Jesus came into His temptation from Satan, how did He meet that? By answering him with the Word of God. And when the devil was talking to Him, the devil never raised any question about the validity of the Word of God. That's interesting! Why didn't he say, "You just wait until the great minds of Europe and America come along, and Doctors So and So of Yale. Wait till those fellows come along. They're going to show that the Bible is not true." Well, the devil didn't say that, and the reason he didn't say it is because these fellows could not, and they have not, and no one else has been able to disprove the accuracy of the Word of God.

May I say to you, again and again our Lord Jesus quoted from the Old Testament. For instance, "When you see the 'abomination of desolation,' spoken of by Daniel the prophet . . . ," Christ did not finish the sentence by saying, "Well, you know that Daniel was not really written by Daniel, it was written much later." He didn't say that. He said "Daniel the prophet." May I say to you, the Lord Jesus Christ is my final authority. He put His seal of approval upon it, and that's good enough for me.

My beloved, this which I have presented to you is probably the most controversial subject that there is today: the inspiration of the Scriptures. And may I say that this subject is all-important. Especially would I say this to young preachers. Now I was young once, and I, like you, felt it was important to spend a lot of time proving that the Bible is true. I remember hearing a great preacher a few years ago say that nothing will kill a church like a series of messages proving the Bible is the Word of God. It doesn't need proving, it needs preaching today!

The new book I purchased on archaeology is only a human book. It may or may not be true. It can be questioned. I myself question two or three of the contributing authors. It is a human book, written by fallible humans. But the Bible is a Book that not only *has* the facts but examines them. And not only will it appeal to the intellect, but the Holy Spirit has confirmed these things and given to my heart an assurance that this is the Word of God. I like it that way, my beloved.

A young theology professor whom I bumped into at Winona Lake this summer said to me that he was giving a series of messages on proving the Bible is the Word of God. I said, "Are you still doing that? You know that the professor whom you are studying under has been doing it for fifty years! Aren't you fellows convinced yet?" Then I told him this, "You know, I went through the same machine that you are going through and the same little ordeal. It's nice to go through it, but I do hope that someday you come to the place where the Holy Spirit is going to give your heart an assurance that it is the Word of God."

God's Word will stand all of the acid tests you put to it. Oh, my friend, here is a Book that will still appeal to your intellect. It will appeal to all the mental acumen you've got. But it's also going to appeal to something else. If you examine the facts and examine its truths, then the Holy Spirit is going to make this thing *real* to you. Then, honestly, you will be surprised how unimportant the shovel of the archaeologist really is to your faith.

CHAPTER 4

THE DOCTRINE
OF ORIGINS

In the study of man there are two great themes that we shall consider, both the origin and the nature of man.

Man has been engaged in speculation concerning himself from the very beginning. I'm of the opinion that all of us like to talk about ourselves. Someone has described the boor as a person who talks about himself and won't give you an opportunity to talk about yourself. So since we do like to talk about ourselves, this subject about the origin of the human family, about where we began, and about our nature—how we are made—is a subject that interests us. Certainly it is very close to us, pertaining to our very being.

We are going to see that there are actually two viewpoints. One is a theory of man and it is called philosophy. The other, while considered a theory by the unbeliever, we perceive to be the truth, that which is stated in the Word of God. Philosophy is a theory, and truth is the Word of God.

Philosophy has attempted to find the origin of man in some other area and some other place than in creation by a Creator. Also the philosophy of man not only disagrees with but is diametrically opposed to the Bible teaching on the nature of man. And we need to face up to that fact and take a closer look at these two subjects.

The Origin of Man

First of all, we want to look at the origin of man. What do we know about it? Where and how did he begin? As you know, there are several theories that are abroad today, and right now there are four theories that probably encompass the thinking of every person.

NATURALISTIC EVOLUTION

The first one is *naturalistic evolution*—or you may want to call it biological evolution. Biological evolution has no place for creation. It has no place for God whatsoever. The thing that characterizes it is that it is godless, which is one of the reasons it has been so popular. It has afforded man in the twentieth century an explanation for the origin of man without having to acknowledge God. In fact, it is so popular that most of what is taught in the schools today is from the evolutionary viewpoint. It's amazing that it is so popular in view of the fact that it can explain very little. It cannot explain religion today. It cannot explain history, and there are many more things, even scientific things, that the theory of evolution cannot explain, and yet today it is so entrenched that some are demanding it be called not a theory but a *fact*.

Actually, some of the theories which have been advanced are utterly ridiculous and preposterous. In fact, biological evolution has many problems. I wonder if you realize that. Biological evolution, for instance, has the gap theory. In other words, there are certain gaps in biological evolution that evolutionists cannot fill, and it creates a problem for them. And any honest evolutionist who is a scientist will tell you that they do not know how to fill in these gaps now and they accept by theory that sometime in the future they will be able to fill them. This is the reason you hear them speak of "the missing link." Actually, there are many missing links, not only one, in this theory of evolution, but they feel that somewhere along the line they will be able to fill them in.

Some years ago Dr. Louis Leakey, a British paleontologist (the son of missionaries, by the way), claimed that down in Tanzania he had found something he felt could fill in one of these gaps. He was certain that this was the connecting link between South African ape-men and true men. He found a skull that he called the "nutcracker skull" because the teeth in it were so set and were in such good condition that the fellow could crack a nut. And the amazing thing is, he didn't find an entire skull, he found only part of a skull. Well, we have had theories like that before, and since we have heard no more of this one since 1961, I guess the scientific world didn't fall for it.

The origin of life is a real problem for the evolutionist. I have several clippings about a whole crew of scientists working on the problem of how life originated. You see, it's one thing to trace back and claim this came from that and that came from the other thing, but where did the first thing come from? You've got to go back to a place where life started.

Now how did it begin? Any honest evolutionist will tell you, "We haven't solved that problem yet; we don't know how life began." Many scientists are working in the field of theoretical science, attempting to come forward with the answer to that particular problem. I remember a British scientist who believed that mankind came from seaweed. He advanced his theory as being really a sensible solution. So, my friend, when you go down to the beach now, and you see some seaweed there, you ought to be careful how you treat it because you could have evolved from it!

Well, if you think that's ridiculous, listen to this. I tuned in a television program during the summer on this matter of man exploring in space, and a young scientist out of Massachusetts Institute of Technology was trying to explain why they wanted to get to other planets. He said, "We do not know how life began. But it looks like it might be plausible that millions of years ago some intelligent prehistoric creature came to this earth, he just stopped off, camped here for the night, and left his garbage. And man came out of the garbage can!"

Honestly, I thought I'd tuned in a comedy program! I was waiting for everybody to laugh, and I found that I was the only one laughing. The man was serious! And that's not all. He continued by saying that what we need to do is to go to some of these other planets and leave *our* garbage cans. May I say to you, what audacity, what arrogance of man, thinking he can go to another planet and propagate our race over again! I think we'd better leave man on this little earth and not let him track his sin all over God's universe.

These are actually theories that are put forth by intelligent folk today. Now let me just say that there have been other theories of the past that were in their day scientific, and many intelligent people accepted them; and there were others who pointed out that they contradicted the Bible. For instance, there was a time when intelligent men accepted certain scientific views of the Ptolemaic theory, which says that the earth is at the center with the sun, moon, and stars revolving around it. These were intelligent men like Augustine—men with amazing I.Q.s. But, my friend, today that theory has been exploded and is out. I do not know of an intelligent person holding it now.

Then there was the Newtonian science that came in, and you'll find that not only Sir Isaac Newton but other intelligent men of his day held that theory. While some of his hypothesis was true, the absolutes such as time, mass, and space have been rejected. Even men like Albert Einstein have rejected part of it. Later research has shown its application to sub-atomic particles to be an impossibility.

Now if you want to know the main reason that I would not accept biological evolution, it is that in the final analysis it's merely a theory that attempts to explain the origin of life, and especially of man. I do believe that eventually evolution will go out. It's the popular thing right now, and we're down in that trough today where we are branded unscientific for not going along with it. It has always been said that you are not intelligent if you don't follow the theory that's in vogue. Well, brother, I'll just have to appear unintelligent. I refuse to accept any theory just because it happens to be popular today. Biological evolution is a theory, not a proven science at all.

There are certain things that science does not know, and we're going to make reference to that. But I want to make this statement right here. The reason that we as Christians reject biological evolution is threefold:

First, we believe that biological evolution has no explanation for *from nothing to the inorganic*. In other words, where did matter begin? I honestly believe that this universe is far more vast than is thought today, as far as expanse and time are concerned. I believe that it has been in existence literally trillions of years. You see, we have a God of eternity. And He is an infinite God without limits of any kind. But evolution must be able to fill in the gap from nothing to matter, and its proponents have no explanation for that at all. It's one thing to say that a little cell developed and eventually became a man over a long expanse of time. Granted, if that were true, where did the little cell come from? How did it begin? You have to go back to the time somewhere in the past and tell how it came into existence.

Actually, my friend, the only way that you can explain matter is by creation. "In the beginning God created the heavens and the earth" (Genesis 1:1)—that's the only logical explanation there is. Biological evolution has no explanation for from nothing to the inorganic. And therefore we reject it because the Bible has the only record that will explain from nothing to the inorganic.

The second problem is going *from the inorganic to the organic*. Now up to today neither evolution nor science can bridge that gap from inorganic to living organisms. How does life begin? What is behind it? And how can you take that which is inorganic and make it live? There are several foundations that are supplying millions of dollars for research in this area, but they haven't come up with the explanation for the origin of life. Biological evolution has no explanation for that. Just to push our thinking out there in the ocean and claim our ancestors came from seaweed millions of years ago doesn't answer anything at all. If you want to know the truth, no theory has solved the problem.

Then there is the third step—going *from organic to man*. God created the whales. God created the fish. God created the animals. But the creation of man is a separate creation. And there is no natural transition from the animal to man. The very fact that man has a chassis that is similar to an animal's does not prove that they have a common ancestor. It merely proves that they move in the same environment. We live in the same world that the animal lives in, and therefore we have to have feet, and we have to have a head—we must have many things that the animal has. Likewise the animal has to have many things that we have. But there is no such thing as a bridge between man and animal.

There are many questions biological evolutionists have not answered. They have not proven anything. Therefore you will find that in the Word of God is the only explanation:

> **And the LORD God formed man of the dust of the ground, and breathed into his nostrils the breath of life; and man became a living being.**
> (Genesis 2:7)

God created man from the dust of the earth, and He breathed into his breathing places the breath of life. My beloved, that's the only explanation of life.

Evolutionists have never been able to bridge that gigantic gap between inorganic dust and human beings. Even the old Piltdown man, which was found in Great Britain, you'll remember, was proved a forgery. How do you know that the others are not forgeries? How do you know that other so-called missing links, the Java man for instance, are genuine? Years ago I visited the Field's Museum of Natural History in Chicago, where they had all the steps of the evolution of man set up. Their story of the development of man is all myth, it's fairy stories. When we came to the

Java man, I asked the curator the question, "How do you know that the Java man is not really a myth?" He said, "If you want to know the truth, we don't know." When you come down to facts, evolution is all something which has just been constructed. You see, when you start out with a certain thesis, it's amazing how men's imagination can fill it in.

Now there is no question but that there is development within phyla or families in which the members are assumed to have a common descent. In other words, I am of the opinion that all horses came from one pair of horses. I'm of the opinion that probably all monkeys came from one monkey and its mate. But I don't think any of *you* came from a monkey! But there are certain great families, and their development within the phylum can be found in many, many places today. However, friends, there is no transition from animal to human here at all. *Homo sapiens* is a separate creation of God.

Therefore, for these three reasons we reject what is known as naturalistic or biological evolution. And I believe that Christians today ought to stand on their two feet and say they reject it and be able to give a reason why.

Listen to this statement by Swedish botanist Dr. Heribert Nilsson, who is an evolutionist:

> My attempts to demonstrate evolution by experiment carried on for more than forty years have completely failed. . . . At least I should hardly be accused of having started from a preconceived anti-evolutionary standpoint. . . . It may be firmly maintained that it is not even possible to make a caricature out of paleobiological facts. The fossil material is so complete that it has been possible to construct new classes, and the lack of transitional series cannot be explained as due to the scarcity of material. Deficiencies are real. They will never be filled. . . . The idea of an evolution rests on pure belief.[1]

May I say to you, he is moving into the realm of religion! My friend, to be an evolutionist you have to take it by *faith*. Evolution is speculation and always has been. But, unfortunately, a great many folk have accepted it as fact.

THEISTIC EVOLUTION

We come now to the second view, which is the most illogical one that anyone can have. In our day a group of theologians (young theologians, for the most part), not wanting to be called intellectual obscurantists, have adopted what is known as *theistic evolution*. They are trying to run with the hare and the hounds, and they take the position that God created the amoeba to begin with, but from there on He went off and left the little amoeba and it did its own developing. That's theistic evolution.

Unfortunately, the men who hold this view have gotten into many of our so-called Christian schools. They have been able to worm their way into an amazing number of places. I could tell you many places where you'd really be surprised to know that theistic evolution is held as being the teaching of the Word of God.

Now I want to pass on from that because I do not think that you can logically believe in theistic evolution. You're either going to accept the Bible account or you're going to reject the Bible account. I can understand how an unbeliever can reject the Bible account, but I cannot understand how a so-called Bible believer can say, "I'm a theistic evolutionist." It's impossible. You either believe the Bible or you don't believe the Bible, and these two views are certainly in conflict. This idea today that you can reconcile them—well, it's a sad thing.

PROGRESSIVE CREATIONISM

Now here is a third viewpoint which is to my judgment dangerous. It is known as *progressive creationism*. Probably ninety percent of our Christian schools are teaching progressive creationism. I will be giving you quotations from Dr. Bernard Ramm. I knew him when we taught for a time at the same school. I consider him a friend, and I think he is a fine Christian gentleman who has, in my opinion, very high principles. But I do not agree with his viewpoint of progressive creationism. Several times in his book he makes the statement that this is the view he holds. It's called, and this is his definition, "development from vacancy."[2]

Dr. Ramm takes the position that Genesis 1:2 does not refer to any kind of a cataclysm or catastrophe, but actually speaks only of vacancy. That is, God started off with a lot of raw material, which He developed by evolution—or you can call it something other than that if you want to. Dr. Ramm uses the illustration of an artist who gathers his canvas, brushes, and paints, and then he starts painting. Likewise God first created all the materials, and then He began to work them over, and after a few thousand years, a million years for that matter, He came out with man. That is the view, generally speaking, of going from raw materials to finished product. It would be a very difficult viewpoint to defend.

Someone has made the statement that progressive creationism is disguised theistic evolution. It's very close to it. The fact of the matter is, you have to be an intellect like Dr. Ramm to make the distinction. And there are not many able to make the distinction today. As a result, most of them end up in theistic evolution. I have found that many who are coming out of even our so-called Christian schools today are really holding the theistic evolution view rather than that of progressive creationism.

Now having said that, may I go on to say that the theistic evolutionist and the progressive creationist both believe that the soul and the spirit of man were created. But they think the physical, or the body part of man, was evolved. And they see the six days of Genesis as being long aeons of time and periods in which that took place. I believe the Scripture makes it clear that this is not what happened but that man was created not only soul and spirit, but also body, and that he was fully created at the same moment. It was not something that developed over a period of time.

Here is Dr. Ramm's view in his own words: "We believe Genesis 1:2 is not referring to ruin and destruction but to vacancy awaiting in forming."[3] According to his theory, "in forming" means that the Holy Spirit worked from within and developed man from within—that God did not form him from without, but that the Holy Spirit formed him from within. And, of course, that viewpoint takes the position that the six days of Genesis are not twenty-four-hour days, but that they are aeons or periods of time which cover thousands, perhaps millions, of years.

Now I feel that many keen-minded professors, in attempting to hold an intellectual position with their counterparts in the universities, adopt this viewpoint because they feel it will enable them to answer the evolutionists. Certainly they do have an interpretation for the gap theory, because the minute the evolutionist finds a gap, these folk come along and say, "Well, that's where God stepped in and created." The only difficulty with this is that we don't always have a specific Scripture to answer all the different gaps that are found in the evolutionary theory. You can see progressive creationism as a desperate attempt by intelligent people today to give a scientific explanation for creation.

To summarize: May I say, we totally reject evolution. We reject it for three reasons. We reject it first of all because it is unscriptural. You cannot reconcile evolution with the Word of God. The idea of being a theistic evolutionist is as inconsistent with the Word as any position can possibly be.

Actually, evolution is more of a philosophy than it is a proven fact. It is a system of the interpretation of origins. Evolutionists do have a certain amount of information, and because of this they have applied that philosophy to all walks of life.

We also reject evolution because of the fact that all theories of the past have eventually been proven untrue. The Scientific Bureau of Paris lists seventy-nine theories for the origin of this universe which at one time were considered scientific, and all of them are rejected today. Therefore, evolution, though it may be popular now, and it may be the thing in our universities, if it runs its course as other theories have, it will be as dead as a dodo bird. So I don't want to hang onto a theory that will be as much of a back number as that. It, too, will be exploded, just as these other theories have been.

Now we reject evolution for another very definite reason: It has no explanation in three fields. That is, evolution cannot explain going *from nothing to the inorganic*. It has no explanation for the origin of matter. Neither can it bridge the gap between the *inorganic and the organic*—that is, how life began. And then, this third, from the *organic to mankind*. There are too many gaps in that, so we reject it altogether.

FIAT CREATION

We come now to the fourth viewpoint, and the one that I hold, which is that of a *fiat creation*—that God spoke, and when He spoke, matter came into existence! And I believe that God brought into existence an original creation.

Now I do not think that man was in the original creation in any form whatsoever. And I hold that when you come to the first six days recorded in Genesis 1, you come to a time actually of renovation rather than creation, and when you come to the creation of man, he is something brand new. Physically man was created of the ground. But man is more than dust. God "breathed into his nostrils the breath of life; and man became a living being" (Genesis 2:7). He became something new that had never before been on this earth.

Who? When? Why?

There are three questions we want to investigate about creation, and especially the creation of man: Who created man, when was he created, and why was he created? I think any intelligent person ought to be able to answer these three questions. The interesting thing is, I believe God has given us reasonable answers.

Actually the last question is the most difficult, so let's ask the question of *who* first. And we believe the Scripture offers the only explanation. Let's go to Genesis 1:1, the very first verse of the Bible.

In the beginning God created the heavens and the earth.

"In the beginning God"—in the Hebrew, *Elohim*—"created," *bara,* which means He created out of nothing. The other word that is used later in Genesis 1 is God "made," *asah,* and that means out of existing matter. And you'll find that is true of many things. I do not think God created the plants at this time. The seed was already in the earth, we are told. All it needed was the proper kind of atmosphere and climate in which it could fructify and grow. And I think that's exactly what happened as far as Genesis is concerned. But the interesting thing is that when you come over to Genesis 1:21 and see the word *create,* there the Hebrew is *bara* again—but you don't find *bara* between verses 1 and 21.

We could spend a week or more just talking about Genesis 1:1. I had the privilege of hearing lectures by Dr. A. B. Winchester of Canada, and I heard him speak for one whole month on the first chapter of Genesis, speaking three days a week for a period of fifty minutes. And he apologized at the end of the series that he had not finished the first chapter! He said he had hoped to be able to do it in one month. Oh, so much can be said about this!

Now in Genesis 1:1, we have all of the actual creation with the exception of the creation of animals and man as we know them today. However, there is abundant evidence that there were animals at the beginning of creation which have disappeared, for instance, the dinosaur. Perhaps they were in this original creation and then disappeared off this earth. In fact, verse 2 indicates that the entire creation of that time disappeared. During that period did God have an intelligent creation on this earth? I do not know, but there seems to be evidence that there was an intelligent creation on this earth before man was ever put here.

Creation's Three Bridges

And all of that is in Genesis 1:1: "In the beginning God created the heavens and the earth"—there is the creation. And when you get to the creation of animals and of whales and of fish, that is a separate creation. The Hebrew states it very carefully. *Bara* is the word for "create." *Asah* is the word for "make." And all the way through the six days you have, "God *made* this, God *made* that." On the first day, He *made* light appear. He didn't create light on that day. Light was already in His universe. He made it break through the darkness on "the face of the deep." And you do not find the word *bara* until you get to the creation of animals—life, you see.

Then, when you come to the creation of man, *bara* is used again, so that there are three acts of creation in Genesis 1, and *only* three acts of creation. They are very important because they bridge the three gaps. They bridge the gap from the nothing to the inorganic: "In the beginning God created the heavens and the earth"—matter. Then from inorganic to organic, life—"God created great sea creatures and every living thing that moves." God created the animals—life appeared.

Then from organic to man:

> *So God created man in His own image; in the image of God*
> *He created him; male and female He created them.*
> (Genesis 1:27)

You have here in Genesis that bridge which evolution cannot find. That bridge in the Book of Genesis in chapter 1 is in the word *create*, you see. This is a reasonable explanation of the origin of things, my beloved. And may I say that I think it's God appealing to the intelligence of man.

THE BIG BANG THEORY

The earth was without form, and void; and darkness was on the

> *face of the deep. And the Spirit of God was hovering over the*
> *face of the waters.*
> (Genesis 1:2)

Some years ago I was very much interested in this news item: "The universe began in a mighty atom blast, British scientists believe." It goes on to explain that a team of six British scientists say they've obtained proof to explain how the universe began. They say that the positions of unknown stars and planets far out in space, and the way they're receiving radio signals rushing in every direction, means that at some time in the past there was a great blast. Well, that's what Genesis 1:2 says. The earth was "without form, and void," *tohu wa bohu* in the Hebrew. Some great catastrophe took place. The earth "became" without form and void, if you please. But Isaiah says God did not create the earth *tohu wa bohu* "without form and void." This is very interesting. Since God did not create it without form and void, something happened to make it so. "Without form" is the Hebrew word *tohu*, meaning "a ruin," "vacancy." "Void" is the Hebrew word *bohu*, meaning "emptiness." Notice this statement in the prophecy of Isaiah:

> *For thus says the LORD,*
> *Who created the heavens,*
> *Who is God,*
> *Who formed the earth and made it,*
> *Who has established it,*
> *Who did not create it in vain,*
> *Who formed it to be inhabited:*
> *"I am the LORD, and there is no other."*
> (Isaiah 45:18)

Here God says that He did not create the earth "in vain," and the Hebrew word is *tohu*, which we find in Genesis 1:2. God did not create the earth without form and void. God created this universe a cosmos, not a chaos. This is what Isaiah is attempting to make clear. He created it not *tohu wa bohu*, but the earth became *tohu wa bohu*. God formed the earth to be inhabited, and it was God who came to this wreck and made it a habitable place for mankind.

Our current study and exploration of space has revealed, so far, that you and I live in a universe in which only the earth is habitable for human beings. I believe Genesis is telling us that this earth *became* without form and void, that it was just as uninhabitable as the moon when the Spirit of God moved upon the face of the waters.

I believe that the entire universe came under this great catastrophe. What was the catastrophe? We can only suggest that there was some pre-Adamic creature on this earth. And it seems possible that all of this is connected with the fall of Lucifer, "son of the morning," who became Satan, the devil, as we know him today, but God has not given us details. The fact of the matter is that He has given us very, very few details in the first chapter of Genesis.

Why didn't God tell us more? I think primarily because it's none of our business. The second reason I think He didn't tell us is because He's attempting to give us a Book for guidance so that, though we are fools and wayfaring men, we needn't go astray (see Isaiah 35:8). God is giving us the way of salvation, not a book on geology or origins. Yet He gives enough to appeal to the intellect of man. So in Genesis 1:2 we are told what the earth became. Something happened to this earth, and it *became* without form and void.

AND GOD SPOKE!

Now into this picture God moved. And when He moved into the picture we find the Spirit of God brooding or hovering over it, and He moved upon the face of the waters. It is a picture of a mother hen getting her little chicks under her wings. And the Spirit of God brooded in that darkness over the face of the deep.

Will you notice now the thing that happened on the first day,

> *Then God said, "Let there be light"; and there was light.*
> (Genesis 1:3)

Candidly, they can't tell us much about light even today. They don't quite know what light is. But God said, "Let there be light," and in light there's tremendous energy and sometimes heat. When God spoke, these things came into existence. Oh, the power of the Word of God! And this is the thing which answers the old nebular hypothesis which opposed biblical teaching.

The nebular hypothesis says that matter is indestructible and therefore Genesis is wrong. The Bible says God spoke and matter came into existence—but that can't be if matter has always been here. Well, what do they do today with atomic fission? They take matter and translate it into energy, and poof, it's gone! You see, they reverse God's process. They did find out His secret. He took nothing and spoke and made energy into matter, and today man takes matter back out through energy, and that's atomic fission. Do you see that it has upset man's nebular hypothesis? Let's wait till they get something permanent, something that's satisfactory today. A great many theologians at that time tried to reconcile the nebular hypothesis with the Word of God. Well, they couldn't do it then, and you can't reconcile evolution with the Bible today.

Dr. Werner Von Braun, who worked in developing space travel, said that space is revealing the hand of a Creator. That is interesting. I think one of these days they are going to move into a pocket that will upset evolution and tear it to pieces. Then you'll find another theory coming along to replace it. That's the reason I'm not hanging onto evolution, nor am I hanging onto this theory of progressive creationism, because I do not believe they offer satisfactory explanations.

Six Days of Renovation

Genesis began with six days of renovation, and I personally believe they were twenty-four-hour days. If you think they were longer periods of time I won't fall out with you, but I can't understand what "the evening and the morning" mean unless they are twenty-four-hour days. Oh, I know they say that morning is the beginning of a period, and there was an evening of it, of going down, and then a morning of it coming back. Well, Genesis says, "The evening and the morning were the first day." I understand it as a twenty-four-hour day.

Notice, if you will, that in the six days only two things are created: One is life and the other is man. What you have is God beginning to make a place for man to live. To me that's the most wonderful thing in the world. He begins to separate the firmament or expanse. He divides the water above from the water beneath. He was making air spaces here for man to live. He was preparing the way. And we are told that plant life appeared.

> *Then God said, "Let the waters under the heavens be gathered together into one place, and let the dry land appear"; and it was so. And God called the dry land Earth, and the gathering together of the waters He called Seas. And God saw that it was good.*
> (Genesis 1:9-10)

Notice in verse 11 that He did not *create* plants at this time. All they needed was for water to be brought, and then they would come up again.

Honestly, when I've traveled across West Texas and have seen that barren land, especially around Sera Blanca, I never believed that anything would ever grow there. But when I went back the other day after they had an abundance of rain, it was as green as a golf course! That's what Earth needed—only rain, a favorable environment for growth.

Looking back at verse 2, when presumably this great catastrophe had occurred, all life had disappeared, even the plants couldn't grow.

But when God separated the waters from the waters, then gathered the waters together, and the dry land appeared, then plant life began to grow.

Then on the fourth day the sun, moon, and stars became visible. God didn't create them at this time. They probably had been created billions of years before. He simply made them shine through at this time.

Then we find in verse 21:

> *So God created great sea creatures and every living thing that moves, with which the waters abounded, according to their kind.*

There is the word for *create, bara,* again. It appears also in verse 27:

> *So God created man in His own image; in the image of God He created him; male and female He created them.*

May I say that it makes it very clear here that God created man as a separate creation. Progressive creationists and theistic evolutionists come along and say, "That means God created the soul and the spirit, but the body was already here." Let's see if you can draw that conclusion from what is said:

> *And the LORD God formed man of the dust of the ground, and breathed into his nostrils the breath of life; and man became a living being.*
> (Genesis 2:7)

He didn't make man's soul out of dust, and He didn't make his spirit out of dust. Notice that God created the physical part of man at the same time He created the spiritual part of man. It was all one operation.

> *And the LORD God caused a deep sleep to fall on Adam, and he slept; and He took one of his ribs, and closed up the flesh in its place.*
> (Genesis 2:21)

(And that has been a rib-tickling story ever since!) The Hebrew means God took a side of man. (And that's the reason some believe a man is just half a man until he gets married!) That's also the only time that a woman has been taken from a man. Now it's the other way around, the man comes from the woman. But here it's different; this speaks of the creation of a man and a woman.

> *And the LORD God caused a deep sleep to fall on Adam, and he slept; and He took one of his ribs, and closed up the flesh in its place. Then the rib which the LORD God had taken from man He made into a woman, and He brought her to the man. And Adam said:*
> *"This is now bone of my bones*
> *And flesh of my flesh."*
> (Genesis 2:21-23)

She wasn't just a rib, she was one-half of him. "Here's my other half—she belongs to me, she's part of me."

Adam, I think, understood that there was no development. Will you notice verse 23: "Adam said: 'This is now bone of my bones and flesh of my flesh; she shall be called Woman, because she was taken out of Man.'" Not evolved, but taken out of man.

From my viewpoint you cannot support theistic evolution or progressive creation from the Genesis account. And I have concluded that the creation of man was an act of God that took place. But I'm not through. Let's look at Genesis 3:

> *Then the LORD God said, "Behold, the man has become like one of Us, to know good and evil. And now, lest he put out his hand and take also of the tree of life, and eat, and live forever"—therefore the LORD God sent him out of the garden of Eden to till the ground from which he was taken.*
> (Genesis 3:22-23)

Man, created in the Garden of Eden, is now sent forth from the garden into an altogether different environment, if you please.

Now there are other Scriptures we could give—you remember the Lord Jesus made this statement:

> *And He answered and said to them, "Have you not read that He who made them at the beginning 'made them male and female'?"*
> (Matthew 19:4)

He made them male and female. Our Lord, when He was here among us, put His seal upon the creation account in the Book of Genesis that, separate from everything else, it was a creative act of God that brought Adam and Eve into existence. May I say as a Christian, I hold to that. And I think it's to run down the flag to yield to any kind of theory—and after all, that's all evolution is in its final analysis. The theory of evolution has problems. It's the flimsiest sort of thing, yet they are holding on with the idea that all the gaps will be filled in time.

We reject it, therefore, because Scripture makes the fact of creation clear. Note this additional Scripture penned by Paul the apostle:

> *All flesh is not the same flesh, but there is one kind of flesh of men, another flesh of animals, another of fish, and another of birds.*
> (1 Corinthians 15:39)

Paul says there are several kinds of flesh, flesh of animals, of birds, of fish, and the flesh of man. One did not evolve from any of the others. I do not see how you can hold to any kind of theory that the physical part of man has evolved. It has not evolved according to the Word of God.

When did God do all this? I cannot date it. May I say that I think the biggest problem before theologians is to try to arrive at a more satisfactory dating of the origin of man. I do not know this, but I believe that man has been on this earth a lot longer than originally was thought. Any dating before David is difficult. Any dating before Abraham is hazy, and dating before the Flood is pure guesswork. So we cannot do anything but speculate, and my speculation is as good as anybody's. Some Bibles print a timetable dating creation at 4,004 B.C., but no one knows about dating back that far. There's plenty of room in the genealogies to move man as far back as you need to take him.

And now we leave the questions of when and how to discuss *why* God created man. And here is the real problem. Why did God do it? Well, I think there are several reasons, and we will discuss them in the next chapter.

CHAPTER 5

THE PURPOSE AND NATURE OF MAN

We've been investigating the great questions of the creation of man—who created him, and when? We want to look now at the question of why man was created, and this last question is the most difficult one of all. Man is here today but the question is, why? And that's hard to explain. Why would a perfect God, a God who loves, continue with the human race the way He has in this world today?

Why Man?

So God created man in His own image; in the image of God He created him; male and female He created them.
(Genesis 1:27)

The greatest blow man's ego ever received was when he found out that this little earth was not the center but on the side of this galactic system in which we are. We're just a sideshow. Nevertheless, we are here because we are the beloved of our God, and we are here for His good pleasure.

FOR HIS PLEASURE

You are worthy, O Lord,
To receive glory and honor and power;
For You created all things,
And by Your will they exist and were created.
(Revelation 4:11)

God does not exist for our pleasure. We exist for His pleasure. He created us because He wanted to create us. The explanation is found in Him, not in us. We think we're the center of this universe. We are not.

God has created everything for His pleasure. This universe is not, as early scientists thought, geocentric, that is, earth centered. Now they've found out that the universe is too big to even be uranocentric, that is, heaven centered. The heavens are too big. My friend, this universe is Theocentric, it is God centered. This universe exists for Him.

I looked last night at the evening star. Have you seen the evening star recently? And then the other morning I got up early before the sun came up, and the morning star was there. It was really bright. Do you know why it is there? (By the way, our Lord is called in Revelation 22:16 the "Bright and Morning Star." He uses that title.) The morning star is in that position because that is where He wanted it. If the Lord Jesus wanted it moved one inch, He would move it one inch! Man needs to learn that. God didn't create this universe for man. Man was created for God. We exist for Him. We were created for *His* pleasure.

If you take the position that the God of this universe has no right to do whatever He wants with that drunkard who is going down the street blaspheming Him, then, my friend, you don't know much about God. This universe exists for Him, and for His pleasure.

"You are worthy, O Lord, to receive glory and honor and power; for You created all things" (Revelation 4:11). Why? "For thy pleasure they are and were created" (KJV). That is one of the songs we'll sing in heaven when we get there. God didn't need a universe to juggle. He didn't create it for a utilitarian purpose. He created this universe for *His* pleasure. And, friend, that's a good enough reason.

When I was a boy, my dad was the authority. I know today we've moved away from that principle, but in my home he was the boss. He used to make me cut wood, especially on a Saturday morning, and I'd say I wanted to fish if it was summertime, and in the fall I wanted to hunt.

"Cut wood!" he'd say.

"Why do I have to do this?"

"Because *I want you to.*"

That ended the argument for me. I did it because he wanted me to do it, and that was satisfactory. Ooh, boy, I never talked back! I went to get the ax and I cut the wood. I did it because *he* wanted it done.

Now today we have a lot of people, even Christians, who ask "Why?" about all manner of things. Well, it's because God wants it, that's the first reason, and that's good enough.

FOR GOD'S GLORY

The second reason God created the universe was for His glory. "When the morning stars sang together, and all the sons of God shouted for joy . . . " (Job 38:7). Way back yonder at the beginning when God created everything, all creation was singing praises to Him, all creation was for His glory. And that's exactly what God intends for all eternity. He's working today on a plan whereby, through redemption, He is going to bring this little earth on which we live—now in rebellion against Him—back into line with His program, which is:

> *That at the name of Jesus every knee should bow, of those in heaven, and of those on earth, and of those under the earth, and that every tongue should confess that Jesus Christ is Lord, to the glory of God the Father.*
> (Philippians 2:10-11)

You see, God the Son came down to earth and became the man Jesus so that at the name of Jesus every knee must bow and every tongue must confess that He is the Lord. Creation is for the glory of the Lord Jesus.

FOR FELLOWSHIP WITH GOD

The third reason for creation is, and I think this is the most wonderful one of all, for God's fellowship. We see this throughout the entire story of God's relationship with man. It's a lovely thing that's said here, and I think we miss a great deal of this because we rush over Genesis too hurriedly.

> And they heard the sound of the LORD God walking in the garden in the cool of the day, and Adam and his wife hid themselves from the presence of the LORD God among the trees of the garden. Then the LORD God called to Adam and said to him, "Where are you?" So he said, "I heard Your voice in the garden, and I was afraid because I was naked; and I hid myself."
> (Genesis 3:8-10)

It says that in the cool of the day God came down into the garden. Imagine, the God of this universe condescended to visit the garden! Why did God come? He had creatures there who were precious to Him. And listen, man is a little lower than the angels, but he's different from the angels. God summons the angels—they are His servants—and they respond immediately. He says, "Bow," and they bow. But this little man, he has a free will of his own. He's different. God wants to have fellowship with him. So God came down every day to have fellowship.

I don't want to appear sentimental, and I hesitate going beyond Scripture, but I wonder—that day when God came down, and Adam hid himself from Him—I wonder if God felt lonesome. He called out, "Adam, where are you?" I say it reverently but I want to say it: I think God is lonesome for you and me sometimes. I wonder if this was His feeling, *I created him so as to have fellowship with him. I wanted to share, and I can't share with him.* Why? Because he is over yonder hiding. *He's out of fellowship with Me.*

The Nature of Man

That brings us to the nature of man. Philosophy and psychology have their explanations for man. Philosophy today says that man is essentially good, that he is innately and inherently good. He can be improved upon, but he's good. And psychology brings in the human factors of heredity and environment, and they contribute unlimited possibilities to what you can do with man. The fact of the matter is, it's the same old story that Adam and Eve heard in the Garden of Eden: "You can become as gods." That is the same story you find today. In fact, it is the whole theory of communism and socialism—which are essentially the same. They seek to improve man. They say, "Man can be improved, and we want to improve him." And look at the results!

Some forms of theology imply that man can assist in his own salvation because there's a spark of good in him, and man can be improved. The do-gooders and liberal politicians said that we ought to get rid of the slums and put people in a nice environment. Now you see what these eggheads accomplished. The new areas that they built to get rid of old slums have become new slums. A newspaper clipping tells of one woman on a committee who thinks the mistake they made was failing to put candy stores and ice-cream parlors on the corners—they forgot to do that! You see, they are still working from that old theory that you can improve man.

A liberal who switched to the conservative view over in Chattanooga, Tennessee, told me, "I used to head up the Community Chest program, and I remember that one of our projects was 'a bathroom in every home.' So we went down to the slums and put in those bathrooms. The next year we went back to see the results. Do you know what had happened? The bathtubs had served as coal bins. They stored their coal in them to build their fires. Some of the tubs had never been used for a bath! We thought if we just put bathtubs in we'd get a bunch of clean people, and all we did was provide some very expensive coal bins."

Now may I say that theology has another theory, first called modernism and now called liberalism. The theory they hold is that man can save himself. All he needs to do is just get hold of himself. Liberalism is sort of a do-it-yourself kit. They say, "You don't need God, you can do it yourself. And there's nothing that you can't do yourself."

Christian Science says that human nature is totally good.[1] What you think is bad is not bad. One big difference between Christian Science and myself is this: They look at mankind and they say that bad is not really bad, that the bad is not there. And I say to them, "The good you see is not really there. If the bad is not there, the good is not there either." But they insist that man is totally good. And that is very appealing to mankind! All he needs to do is think positively. What does that mean? Well, all you have to do is get hold of yourself. Once you get hold of yourself you've pretty much solved your problem.

In our day we have a great many Christians who are going to psychiatrists, thinking they can solve their problems that way. Why? Because fundamentally they are missing what the Word of God has to say. The Word of God tells us that the human family is totally depraved. The Bible says there was a fall, and in the third chapter of Genesis you read of it.

> *Now the serpent was more cunning than any beast of the field which the LORD God had made. And he said to the woman, "Has God indeed said, 'You shall not eat of every tree of the garden'?" And the woman said to the serpent, "We may eat the fruit of the trees of the garden; but of the fruit of the tree which*

is in the midst of the garden, God has said, 'You shall not eat it, nor shall you touch it, lest you die.'" Then the serpent said to the woman, "You will not surely die. For God knows that in the day you eat of it your eyes will be opened, and you will be like God, knowing good and evil." So when the woman saw that the tree was good for food, that it was pleasant to the eyes, and a tree desirable to make one wise, she took of its fruit and ate. She also gave to her husband with her, and he ate.
(Genesis 3:1-6)

If you want to know the results of that fall, turn over to the fifth chapter of the Epistle to the Romans:

Therefore, just as through one man sin entered the world, and death through sin, and thus death spread to all men, because all sinned.
(Romans 5:12)

Now when Paul says all men have sinned, he doesn't mean they've committed an act of sin. He means that in Adam they sinned; that is, what Adam did, they did. Adam's sin has been made over to the human family.

Somebody says, "Well, I don't think that's quite right." I've used this illustration at other times, and let me use it again here because it does illustrate the fact that what Adam did, I did, and what Adam did, you did. All have sinned in Adam. If that doesn't seem fair to you, let me tell you my story, which is probably similar to yours. On my father's side, my grandfather lived in North Ireland. He was a Scotsman, and probably had itchy feet, because he left Scotland and went to North Ireland. He and his wife walked into a lot of trouble over there. Finally he said to my grandmother, "We're going to the new country." So they boarded a ship and came over to Georgia.

Well, when my grandfather made up his mind over in North Ireland to come to this country, I made up my mind that I was coming to this country. Yes, I did. What he did, I did! Listen, if Grandpa had stayed in North Ireland, I would be there today. But he said, "I'm going to a new country," and he came to Georgia. He didn't like Georgia. He went over to Mississippi, and he had a plantation there. Then after the Civil War they lost everything and went to Texas. And that's where I was born.

Look—what my grandfather did, I did. You see, when he left that country, I left that country. When he left Georgia, I left Georgia. When he left Mississippi, I left Mississippi. And the reason I was born in Texas is because what he did, I did. I'm glad he came to Texas. It wouldn't do me any good if I didn't like it, but I do approve of every move he made.

Now may I say that what Adam did, we did. Back yonder in the Garden of Eden this man sinned, and when he sinned he plunged all who came from him into sin—every one of us. Now, friend, this is what the Word of God has to say, and actually this is the thing that's wrong with the human family today: We were born with a sinful nature that we inherited from Adam.

Let's continue now with the historical event recorded in the third chapter of Genesis:

> *And they heard the sound of the LORD God walking in the garden in the cool of the day, and Adam and his wife hid themselves from the presence of the LORD God among the trees of the garden. Then the LORD God called to Adam and said to him, "Where are you?" So he said, "I heard Your voice in the garden, and I was afraid because I was naked; and I hid myself." And He said, "Who told you that you were naked? Have you eaten from the tree of which I commanded you that you should not eat?" Then the man said, "The woman whom You gave to be with me, she gave me of the tree, and I ate."*
> (Genesis 3:8-12)

Well, that's the sorriest thing that Adam did. And that's the fruit of his fall, by the way.

> *And the LORD God said to the woman, "What is this you have done?" The woman said, "The serpent deceived me, and I ate."*
> (Genesis 3:13)

That's passing the buck, is it not!

> *So the LORD God said to the serpent:*
> *"Because you have done this,*
> *You are cursed."*
> (Genesis 3:14)

Then in verse 15 we have the first prophecy regarding Christ:

> *And I will put enmity*
> *Between you and the woman,*
> *And between your seed and her Seed;*
> *He shall bruise your head,*
> *And you shall bruise His heel.*
> (Genesis 3:15)

But God didn't let the woman off, and He certainly didn't let the man off. "To the woman He said: 'I will greatly multiply your sorrow and your conception,'" and so on.

> *Then to Adam He said, "Because you have heeded the voice of your wife, and have eaten from the tree of which I commanded you, saying, 'You shall not eat of it':*
> *Cursed is the ground for your sake;*
> *In toil you shall eat of it*
> *All the days of your life."*
> (Genesis 3:16-17)

That is an historical event that took place: the fall of man.

The result of the fall is that man has been brought to the place of death. That, after all, is the final proof. By man came death. In Adam all die. We are tied up with Adam whether we like it or not. And this is the reason a little infant dies who has not *committed* a sin. He is a sinner in Adam.

> *Therefore, just as through one man sin entered the world, and death through sin, and thus death spread to all men, because all sinned.*
> (Romans 5:12)

Because of Adam's sin the little infant will die—and death has passed on to all men because all have sinned.

Three Proofs

Now briefly, what's the proof of that? I want to give you three proofs.

HISTORICAL PROOF

History has proven that man is fallen and totally depraved. I do not see how anyone can miss this today. Someone asked the novelist William Thackeray one day, "Why is it that you do not have any paragons of virtue as your heroes? Why is it that your heroes and heroines are so fallible and so filled with faults?" He replied, "My business as a novelist is to hold up a mirror to nature, and I attempt to portray human nature as I see it." Then he added, "I see no heroes among mankind."

Thackeray was a Christian and a very astute judge of human nature, by the way. Have you read his *Vanity Fair*? What a takeoff on the human family! Little Becky, the heroine—boy, is she out for herself! And the hero? Well, who in the world is the hero? The young man who died on the battlefield of Waterloo, with his face down in the mud that night? He was the biggest coward of all. And his little wife, he two-timed her. Thackeray said, "There are no heroes." George Eliot agreed with that. She said that was the reason she had none in her writings.

The other day someone handed me a printed message by Dr. Lloyd-Jones of Westminster Chapel in London. I'll give you only a brief synopsis of his message:

> The first is, that here we are given, as I have said, the only real and adequate explanation of why there are such things as wars. Armistice Sunday, two World Wars, why have we had them? Why is man guilty of this final madness? Why is it that men kill one another and have even gloried in war? Why? What's the explanation of it all? There's only one answer: It's because men are as the apostle Paul describes them, "enemies and aliens in their minds." It is not only the teaching of the apostle Paul. You remember how James puts it in the fourth chapter of his epistle: "Whence come wars among you?" and answers the question, "even lusts that war in your members."[2]

What's wrong with men today? Well, our father Adam sinned, and he plunged the entire family into sin, and every one of us is tinctured with this thing. There's not a good one in the lot. You may think you are, but you are not. You're a sinner in God's sight.

At a summer Bible conference a couple came to me and said, "We are the couple who got so tired of hearing you on the radio tell us we were sinners, although we were active in the church, that we wrote to you about it. We even went to talk to our preacher about it. And he said, 'Don't pay any attention to that fellow McGee. He emphasizes that.'" Yet they kept listening. And when they came to me at that conference, they said that they had gotten gloriously and wonderfully saved because they had come face-to-face with the issue that they're sinners.

My friend, until we see our true selves as sinners, we can never know Christ as our Savior. There are too many people who say, "I've come to Jesus." But they have never come to Him as sinners. You have to come as a sinner, because you and I belong to a family that's sick—not only sick, we're incurable. Christ alone has the cure. History proves it.

THE CONSCIENCE OF MAN

Do you know that the conscience of man tells him he's guilty? I have a little clipping titled *Guilt* in which the psychologist William James writes, "One single word which torments more Americans in more unsuspected ways than any other disease of the mind or body, one word, *guilt*." And you know, when you lie on the psychiatrist's couch, that's what he is after. He starts probing around to find out where that tender spot is, what it is back in your childhood that causes you to feel guilty today.

I don't care who you are, you are guilty and you know you're guilty. Your conscience bears witness to that fact. Do you know that the only place that you can unburden your guilt is at the Cross of Christ? That's the one place you can lay down a burden of sin and know that you stand justified before God. And, my Christian friend, you'd better stay off the psychiatrist's couch. You'll never get cured there.

I talked to a woman the other day—oh, was she guilty! She may even be guilty of murder! She's not sure whether she is or not. She did an awful thing, and she has tried everything to rid herself of the guilt. She has been to the authorities, and she's been to the psychiatrists. I said, "Oh, if you'd only bring it to the Lord Jesus Christ! He said to that woman caught in adultery, 'Neither do I condemn thee: go, and sin no more.' That woman, a sinful woman, left cleansed because she came to the Lord Jesus Christ." Oh, my friend, if we would only learn where to take our sins! But thank God for a conscience that tells us we are guilty.

THE WORD OF GOD

Now let me move to the third proof. The Word of God is the final proof that mankind is fallen and totally depraved. "All have sinned and fall short of the glory of God" (Romans 3:23).

Listen to David as he confessed his sin to God:

> *Behold, I was brought forth in iniquity,*
> *And in sin my mother conceived me.*
> (Psalm 51:5)

In other words, David said, "I started off as a sinner. I have a sinful nature, and it came to me even when I was conceived." May I say to you, as you move through the Word of God, that's what you find everywhere you read.

Job in despondency prayed, "Who can bring a clean thing out of an unclean? No one!" (Job 14:4). Let me say this, there are many parents today who think they are raising carnations instead of stink-weeds. But let me give you this verse again: "Who can bring a clean thing out of an unclean?" Do you think your child is any different from you? Are you a perfect individual? Do you always tell the truth? What is *your* past? Your child is just like you. "Who can bring a clean thing out of an unclean?" You cannot and you did not. So your child is guilty just like you are.

The Lord Jesus said to Nicodemus in John 3, "You must be born again." Then He added, "That which is born of the flesh is flesh," it always will be flesh, it's nothing else but flesh. You can't change it. And God never changes it. Some people say, "He changes human nature." No, He never changes human nature. But He will give you a *new* nature—you must be born again. He doesn't even intend to salvage the old nature.

May I say to you, friend: This old nature that we have—we need to *judge* it as God is judging it. Will you listen to His injunction?

> *. . . that you put off, concerning your former conduct, the old*
> *man which grows corrupt according to the deceitful lusts.*
> (Ephesians 4:22)

That's *you*, my beloved, and I'm just like you are. I'm a sinner saved by grace. That's all. Take a look at Colossians 1:21:

And you, who once were alienated and enemies in your mind
by wicked works, yet now He has reconciled.

You can hardly turn anywhere in the Word of God without finding
that concept.

The heart is deceitful above all things,
And desperately wicked;
Who can know it?
(Jeremiah 17:9)

Certainly every man at his best state is but vapor.
(Psalm 39:5)

Even when you are at your best, you are only vapor or breath or vanity.
Have you ever noticed that when you try to be your best, you become
your worst? That's one reason that Bahaism never appealed to me. I
was in Chicago when it started, and there was a lovely temple with
little booths in it, and you could go in and look at the beautiful
pictures. The idea was to sit down and think beautiful thoughts. Have
you ever tried that? Well, if you haven't, when you get home tonight
get in your room and say, "I'm going to think some beautiful
thoughts." And you will think of the dirtiest things you ever thought
of. Why do we do that? It's because we are sinners. That's our problem.
But notice our Lord said:

If you then, being evil, know how to give good gifts to your
children, how much more will your heavenly Father give the
Holy Spirit to those who ask Him!
(Luke 11:13)

Look again to the psalmist:

They have all turned aside,
They have together become corrupt;

> *There is none who does good,*
> *No, not one.*
> (Psalm 14:3)

And Isaiah wrote this:

> *But we are all like an unclean thing,*
> *And all our righteousnesses are like filthy rags;*
> *We all fade as a leaf,*
> *And our iniquities, like the wind,*
> *Have taken us away.*
> (Isaiah 64:6)

And note this from Ecclesiastes 7:20: "For there is not a just man on earth who does good and does not sin." The New Testament confirms it:

> *For all have sinned and fall short of the glory of God.*
> (Romans 3:23)

> *If we say that we have no sin, we deceive ourselves, and the truth is not in us.*
> (1 John 1:8)

> *He who is without sin among you, let him throw a stone at her first.*
> (John 8:7)

Oh, that was a magnificent response by our Lord when the crowd of religious rulers flung down before Him a woman whom they said had been taken in adultery. He picked up a stone and said in effect, "Here, the one who is without sin among you, throw it at her." It wasn't thrown. Dr. G. Campbell Morgan remarked, "That took me out of the stone-throwing business," and it ought to take you out of it, friend.

You ought to quit criticizing other people, because you too are a sinner. If you're without sin, then you can throw stones, but I don't think you are without sin. The Lord Jesus said to His unbelieving brothers, "The world cannot hate you, but it hates Me because I testify of it that its works are evil" (John 7:7).

This teaching on the sinful nature of man won't make me the most popular preacher around, but I'll tell you this: It will cause unthinking people to think! And there will be folks who will get saved. Although it won't be popular, folks need to be told today that they are sinners and that there is no spark of good in them. Oh, how they need to know Christ who came and died on a cross for no other reason than that man is a sinner. And God, who created man, wants to bring him back into fellowship with Himself.

CHAPTER 6

ANGELS

We move now to a theme which is different from any we've had heretofore. This theme deals with that which you and I can know nothing about by sense perception. Now, it is entirely possible that you think you have seen an angel. There are men who have thought they've seen angels and then married them and found out differently after they got married—or at least they found out there are two kinds of angels, good angels and bad angels! But none of us has ever seen an angel.

However, the Word of God moves back and forth from earth to heaven without any strain or difficulty. And it speaks of things in heaven as easily as it speaks of things on this earth. It moves back and forth and shifts from the seen to the unseen.

You remember the story in Luke 16 about Lazarus, the beggar who died, and the rich man who also died. Jesus told about their lives down here, and then with no strain or hocus pocus or abracadabra at all, He moved from this life right over to the other side. Our Lord spoke as comfortably of the things there as He did of the things here.

We need to recognize that creation is not limited to our sense perception. It's not limited to what we can see or feel or what is tangible. Actually, there are a great many things that are in the physical world that you and I have to take by faith.

For example, when I studied chemistry, my professor talked about atoms. He talked about atoms, and he talked about atoms. I thought that he was acquainted with them, the way he talked about them— that they just were little fellows he tamed and kept in cages, that sort of thing! But I was amazed to discover that he had never seen an atom. And neither have you nor I ever seen an atom, but I am confident that you would not doubt that there is such a thing as an atom. It is a reality today. But the atom, although we don't see it, is, of course, in the physical realm.

However, there are things that exist which are unseen, as we're going to discover. Creation therefore is not limited to only what you and I know and understand. I get rather amused at the liberals today who say, "We have a broad faith, we are broad-minded—we encompass everything." But when they begin to narrow the thing down, you wonder if they believe in anything. This is what I mean: Is it a broad faith to say, "I don't believe in angels; I don't believe in miracles; I don't believe in the supernatural; I don't believe in the Bible"? Well, when you talk like that you don't have a broad faith, my brother, you have a narrow faith. And, friends, we do need to have a broad faith.

The Word of God is our only reliable source; it is our only authority. The only way you and I can know about angels is through what the Word of God has to say.

What Are Angels?

The Greek word for angels is *angelos*, which means messenger or envoy. It could refer to either human or supernatural beings. It is used sometimes, as we shall see, for human messengers. But in the Scripture, practically all instances refer to a creation of God which is above man.

The word *angelos* occurs 108 times in the Old Testament and 165 times in the New Testament, totaling 273 times in the Word of God.

So you see that the Bible does have a great deal to say about these creatures.

Now let's see if we can find out something more about them. First of all, we want to know about their origin. Angels are created, they are part of the creation of God. Let's look at a number of Scriptures, first, Nehemiah 9:6:

> *You alone are the LORD;*
> *You have made heaven,*
> *The heaven of heavens, with all their host,*
> *The earth and everything on it,*
> *The seas and all that is in them,*
> *And You preserve them all.*
> *The host of heaven worships You.*

That is one reference to angels in Scripture. Then let's take a Scripture in the New Testament, speaking of the Lord Jesus:

> *For by Him all things were created that are in heaven and that are on earth, visible and invisible, whether thrones or dominions or principalities or powers. All things were created through Him and for Him.*
> (Colossians 1:16)

The next Scripture is rather conclusive in this connection:

> *Praise Him, all His angels;*
> *Praise Him, all His hosts!*
> *Praise Him, sun and moon;*
> *Praise Him, all you stars of light!*
> *Praise Him, you heavens of heavens,*
> *And you waters above the heavens!*
> *Let them praise the name of the LORD,*
> *For He commanded and they were created.*
> (Psalm 148:2-5)

In this creation of heavens and of earth and waters we have the creation of angels—in fact, they are mentioned first. Angels are a creation of God. That's the first thing we learn about their origin.

The second thing we find is that angels are invisible. That is, they are invisible as far as we are concerned. The passage in Colossians says that "by Him [the Lord Jesus] all things were created that are in heaven and that are on earth, visible and invisible." There are things that are seen and things that are not seen—angels come under the category of those which are not seen.

We have another Scripture along this same line:

> *. . . Who makes His angels spirits,*
> *His ministers a flame of fire.*
> (Psalm 104:4)

And we find it repeated in Hebrews 1:14 that His ministers are spirits. So it is clearly stated the angels are invisible.

We know now that angels are created of God and that they are invisible. We know something else about them from Scripture. They are higher than man. They were created before man, and they are a higher creature than we are. And, may I say, that would stand to reason, would it not? In this earth on which we live, we find a creation beneath us, the animal world; and since we have this creation beneath us, it's reasonable to conclude that there is a creation above us, you see.

Now I want you to notice several Scriptures which pertain to this.

> *What is man that You are mindful of him,*
> *And the son of man that You visit him?*
> *For You have made him a little lower than the angels,*
> *And You have crowned him with glory and honor.*
> (Psalm 8:4-5)

God has made the angels higher than man, or to put it like the psalmist did, man has been made a little *lower* than the angels. You may recall what was said to King David by the woman of Tekoa as recorded in 2 Samuel 14:20: "My lord is wise, according to the wisdom of the angel of God, to know everything that is in the earth." There was attributed to David a wisdom like the wisdom of an angel, which was quite a compliment.

It's interesting to note that after our Lord had been tempted by Satan in the wilderness, He was with the wild animals, and the angels ministered to Him (see Mark 1:13). We assume it's the angels alone who ministered to Him, but I believe that the animals did too. The animals were not there to hurt Him or harm Him in any way. You see, He was the One who recovered what Adam had lost. Adam was given dominion. And if you read the Genesis account very carefully, you will find out specifically that Adam was given control of the animals (Genesis 1:28; 2:19-20).

You talk about domesticated animals, well, this man Adam had control of all of them. And we go to the circus today and see somebody go into the lion's cage, and we see an old shaggy lion without any teeth jump through a hoop, and everybody applauds. Isn't that wonderful to make a lion jump through a hoop! Well, believe me, Adam had what we call wild animals outside his door, running around like pussy cats. They would not harm him at all. He had dominion. That's an important thing.

When man fell, friends, he lost something on this earth. Again, if you read very carefully in Genesis, you'll discover that before he disobeyed God, Adam had authority on this earth over the animals and perhaps over the weather. But he lost that in the Fall. In this day when we talk so much about scientific achievements and how far man has come and how he has conquered the forces of nature, it reminds me of the politician who came down from Washington years ago for the dedication of the third dam on the Colorado River. At this dedication the politician waxed very eloquent, declaring, "Man now has conquered the forces of nature!" Well, before he got back to Washington, we had a heavy rain, and it washed out all three dams!

May I say to you, man does not control the forces of nature, not yet. He's trying to, and I remember when they sent three planes out to try to detour a hurricane, but she had her own way, and she just kept going merrily on her way. Man does not control nature.

So our Lord was ministered to by the animals beneath Him as a man and by the angels which were above Him as a man.

Angels have great power. These two passages of Scripture mention the power of angels. First from the New Testament: ". . . whereas angels, who are greater in power and might [than man] . . ." (2 Peter 2:11). Then from the Old Testament: "Bless the LORD, you His angels, who excel in strength" (Psalm 103:20).

In spite of the fact that angels have great power, we are told specifically not to worship them. The apostle Paul wrote to the Colossian Christians:

Let no one cheat you of your reward, taking delight in false humility and worship of angels.
(Colossians 2:18)

You'll recall that John, on the Isle of Patmos, fell down to worship the angel who was so great and mighty and had revealed so much to him:

And I fell at his feet to worship him. But he said to me, "See that you do not do that! I am your fellow servant, and of your brethren who have the testimony of Jesus. Worship God!"
(Revelation 19:10)

In other words, "I worship God. You don't worship me at all." That is something, by the way, that is quite amazing. If we are not to worship angels, we certainly ought not to worship Mary or any other human being. If an angel appeared before us at this moment, we are not to fall down and worship that angel. In fact, if he was God's angel, he would forbid us to fall down and worship him.

Now there is something else that we need to say about the angels. There are a large number of them. The fact of the matter is, as far as we are concerned, I think they, like the stars, are almost numberless. And this is the impression the Word of God gives constantly concerning them:

> *But you have come to Mount Zion and to the city of the living God, the heavenly Jerusalem, to an innumerable company of angels.*
> (Hebrews 12:22)

"An innumerable company" means you can't number them—there are more than you can count. And you will recall the apostle John's experience recorded in Revelation:

> *Then I looked, and I heard the voice of many angels around the throne, the living creatures, and the elders; and the number of them was ten thousand times ten thousand, and thousands of thousands.*
> (Revelation 5:11)

John said that he saw angels around the throne and then he saw another great circle of them, and beyond them another and beyond them another and beyond them another. John finally finishes by saying, "And there were myriads and myriads of angels." Again, you could not count them, there were so many. They are also called in the Old Testament "the hosts of heaven." It's a term that would indicate a great army.

Now we want to know something else about them. They are sexless. Angel pictures showing a woman with wings are not pictures of any angel mentioned in the Word of God. Instead, the gender that is used in Scripture—ladies, forgive me—is masculine. If you are going to attach a gender to angels, it would have to be masculine. However, the reason the masculine word is used is because it is in the generic sense of mankind. *Anthropos* means man, and we get our word *anthropology* from it, but that does not denote that it means male. The angels, as our Lord said, neither marry nor are given in marriage (see Mark 12:25). As far as we know, they do not propagate themselves. We assume from Colossians 1:16-17 that the number never has increased nor decreased. There have always been the same number, and probably always will be the same number of angels.

Who Are Angels?

It is important to see the term *angel* used in other connections. The word *angel* applies actually to God on certain occasions. When you go back into the Book of Genesis, you will find the term *the Angel of Jehovah*. There was the appearance of the Angel of the LORD, or the Angel of Jehovah, to Hagar. Let me give some background first from Genesis 16:

> *Now Sarai, Abram's wife, had borne him no children. And she had an Egyptian maidservant whose name was Hagar. So Sarai said to Abram, "See now, the LORD has restrained me from bearing children. Please, go in to my maid; perhaps I shall obtain children by her." And Abram heeded the voice of Sarai. Then Sarai, Abram's wife, took Hagar her maid, the Egyptian, and gave her to her husband Abram to be his wife, after Abram had dwelt ten years in the land of Canaan. So he went in to Hagar, and she conceived. And when she saw that she had conceived, her mistress became despised in her eyes. Then Sarai said to Abram, "My wrong be upon you! I gave my maid into your embrace; and when she saw that she had conceived, I became despised in her eyes. The LORD judge between you and me." So Abram said to Sarai, "Indeed your maid is in your hand; do to her as you please." And when Sarai dealt harshly with her, she fled from her presence.*
> (Genesis 16:1-6)

We see now the ministry of the Angel of the LORD:

> *Now the Angel of the LORD found her by a spring of water in the wilderness, by the spring on the way to Shur. And He said, "Hagar, Sarai's maid, where have you come from, and where are you going?" She said, "I am fleeing from the presence of my mistress Sarai." The Angel of the LORD said to her, "Return to your mistress, and submit yourself under her hand."*
> (Genesis 16:7-9)

Then when Hagar's son was a teenager, they both were sent away from the home of Abraham.

> *And God heard the voice of the lad. Then the angel of God called to Hagar out of heaven, and said to her, "What ails you, Hagar? Fear not, for God has heard the voice of the lad where he is. Arise, lift up the lad and hold him with your hand, for I will make him a great nation." Then God opened her eyes, and she saw a well of water. And she went and filled the skin with water, and gave the lad a drink. So God was with the lad.*
> (Genesis 21:17-20)

The Angel of the LORD here, you see, is God, and many of us believe that the term *Angel of Jehovah* in the Old Testament is none other than the preincarnate Christ. However, I am not going to develop that particular theme now.

I want you to notice another connection in which the word *angel* is applied. Men are called angels. You will find this occurring in several different Scriptures, although we'll quote only one.

On one occasion John the Baptist sent two of his disciples as messengers with a question for Jesus. When it was answered to their satisfaction, the messengers returned to John with the answer.

*When the messengers of John had departed, He [Jesus] began
to speak to the multitudes concerning John: "What did you go
out into the wilderness to see? A reed shaken by the wind?"*
(Luke 7:24)

Now the thing I want you to notice is that the word for *messenger* here
is the Greek word *angelos*. And you could translate it, "When the
angels of John had departed," indicating that the word *angelos*, angel,
also applies to men. Let me give you some other Scripture references
that illustrate this: In James 2:25 the word is translated *messengers*,
and all of the salutations in chapters 2 and 3 of the Book of Revelation
are directed to the "angel of the church" in all seven churches. "To
the angel of the church in Ephesus write. . . . To the angel of the
church in Smyrna write . . ." and so on. Well, the angel is evidently
the pastor of the church, not a supernatural creature. And, of course,
I like it that way because it is the only place that you will find a
preacher called an angel, and I'm going to hold to that interpretation!
They call pastors other things sometimes.

There is something here that I want to dwell on for just a minute,
because this is rather important. The departed spirits of men have
been called angels. That is where the notion has arisen that we
become angels when we die. But a close examination of these Scriptures reveals that you couldn't press it to that point at all. Again, I'm
only going to make reference to these. Acts 12:15 refers to Peter's
having been put in prison and the angel freeing him. Keep in mind
how the angel ministered to Peter in that connection—opened the
prison doors and led him out of prison. Then Peter came to the place
where the church was assembled and knocked on the door. The
people inside were praying. Do you want to know the kind of faith
they had? It was like our faith. They did not believe God would let
Peter out of prison, yet they were praying for that! And when the little
maid came running in, saying, "Peter is at the door," they said, "Can't
be true. It must be his angel." And when they said "his angel," they
meant his spirit. And that is the way in which *angelos* is used.

Here is another example of *angel* referring to a person's spirit. Our Lord said:

> **Take heed that you do not despise one of these little ones, for I say to you that in heaven their angels always see the face of My Father who is in heaven.**
> (Matthew 18:10)

Their angels are their spirits which are always before God the Father. By the way, this is the passage that brutal parents ought to look at. Do you want to know whether a child who dies is saved or not? The spirit goes immediately into God's presence. How do you think God feels toward the one who sent the spirit of that little one into His presence? I think you may be able to get by with some things, but I would hate to be either a parent or any other person who killed or mistreated one of these little ones in a fit of anger. Our Lord says their angels (or spirits) are in the Father's presence always, and from 2 Corinthians 5:8 we can conclude that their spirits go to Him immediately when these children die. That very solemn Scripture in Matthew 18 probably should be given to some of these folk today, that is, if anything would impress a brutal and almost senseless person who would mistreat a little one like that.

Now, I want to be very careful here to give you another Scripture that shows that the departed spirits and the angels are not the same—that departed spirits do not become angels at all. I turn to Hebrews:

> **But you have come to Mount Zion and to the city of the living God, the heavenly Jerusalem, to an innumerable company of angels, to the general assembly and church of the firstborn who are registered in heaven, to God the Judge of all, to the spirits of just men made perfect.**
> (Hebrews 12:22-23)

These verses make it clear that the angels and the spirits of righteous men who have been brought into God's presence are separate. Departed spirits of people do not become angels.

Those are the three ways in which the term *angel* is used in Scripture that we need to note. They will keep us from getting detoured when we come to a passage and wonder what in the world the writer is talking about. It is quite clear that there are occasions when God was spoken of as an angel, when He appeared as an angel to man. And men, when they became messengers (like the disciples of John the Baptist), are called angels, or even the pastors of the churches in Revelation could be called angels. And on two occasions the word *angel* was used for departed spirits, first of children (Matthew 18:10) and then of Peter (Acts 12:15). But let me repeat, angels are not the departed spirits of people.

Where Are Angels?

Now I want you to notice something else that is rather striking. It would seem that the sphere in which the angels move is the second heaven. As you and I live here on earth we see above us the realm where the birds of heaven fly, which is the first heaven. The second heaven, the stellar spaces, seems to be the place where the angels are. And out beyond is the third heaven, the place to which the apostle Paul was caught up. I want you to notice several passages of Scripture in this connection. One is in Ephesians, speaking of the mighty power of God:

> *which He worked in Christ when He raised Him from the dead and seated Him at His right hand in the heavenly places, far above all principality and power and might and dominion, and every name that is named, not only in this age but also in that which is to come.*
> (Ephesians 1:20-21)

Paul is speaking of the place above where the angels are, for there are gradations of angels, as we're going to see. But when God raised our Lord from the dead He took Him, the resurrected Man, the glorified

Christ, back above and through the second heaven, the abode of the angels, clear back to the throne of God itself.

Now notice that the Epistle to the Hebrews also has something to say in this connection:

> *But we see Jesus, who was made a little lower than the angels, for the suffering of death crowned with glory and honor, that He, by the grace of God, might taste death for everyone.*
> (Hebrews 2:9)

You see, when Jesus came to this earth as a man He put Himself below the place of angels. Now this innumerable company had seen Him become the Angel of Jehovah in Old Testament times. And they probably were surprised to see Him leave His throne in heaven because He didn't do that very often. I'm confident that at His incarnation they did not know His mission since we're told in 1 Peter 1:12 that even today "angels desire to look into" these things. They were absolutely breathless—if angels can be breathless—when they saw Him descend through their host, come down to earth, and become a man!

I think that they are learning something about God even today, because Jesus left their sphere altogether, the stellar spaces, and came down to this earth and entered the human family as a baby. You and I have no notion of what was involved in the Lord Jesus Christ becoming a man. I wish an angel could come now and tell you something about how surprised they were. And they could tell you what humiliation it was for Him to become even an angel. But how much more to become one of us "worms"—and that's what we are in contrast to angels. Look at the little ant that's crawling around your home somewhere. Take a good look at it. Do you want to be one of them? Of course you don't. Do you think an angel wants to become one of us? He looks down at us and says, "Be a man? No, never!" He doesn't want to be a man any more than you and I want to be an ant. And when the angels saw Him, the mighty

Creator, leave heaven's glory and become a man, that to them was incomprehensible!

Will you notice just one more Scripture in this connection:

> *Seeing then that we have a great High Priest who has passed through the heavens, Jesus the Son of God. . . .*
> (Hebrews 4:14)

Jesus came down through the heavens, you see. And the picture is this: through the third heaven, the throne of God; through the second heaven, the stellar spaces; through the first heaven where the flying creatures move. They saw Him leave heaven's glory. Instead of becoming an angel, Jesus came all the way down through their habitation to this earth. He became a man. And when He had finished our redemption, He went back up there so that He might become our High Priest. Oh, my friend, we have Someone up there who is just like we are—He's a man, you see. The wonder of the incarnation of Christ is that you and I have Somebody in heaven who has lived through what we are going through. An angel does not understand us. He can't enter into our lives at all.

How Do Angels Relate?

What is the angel's relation to the earth and to the human family? I'll have to slight this, but let me mention some things. They desire to look into the gospel (1 Peter 1:12). They were present at the giving of the Law (Galatians 3:19). They were present at the birth of Christ—"a multitude of the heavenly host praising God" (Luke 2:9-14). I mentioned a moment ago an angel who freed Peter from prison. And an angel ministered to the exhausted Elijah when he was running for his life. The writer to the Hebrews says angels are "ministering spirits sent forth to minister for those who will inherit salvation" (Hebrews 1:14).

Let me say that at one time I believed this verse indicated that God has put an angel with every person whom He has created in this world, a guardian angel to watch over and guard us. I no longer hold that view. Right away somebody is going to say, "Doesn't it say here that the angels are going to minister to the heirs of salvation?" Let's read the verse like it is. The angels are going to minister to those "who *will* inherit salvation." This verse is looking forward to the time when God turns again to the nation Israel and to the gentile world—*after* the church is removed from earth. Notice that it does not say that the angels are ministering to those who are *right now* the heirs of salvation. You see, God is moving according to His program, and He has a purpose for everything He does.

Christ is the Son; angels are servants. Christ is King; angels are subjects. Christ is the Creator; angels are creatures. Christ at this moment is waiting until His enemies will be made His footstool. The Father never gave such a promise to an angel, but He says that someday His Son shall rule. This tremendous passage, Hebrews 1:5-14, sets before us the deity of the Lord Jesus Christ and the exaltation of the Lord Jesus Christ. He is higher than the angels. The Word of God does tell us that when the Lord Jesus returns to the earth, His holy angels are coming with Him. And, under His command, they are to war with the enemy.

When Did Some Angels Fall?

There was a fall of angels. They had a fall just as man had a fall, although theirs was different in many ways. When did it take place? I can make only a suggestion. We will go into more detail in the next chapter when we see how the archangel Lucifer became Satan. I hold the view that it took place between Genesis 1:1 and Genesis 1:2, when this earth became without form and void. It goes back to the sin of a great creature who with a third of the angelic hosts rebelled against God and was plunged to earth. There is apparently no redemption for them. And the reason there's no redemption for them is that each one was created as a free moral agent, and each one made his own decision. I think the final judgment of angels ought to make it clear that you would not want God to deal with the human family other than the way He arranged it in the Garden of Eden: that we were all in Adam, we all sinned in Adam, and Adam's sin has been made over to us. Since that is true, the righteousness of Christ can be made over to us, and we can now be a new creation in Jesus Christ. Otherwise, if we were like the angels, there would be no redemption for us when we should fall.

Also we're told that certain angels are reserved in chains:

> *For if God did not spare the angels who sinned, but cast them down to hell [tartarus] and delivered them into chains of darkness, to be reserved for judgment. . . .*
> (2 Peter 2:4)

> *And the angels who did not keep their proper domain, but left their own abode, He has reserved in everlasting chains under darkness for the judgment of the great day.*
> (Jude 6)

Apparently, when the angels fell, the sin of some of them was so great that they immediately were put in chains and are held for judgment.

Other angels are probably the demons that the Scriptures speak of. Those angels were never chained, and they are the emissaries of Satan today and still have a freedom. They are disembodied, but they want to be in a body. Why? That's a strange thing, but I think in the next chapter we can come to some conclusion on that.

Therefore there are two classes of angels, good angels and bad angels. There is a tremendous warfare going on between light and darkness, heaven and hell, God and Satan. That warfare is not confined to this little earth or to man. It's much bigger than this little earth. It reaches out yonder and touches the innumerable host of angelic creatures. In other words, God is resolving a great issue during this time in which you and I live.

How Do Angels Rank?

Now angels are in gradations of rank. They are arranged according to orders, and we see them mentioned this way in the Scriptures.

Michael is the archangel. He's the mighty one who stands for the children of Israel. He is mentioned in the Book of Daniel and again in the Book of the Revelation.

Gabriel is not an archangel. Gabriel is an angel who is apparently a special messenger for God. He came to Daniel to explain the vision of the end times which God had given him. He also announced the births of John the Baptist and our Lord Jesus Christ.

And the cherubim who protect the holiness of God were placed in the Garden of Eden. They did not use the sword to keep man out of the garden. Rather, they made a way for our first parents to return to God through the shed blood. Later in the tabernacle, cherubim fashioned of gold were placed over the mercy seat for that very reason. It is the same picture we saw in the Garden of Eden of cherubim looking down at the mercy seat.

The seraphim are seen in Isaiah 6:1-8. They are standing about the throne of God engaged in worship and service.

Then another is the Angel of Jehovah which we have referred to previously.

Now turning to Ephesians 1:21, notice that we are told of "all principality and power and might and dominion." These are gradations of angels.

Then you will find that the devil has his angels arranged in the same kind of order:

> *For we do not wrestle against flesh and blood, but against*
> *principalities, against powers, against the rulers of the darkness*

of this age, against spiritual hosts of wickedness in the heavenly
places.
(Ephesians 6:12)

These are also gradations, you see. Other armies have generals; we
have generals. Other armies have colonels; we have colonels. And
long before we thought of doing it, God had His angels arranged in
orders, and Satan had his arranged the same way. Apparently God
created them in different orders, and they function according to His
arrangement.

We have a fine example of how this works in the tenth chapter of
the Book of Daniel. Now you will notice Daniel is in prayer. By the
way, chapters 10, 11, and 12 constitute one vision, and it's probably
the most important vision in the Book of Daniel.

Daniel had been praying to God. And he says:

> **In those days I, Daniel, was mourning three full weeks.**
> (Daniel 10:2)

Why? Because he had been praying, and he was not getting an answer
to his prayers. This was unusual for Daniel, because when he prayed
he got an answer. But on this occasion he did not get an answer to
his prayers. So what happened? Well, he kept on praying and fasting
for three full weeks. Then an angel came to him.

> **Suddenly, a hand touched me, which made me tremble on my**
> **knees and on the palms of my hands.**
> (Daniel 10:10)

He's down on all fours.

> **And he said to me, "O Daniel, man greatly beloved, under-**
> **stand the words that I speak to you, and stand upright, for I**
> **have now been sent to you." While he was speaking this word**
> **to me, I stood trembling. Then he said to me, "Do not fear,**

> *Daniel, for from the first day that you set your heart to under-*
> *stand, and to humble yourself before your God, your words were*
> *heard; and I have come because of your words."*
> (Daniel 10:11-12)

I have a notion that Daniel would say, without being irreverent, "Well, where have you been for three weeks? If the first day I prayed you were sent, what has taken you so long?" The angel explains: "But the prince of the kingdom of Persia"—that's one of Satan's angels. Here we see God's angels and Satan's angels. One of them is called the prince of Persia. Now that's interesting! It throws a lot of light on the role of angels in the governments of the world. Satan apparently has an angel for every nation. God, I assume, has an angel to match for every nation. That's an interesting revelation, is it not?

Why did Satan want to withhold God's message from Daniel? Because this vision had something to do with Persia, and Satan didn't want it to get through to him.

> *But the prince of the kingdom of Persia withstood me twenty-*
> *one days.*
> (Daniel 10:13)

That was three weeks!

> *And behold, Michael, one of the chief princes, came to help*
> *me, for I had been left alone there with the kings of Persia.*
> (Daniel 10:13)

In other words, the angel's explanation was something like this: "When God sent me out on this mission, I had only the rank of a sergeant. And when I was bringing to you God's answer, the prince of Persia, Satan's general whom he had set over Persia, withstood me. For three weeks I couldn't get through to you. So I had to get reinforcements, and Michael the archangel came and moved him out of my way so that I could get through to you."

That throws a lot of light on what's happening today. Why are nations that historically reject the God of the Bible having successes in international affairs? Is it because this thing is satanic?

At last, after twenty-one days, the angel says:

> *Now I have come to make you understand what will happen to your people in the latter days, for the vision refers to many days yet to come.*
> (Daniel 10:14)

Why Are We Defeated?

My friend, you and I are so limited in our understanding, in our knowledge, and in our vision. We do not recognize the extent of evil and of this warfare between God and Satan. And today you and I are defeated so many times. Do you know why we are defeated? We are defeated because we don't recognize our enemy. Paul said to the Ephesians:

> *For we do not wrestle against flesh and blood.*
> (Ephesians 6:12)

And, friends, you and I are always fighting flesh and blood, aren't we? I wish the saints would quit fighting each other and quit being so negative. General Robert E. Lee one time found two of his lieutenants arguing with each other; in fact, they were ready to come to blows. General Lee stopped them, and he said, "The enemy's out yonder." We today need to recognize the enemy's out yonder.

There's a great spiritual warfare going on today. This is not superstition. Neither are we long-haired fanatics in saying this. There is something subtle that's going on in this warfare. And we are told to take the whole armor of God, because angels are involved in this. And the armor of God, a spiritual armor, is the only thing that's going to enable you and me to stand today. And the reason so many believers are being crushed is because they are not recognizing this.

> *Finally, my brethren, be strong in the Lord and in the power of His might. Put on the whole armor of God, that you may be able to stand against the wiles of the devil. For we do not wrestle against flesh and blood, but against principalities, against powers, against the rulers of the darkness of this age, against spiritual hosts of wickedness in the heavenly places. Therefore take up the whole armor of God, that you may be able to withstand in the evil day, and having done all, to stand. Stand therefore, having girded your waist with truth, having put on the breastplate of righteousness, and having shod your feet with the preparation of the gospel of peace; above all, taking the shield of faith with which you will be able to quench all the fiery darts of the wicked one. And take the helmet of salvation, and the sword of the Spirit, which is the word of God.*
> (Ephesians 6:10-17)

We also need to recognize this warfare in our prayer life. Have you ever wondered why your prayer life at times becomes so cold and so difficult? Do you find it difficult to pray? Is it easy for you to pray? May I say, it may not be difficult for you to say your prayers, but it's difficult to really lay hold of God in prayer because you've got enemies that will try to keep you from it:

> *. . . praying always with all prayer and supplication in the Spirit, being watchful to this end with all perseverance and supplication for all the saints . . . .*
> (Ephesians 6:18)

Oh, we need to come in the power of the Holy Spirit today. And knowing about angels is very practical in these days in which we live.

CHAPTER 7

SATAN: WHO IS HE?

This is one theme that I approach with mixed feelings. I want to avoid any superstitious and nonbiblical conceptions because there's so much abroad today concerning Satan that is not biblical. Yet I want to be realistic about it. I believe that Satan is a reality. He is a person, and I am convinced that he would like very much to see you skip this chapter. I've prayed more about the preparation of this study than any other in a long time because of that.

He is an enemy. I have never spoken on the subject of Satan when there wasn't something which interrupted in a way that tried to snatch away the seed of the Word that was sown. One thing is obvious: Satan does not want to be identified. Ignorance of his motives and his movements is his chief weapon today. He moves with all subtlety, which is the thing that characterizes him. This is the reason you see him as a serpent in the Garden of Eden. You will see him under different guises as you go through the Word of God. He does this because he does not want his true character to be known. He attempts to conceal that from man.

Let me repeat, ignorance of him is his chief weapon. And if you want to know how well he's done the job, you go out on the streets of your neighborhood shopping area and ask the people who go by for their opinions. Probably one out of ten would say they believe Satan is a reality. The other nine will think that he is merely a myth. I say that he has done a super job of making the average person believe he does not exist.

Paul could write in his day, "We are not ignorant of his devices" (2 Corinthians 2:11). Well, I do not think we can say that today. The average person *is* ignorant of his devices, and I believe even Christians today are not really on the alert. John says in Revelation 12:9 that Satan "deceives the *whole* world" (emphasis added). He is the one who is in the business of deception, and he has done a marvelous job at that.

Paul told the young preacher Timothy:

> *But evil men and impostors will grow worse and worse, deceiving and being deceived.*
> (2 Timothy 3:13)

They are going to deceive others because they are themselves the children of Satan, but in turn, they themselves will be deceived. The world outside, as you well know, is carrying on a racket, seeing who can take more advantage of the other, seeing who can deceive the other fellow. That is the satanic system that exists today. Paul, writing to the Corinthian believers and speaking of nonbelievers, said:

> *. . . whose minds the god of this age has blinded, who do not believe, lest the light of the gospel of the glory of Christ, who is the image of God, should shine on them.*
> (2 Corinthians 4:4)

Now Satan has done and continues doing a masterful job here. He has blinded the minds of multitudes concerning the gospel. That is the only subject on which he will blind the minds of people. Have you noticed that? The "god of this world," which is another name used for Satan, has blinded the minds of unbelievers so they will not believe the glorious gospel of Christ.

Actually, the human family is said to be imprisoned by Satan, so let's use this as an example. Here is a prison house, and it's absolutely invulnerable, you cannot get out any place. There is no way out except through this door—the Lord Jesus said, "I am the door," you see. The only way you get out is through Christ, and you cannot get out any other way.

Satan has a great many people thinking he is down on skid row. Do you think he is fooling around down there where they can't get out? I don't think so. Some think, *Well, he is out here where sin is flagrant.* No, he is not patrolling those areas—nobody is getting out there. The only place he is watching is the one place of escape, and that is through the gospel of Christ. And the only thing he is concerned about in your neighborhood and my neighborhood is that people be blinded to the gospel of Christ.

My friend, Satan has done a good job. I would estimate that last Sunday from 90 percent of the pulpits of Southern California the congregations were told to *do* something in order to get to heaven. Satan likes that—it's his so-called good news. He uses it in a very convincing manner. That is what he told Adam and Eve. He wanted to convince them that by doing what he said, they could become like God! He is telling folks all over the world, "Don't believe the Bible, you will be able to make it by your own efforts. You can do this yourself. You'll become as gods. Don't take the position that Christ shed His blood in order to redeem you. That's not aesthetic. You don't want this business of the gospel of the Cross." Oh, my friend, there is no other way! Jesus is the only way out, and here is where Satan blinds the human family.

I frankly believe that any preacher or any other person who declares the gospel of Christ is immediately under fire. That person is Satan's enemy. Satan uses every possible means to blind men's eyes to the gospel. He is supreme at this business of deception today.

Angels: Two Classes

First of all, we need to note that angels are divided into two classes, those who are obedient to God and those who belong to Satan. We are given that distinction in Revelation 12:7:

And war broke out in heaven: Michael and his angels fought with the dragon; and the dragon and his angels fought.

So we have here good angels and bad angels, God's angels and Satan's angels. And we see Michael who is called the archangel (Jude 9). I personally believe there are other archangels, but as far as we can tell, the holy angels are under Michael. Notice in Revelation 12 that Michael and his angels fought. He is opposed to Satan. Evidently, Satan was an archangel, and when he rebelled against God some unholy angels sided with him. Some of them are already reserved in chains for judgment:

And the angels who did not keep their proper domain, but left their own abode, He has reserved in everlasting chains under darkness for the judgment of the great day.
(Jude 6)

Others of them are called demons, which go about Satan's business. They have not yet been brought to judgment. Why God has made that distinction, I don't know. I suppose there are degrees of responsibility, even among angels, and therefore the responsibility is what made it impossible for some to have any outlet at all. They are reserved in chains.

The Person of Satan

Now when you come to the person of Satan, there are at least forty names given him in Scripture. For instance, you have four names in this one verse in Revelation:

So the great dragon was cast out, that serpent of old, called the Devil and Satan, who deceives the whole world; he was cast to the earth, and his angels were cast out with him.
(Revelation 12:9)

Notice that he's called "the old serpent"; and that, of course, here in the last book of the Bible, takes us back to Satan's first contact with man in the Garden of Eden, for he appeared there as the "shining one," so he is called the "old serpent."

He is also called "the devil," which is the Greek word *diabolos*, meaning *slanderer* or *accuser*. Keep that in mind because it has something to do with his present work, and apparently it also has had something to do with his entire career.

He's also called "Satan," which means *adversary*. He is the awful adversary of God, and he is the adversary of all God's children. We're told:

Be sober, be vigilant; because your adversary the devil walks about like a roaring lion, seeking whom he may devour.
(1 Peter 5:8)

Even there, you see three titles given to him.

Satan is called "the accuser of our brethren" in Revelation 12:10. He is called "Apollyon" in Revelation 9:11, which means "destroyer." He is called "Belial" in 2 Corinthians 6:15, meaning "worthless" or "lawless." He is called "the evil one." You remember that when our Lord taught His disciples to pray, He included "Deliver us from the evil one," which should serve as a warning. And then again Jesus Christ Himself, when He prayed the real Lord's prayer—that is, His own petition to the Father—said:

I do not pray that You should take them out of the world, but that You should keep them from the evil one.
(John 17:15)

Satan is also called "Beelzebub" in Mark 3:22, where the scribes accused Christ of casting out demons by Beelzebub, the prince or ruler of the demons.

These are just some of Satan's names and titles. We won't be going into detail concerning them, though it's a very interesting study in and of itself.

Now this creature known as Satan has the unique distinction of being the originator and the promoter of evil. It is a gross assumption and entirely inaccurate to ascribe grotesque physical forms to Satan. Most of what people envision today, for instance, is Satan as a creature with horns, a forked tail, and cloven feet, which comes from the literature of the Middle Ages. Its origin is Greek mythology and is the description of the god Pan, or Bacchus, the god of pleasure. All of this has shaped the thinking of Christendom concerning Satan more than the Bible has, and it's well to get back to the Word of God and see what God really has to say about him.

Satan is a personality, definitely a personality. You will remember that our Lord, addressing the scribes and Pharisees, said:

> *You are of your father the devil, and the desires of your father you want to do. He was a murderer from the beginning, and does not stand in the truth, because there is no truth in him. When he speaks a lie, he speaks from his own resources, for he is a liar and the father of it.*
> (John 8:44)

This is the way Scripture speaks of Satan. Note that our Lord refers to him definitely as a person, a liar, and a murderer.

Let me repeat this verse:

> *Be sober, be vigilant; because your adversary the devil walks about like a roaring lion, seeking whom he may devour.*
> (1 Peter 5:8)

"Satan," someone has said, "is to be dreaded as a lion; he is more to be dreaded as a serpent; and he is most to be dreaded as an angel." That's the difficulty. We think of him as being a frightful, fearful being. But he was not created a frightful creature. In fact, 2 Corinthians 11:14 tells us that Satan "transforms himself into an angel of light," and if you could see him, you would agree that he is the most beautiful creature you've ever seen. One of the reasons sin is attractive is because Satan is attractive. This idea today that he represents the seamy side of life is not true. He's very much concerned about the things of culture and refinement. He is right in the midst of the things which today are considered the best things in life. And you do not have to go down to skid row to find him at work.

The Origin of Satan

Let's turn back to the Old Testament and see the origin of this evil one. The passage that deals with this is Ezekiel 28. It is a remarkable revelation, and I want us to look at this carefully because here we have the origin of this evil creature.

In this passage, beginning with verse 11, we see Satan behind the king of Tyre. Tyre was the great commercial center. Tyre represents the final Babylon which God will destroy because it is satanic. Notice this:

> *Moreover the word of the LORD came to me, saying, "Son of man, take up a lamentation for the king of Tyre, and say to him. . . ."*

The things that follow could never apply to a human king of Tyre, but they do apply to the one who is behind him. This angel is the highest creature God ever created.

Notice what God Himself says about Satan:

> *Thus says the Lord GOD:*
> *"You were the seal of perfection,*
> *Full of wisdom and perfect in beauty."*
> (Ezekiel 28:12)

Satan was the wisest creature God ever created. No other angel, no other being, was ever created with the intelligence that God gave to this one. He was the seal of perfection, full of wisdom and perfect in beauty. And when God says "perfect in beauty," I can't even imagine what that would be. This creature is today the highest being this side of God. And, thank God, he is not God but only a creature. It would be frightful if he were anything but a creature. However, as a creature compared to you and me, we are no match for him at all.

Billy Sunday made quite an issue of "fighting the devil." But, of course, even Billy Sunday knew he could not fight the devil. You and I cannot fight him. We are told to *resist* him. And in Ephesians 6 we're told to put on the whole armor of God and to *stand*, as we shall see. We are never told to fight. He could overcome you, he could overcome me at any moment he wanted to. Were it not for the grace of God today you and I would be absolutely crushed by him. I have a notion he has more to do with your life than you think he does. He has plenty to do with the lives of believers because he hates believers. By the way, communism certainly must have been spawned in the very atmosphere of Satan, for it's so much like his methods.

Now will you notice the things that are said concerning Satan in Ezekiel 28: "You were in Eden, the garden of God." This is not the Garden of Eden that Adam and Eve were in, although Satan had also been there, but this is a different kind of Eden.

> *You were in Eden, the garden of God;*
> *Every precious stone was your covering:*
> *The sardius, topaz, and diamond,*
> *Beryl, onyx, and jasper,*
> *Sapphire, turquoise, and emerald with gold. . . .*
> (Ezekiel 28:13)

Stop there for a moment. These jewels are found in only two other places. They are in the garments of the high priest, in his breastplate (Exodus 28:15-20). And you'll find them garnishing the foundations of the walls in the New Jerusalem (Revelation 21:18-21). Here in Ezekiel we see this creature covered with all of these precious stones representing that which is highest and *heavenly*.

This gives you some concept of his beauty. And notice this:

> *The workmanship of your timbrels and pipes*
> *Was prepared for you on the day you were created.*
> (Ezekiel 28:13)

He was created an instrument of music, if you please! He didn't carry around a musical instrument, he *was* a musical instrument—perhaps like a mighty pipe organ. Now can you imagine that kind of music, my friend, compared with some of the things we hear in our day which are classified as music? Can you imagine the effect that this creature would have upon all of God's intelligences? He is a walking symphony, and he is perfect in wisdom and perfect in beauty!

That's not all—"You were the anointed cherub" (v. 14). So you see that we're not talking about a man. The word *cherub* is the singular of cherubim. Cherubim are symbolic of God's holy presence and unapproachable majesty. They are celestial beings who guard and vindicate the righteousness of God. Satan was one of the cherubim. Now whether there were others equal to him, I don't know. I assume that all the cherubim are on the same par, but this one—"You were the anointed cherub who covers" (Ezekiel 28:14)—occupied a unique position.

Now, "the anointed cherub who covers" is the picture given to us in the Garden of Eden after Adam and Eve had been sent out of the garden, and God placed the cherubim to guard the way to the tree of life. They were protecting that way of life so that man could come to God, so he would not be destroyed by the holiness of God nor be judged by God. And further on in history, when Moses made the mercy seat and placed it in the tabernacle's Holy of Holies, God's glory dwelt between the cherubim. The cherubim covered it (Exodus 25:20).

Satan was a cherub. And his position was to guard the very throne of God in heaven. He looked down upon it as those cherubim looked down upon the mercy seat in the tabernacle. His position was that of protecting the holiness of God. Satan had occupied this highest of all positions!

And will you notice:

> *You were the anointed cherub who covers;*
> *I established you;*
> *You were on the holy mountain of God;*
> *You walked back and forth in the midst of fiery stones.*
> (Ezekiel 28:14)

This is an Eden, not of green grass and trees and animals, but of stones, *beautiful* stones, if you please.

Now notice this very interesting verse:

> *You were perfect in your ways from the day you were created,*
> *Till iniquity was found in you.*
> (Ezekiel 28:15)

Imagine this highest of God's creatures, perfect in wisdom, beautiful beyond description—there is no way in the world for us today as human beings to conceive of the beauty of this creature—given this high, exalted position, and a musician to top off all that!

But this creature with all of these attributes also had a free will. God had created him, as He did the angels, with a free will—these created intelligences could make a choice. One day God said to this marvelous creature, "Iniquity was found in you" (Ezekiel 28:15).

What Did He Do?

What kind of iniquity could be found in him? Was he going out at night and getting drunk? What was this covering cherub doing? In the Book of Ezekiel God has let us stand with Him at the very beginning, to see the origin, the creation of Satan. But in the Book of Isaiah God lets us see his character.

Now let's look at this creature. What was it he did? What was his sin when iniquity was found in him? He must have done something horrible! Do you suppose he murdered? We could get the FBI on the case and find out if he's guilty of murder or kidnapping or something like that. But, friends, he's not guilty of those things.

> *How you are fallen from heaven,*
> *O Lucifer, son of the morning!*
> (Isaiah 14:12)

He's an angel of light. He is Lucifer. When the sons of God shouted for joy at the creation, Satan was there to shout for joy also, the hypocrite! He was a liar from the beginning. Oh, that same thing is in the human heart. Will you notice it?

> *O Lucifer, son of the morning!*
> *How you are cut down to the ground,*
> *You who weakened the nations!*
> (Isaiah 14:12)

He weakens the nations. He is certainly weakening America today! Now we are going to find out his iniquity. Notice his five "I wills" here:

> *For you have said in your heart:*
> *"I will ascend into heaven,*
> *I will exalt my throne above the stars of God;*
> *I will also sit on the mount of the congregation*
> *On the farthest sides of the north;*
> *I will ascend above the heights of the clouds,*
> *I will be like the Most High."*
> (Isaiah 14:13-14)

"I will go down to *hell*." What? Is that what he said? That's not the direction he wants to go! If you think he's interested in hell, you are wrong. He hasn't been there yet, and he doesn't want to go there. He will resist it until the very end. What he actually said was, "I will ascend into *heaven*." He is mighty interested in that direction.

Listen to his second "I will." "I will exalt my throne above the stars of God—I am going to take over." After all, he is perfect in wisdom and beauty. He has a tremendous following, and he's done some snooping around. Oh, the human heart is like Satan! I suppose he began by stirring up discontent among the angels, approaching them like this: "How do you feel about the way things are being run here? Are you satisfied with your job? Wouldn't you like to have a higher position? Don't you think that you're being a little excluded?" That is the tactic Satan used with Adam and Eve.

Now you may not believe that such a thing could be done in heaven. Well, human beings do that, and they do it right in the church. Anyone on a church staff can tell you about that. Sometimes somebody will take a member of the church staff out to lunch and in the course of the conversation ask, "How do you feel about the pastor?" He is seeing if he can run a wedge in between the pastor and the church staff.

You know, Satan is really clever. He gets into the churches—in fact, he goes to church every Sunday and he majors in sowing discord. He may cause you to feel neglected and unappreciated. Oh, how subtle that is. And how satanic it is! That is a lie which began in heaven among the angels—maybe something like this: "Wouldn't you like to have a better position? I'm thinking about setting up a little kingdom of my own, and I've got you in mind for prime minister. God hasn't given you the chance here that He should have given you. You were created for something better, yet He won't give it to you, and I don't know why He doesn't. But I'll give it to you. I'm making plans to lead a rebellion. Would you like to come with me?"

Again, how subtle! Some of the angels fell for that! You say, "How could intelligent angels fall for that?" Well, I know intelligent human beings today who fall for the same thing! It's satanic, my friend, and this thing does get into the church.

You know, we think the devil is at work when people get into sin, gross sin, or get drunk or steal something. No! They sit in the pew as pious as you please, and they sow seeds of rebellion. That's satanic, that's the way he moves. And you're no better than they are if you listen to them, because the angels who listened to Satan went with him. And in the book of Revelation we are told that Satan took a third of the angels with him when he rebelled. Think of that! A lot of them felt they could get by with it.

Now you may think that Satan's tactics do not work. They worked in the Garden of Eden. And you think they don't work today? You go to the smart men you know, the ones with the high I.Q.s, and they will tell you that they are smart enough to get what they want by themselves—they don't need God. It is the lie of Satan today that you can work out your own salvation, that you're smarter than anyone's given you credit for. All of us want a status symbol of some sort, and we all like to feel that we really are somebody. But when God saves you, He takes you as a nobody. And that's the reason it's not the popular way today. But, friends, it is God's way.

Notice again the "I wills" of Satan. Oh, this is subtle, it's satanic:

> *For you have said in your heart:*
> *"I will ascend into heaven,*
> *I will exalt my throne above the stars of God;*
> *I will also sit on the mount of the congregation*
> *On the farthest sides of the north;*
> *I will ascend above the heights of the clouds,*
> *I will be like the Most High."*
> (Isaiah 14:13-14)

What? The devil did not want to be the devil, he wanted to be God! "I will be like the Most High." But still a great many people think that the devil wants to be the devil. He does not. That's why he led a rebellion against God. And that's the thing he told Adam and Eve—"You will be like God, knowing good and evil" (Genesis 3:5). There are a lot of people who believe that they are good enough for God's heaven. Well, that's Satan's lie, my friend! They have no notion of what the holiness of God is.

Now in the final analysis, what is sin? We have seen the entrance of sin through Satan. He was setting his will against the will of God. *Anything* that is contrary to the will and character of God is sin. Murder is sin, not just because God says it is, but because it is contrary to the will and character of God.

Satan said in substance, "I'm not interested in this job of being the covering cherub. I know I'm the highest creature, but after all, I think I'm pretty enough and I'm wise enough and I'm smart enough and I'm good enough to be God. And I want to be God!" That's what he said to the Lord Jesus in Matthew 4:9, "If you fall down and worship me, I'll give You all the kingdoms of the world." That's what he wants and what he is after.

Oh, that's what so many people are after today—position, power, prestige, status. Things of the world system. Imagine little, puffed-up creature-man who says to God, "I won't do what You want me to do. I am going to do it *my* way." That is exactly what man is saying today. Well, friend, you are not going to do things your way, because God's will is going to prevail in the final analysis.

Therefore, the prayer of all God's people should be "Your will be done / On earth as it is in heaven" (Matthew 6:10). Anything contrary to His will is sin, regardless of what it is.

> *There is a way that seems right to a man,*
> *But its end is the way of death.*
> (Proverbs 14:12)

Mankind sets his will against the will of God.

The will of God is coming down through this world and through His universe like a tremendous steamroller. And any creature that gets in the way of the will of God will be crushed, because God's will must prevail. And anything contrary to that is sin. The sin of Satan was that he set his will against the will of God.

> *All we like sheep have gone astray;*
> *We have turned, every one, to his own way.*
> (Isaiah 53:6)

That's what sin is, basically. What is it that you want above everything else? "My way." Isn't that right? That's all that a human being wants—my way. Oh, my friend, you and I are sinners as long as we put our will against the will of God.

Now will you notice this: The cosmos, the earth, is the place where Satan today has control, and he does have charge of it. When he rebelled against God, he no longer occupied his position, but that's all he has lost. Satan has access to heaven today, as the Book of Job reveals. We find him going into the presence of God, and not an angel turned and said, "What are you doing here?" Nobody said, "You have no business here." He went there because he had a right to be there.

Not only does he have the right to be there, God may give him the right to test us. Our Lord said to Peter in Luke 22:31, "Satan has desired to have you that he might test you." Satan followed the same pattern he had used in Job's case. He went into God's presence and said, "Does Job fear You for nothing? That fellow Job, just give me a chance at him and I will show You that I can make him curse You to Your face!" (Job 1:9-11). And he got a chance at him, if you please. It was terrible what he did to Job.

When the apostle Peter was a target, I think Satan said to the Lord, "You take that fellow Simon Peter. Do You mean to tell me You've called him as an apostle? I know him as well as You know him. I've been watching him, and I can wreck him if You'll just let me get to him." And God permitted it. God said, "I'll let you have him, but only for a little while." Believe me, the time Peter was in the hands of Satan, he certainly was sifted, sifted like grain, was he not? And the experience was tragic for Simon Peter. Satan made him do a dastardly thing—deny his Lord, a thing that he regretted the rest of his life, of course.

___

His Influence in the Cosmos

Satan apparently lost this earth, but he gained it back when man fell. And he is called, if you please, "the god of this world." He's the prince of this world. You may recall how Jesus, at the beginning of His ministry, was tempted or tested by Satan:

> *Then the devil, taking Him up on a high mountain, showed Him all the kingdoms of the world in a moment of time. And the devil said to Him, "All this authority I will give You, and their glory; for this has been delivered to me, and I give it to whomever I wish. Therefore, if You will worship before me, all will be Yours."*
> (Luke 4:5-7)

The fall of man was Satan's gain. He gained the dominion that man lost, so that he is the prince of this world in which we live. Now when we say *the world*, we're not talking about the soil down here, although there's a curse upon it. Terra firma is not Satan's. The world we're talking about is a system, a cosmos, and that is the word used in Scripture. I want to bundle together a whole lot of Scriptures that I hope will help you see what we're talking about now. The cosmos is that which Satan controls today.

Our Lord Jesus said:

> *Now is the judgment of this world; now the ruler [the prince] of this world will be cast out.*
> (John 12:31)

Jesus was looking to the future there, but regarding the prince of this world, this cosmos, Jesus said:

> *I will no longer talk much with you, for the ruler* [the prince]
> *of this world is coming, and he has nothing in Me.*
> (John 14:30)

The prince of this world is Satan.

And John 16:11 says the Holy Spirit will convict the world

> *of judgment, because the ruler* [prince] *of this world is judged.*

Satan is called the prince of the power of the air. He is also called the god of this world.

To the church in Pergamos the Lord Jesus says, "I know your works, and where you dwell, where Satan's throne is" (Revelation 2:13). Satan reigns on this earth today. He controls the system that is known as the world system. But our Lord also says:

> *You are of God, little children, and have overcome them,*
> *because He who is in you is greater than he who is in the world.*
> (1 John 4:4)

And 1 John 5:19 says:

> *We know that we are of God, and the whole world* [the
> cosmos] *lies under the sway of the wicked one.*

In other words, the whole world lies asleep in the lap of the wicked one. And today, this world system is under the control of Satan. That's the reason countries can't have peace. That's the reason the United Nations is not effective. That's the reason for the turmoil on the face of the earth right now. Few of our world rulers today take Satan into consideration, although some have done so in the past. The thing that made certain statesmen in England great is the fact that in their day they not only believed in God and believed in Christ and trusted Him, but they also believed that the devil was a reality, in control of this world system, and that he must be taken into consideration.

Will you notice the admonition of James 4:4:

> *Adulterers and adulteresses! Do you not know that friendship with the world is enmity with God? Whoever therefore wants to be a friend of the world makes himself an enemy of God.*

First John 5:4 says: "For whatever is born of God overcomes the world [the world system]." The Lord Jesus said to His disciples, "I will no longer talk much with you, for the ruler of this world [Satan] is coming" (John 14:30). And 1 John 4:3:

> *And every spirit that does not confess that Jesus Christ has come in the flesh is not of God. And this is the spirit of the Antichrist, which you have heard was coming, and is now already in the world [system].*

Oh my, there are so many other Scriptures regarding this world system.

My friend, what I am going to say now applies to wherever you live, but I'll use Los Angeles as an example. Southern California is a lovely place, but how do you as a Christian look on it? We have fine museums and art galleries in Southern California. There are wonderful places of culture and refinement and great seats of education. How do you look at those? I am saying this carefully now: All of that is part of the cosmos, a world system under Satan's control. And all of that is *judged*. God has condemned it, and it will be going down with Satan when he goes down. How do *you* look upon it? So many Christians think, *If I just don't do this and I don't do a few other little things, that makes me a nice, spiritual Christian,* when in reality you may be as worldly as you can be, and Satan is leading you around by the nose. Why? Because of your attitude and relationship to this world system that we're in today. Paul says we should live like this:

> *. . . those who weep as though they did not weep, those who rejoice as though they did not rejoice, those who buy as though they did not possess.*
> (1 Corinthians 7:30)

"Those who weep, as though they did not weep." Are you going to let some sorrow, some tragedy in your life keep you from serving God? "Those who rejoice as though they did not rejoice." Are you going to let pleasure take the place of your relationship to God, as many do? "Those who buy as though they did not possess." Will you let your business take the place of God? Many a man has made business his god. Paul continues:

> *. . . and those who use this world as not misusing it. For the form of this world is passing away.*
> (1 Corinthians 7:31)

We're in it.

As a pastor I once walked all over Nashville, Tennessee, with a visiting evangelist, because he would not eat where they served beer. So we walked and then drove up one street and down another, and we could not find a place open. Finally we found one, and I said, "Now look here, brother, I'm hungry, you're hungry, I don't drink beer, I hope you don't drink beer, let's go in and *eat!*" This business today of thinking, *Well, if I just don't do this or that, I am a spiritual person.* Oh, that makes us nothing in the world but spiritual snobs—not even knowing what this world system is.

How do you look upon things of this world? Suppose tonight the city of Los Angeles would go up in smoke—and it may very well go up in smoke! Would it break your heart? Are you so wrapped up in this world system, in your business, and in your social life that, if it all were taken out from under you as a Christian today, your heart would be broken? God have mercy on you, because it's going to be taken away from you someday. It is going to disappear. Paul says these things are passing away, and God is going to judge them. And when God judges Satan, it includes all of this world system.

His Influence in Spiritual Warfare

My friend, you and I are in a war, in a conflict, and we are given these instructions. This is mentioned to us at least three times, by the way: Ephesians 6:11—get your armor on and keep it on! James 4:7—submit to God before you try to resist the devil. And 1 Peter 5:8—be watchful because the enemy is stalking you like a hungry lion!

> *For we do not wrestle against flesh and blood, but against principalities, against powers, against the rulers of the darkness of this age, against spiritual hosts of wickedness in the heavenly places.*
> (Ephesians 6:12)

Can you overcome it? No, you can't. You and I are no match for it today. What are we to do? Well, we as believers are given detailed instructions as to what we're to do. We are to "put on the whole armor of God." To fight? No sir, not to fight, because you and I are not going to be able to fight. He says, "And having done all, to stand."

> *Therefore take up the whole armor of God, that you may be able to withstand in the evil day, and having done all, to stand.*
> (Ephesians 6:13)

There is a demonic world around us and it is manifesting itself at the present hour. If I had said this when I was a young preacher, many would not have believed it. Or they would have said as did one dear lady, "Dr. McGee, you sound positively spooky." Today, however, demonism is a popular subject and is plainly exhibited. There is a Church of Satan in many of our cities. There are strange things happening within certain of these weird, way-out groups. A man said to me recently, "Dr. McGee, this thing is *real* today." Who said it wasn't real? If you are an unbeliever in this area, open your eyes and see what is happening about us. People are being ensnared and led into all kinds of demonism. There are spiritual forces working in the world, evil forces working against the church. They are working against the believer, against God, against Christ.

We have the enemy located and identified. The enemy is spiritual. It is Satan who heads up his demonic forces. Now we need to recognize where the battle is. Paul identifies the arsenal which is available for the defense. Nowhere is the believer urged to attack and advance. The key to this entire section in Ephesians is the phrase "to stand."

This is an hour when my heart is sick as I see the attendance way down and the interest gone in churches that at one time were great churches. The members were blind to the fact that a battle was being fought there, a spiritual battle.

Winning the War

Do you pray for your pastor on Saturday night? Don't criticize him, but rather *pray* for him. He needs your prayers. The devil gives him enough opposition. You don't need to join the crowd that crucifies the man who is preaching the Word of God. You ought to uphold his hands as Aaron and Hur upheld the hands of Moses on behalf of Israel. My heart goes out to pastors who are in need of congregations who will stand with them.

Stand therefore, having girded your waist with truth, having put on the breastplate of righteousness, and having shod your feet with the preparation of the gospel of peace.
(Ephesians 6:14-15)

"Stand therefore." This is the fourth time Paul has given this exhortation to the believer. This is the only place that I find him laying it on the line and speaking like a sergeant. Earlier he said, "I beseech you," but now he gives the command to stand. Not only are we to be in a standing position, but we are also to have on certain armor to protect ourselves. We are not to be outwitted by the wiles of the devil; we are to be ready for his attacks.

"Having girded your waist with truth." In the ancient garment of that day, the girdle about the waist or loins held in place every other part of the uniform of the soldier. It was essential. To tell you the truth, if the girdle was lost, you lost everything. The garments would fly open and the pants would fall down. We see this routine in comedies, and people laugh to see a man trying to run or fight with his trousers drooping. It looks funny in a comedy routine, but it is not funny in a battle. We are told to be girded with truth in the face of the enemy. Truth is that which holds everything together. What is that truth? It is the Word of God. We need people to give out the Word of God and to give it out just as it is written. We need people whose loins are girt about with truth. They need to *know* the Word of God. We often hear preaching coming from folks who are standing there about to lose all their spiritual garments! They are not girded about with truth, which is the Word of God.

Every piece of this armor really speaks of Christ. We are in Christ in the heavenlies, and we should put on Christ down here in our earthly walk. Paul has already told us to put on Christ, the One who is the truth, and we should be diligent to put Him on in our lives.

Any testimony that does not glorify Jesus Christ should not be given. There are too many testimonies that glorify self. Jesus didn't get very much when He got you, and He didn't get very much when He got me. This is a day when the little fellow really does not have very much to say. We get the impression that we need to be someone great in the eyes of the world. But what we need is to have our loins girt about with truth so that we can give a testimony that glorifies Christ. Christ is the truth. Truth alone can meet error.

"Having put on the breastplate of righteousness." Christ is the righteousness of the believer. I do think, however, that it includes the practical righteousness of the believer. Let's be clear that the filthy rags of self-righteousness are useless as a breastplate, but I do think that underneath there should be a heart and a conscience that are right with God. Only the righteousness of Christ can enable the believer to stand before men and before God, but the heart that is to be protected should be a heart that is clean before the Lord. It is an awful condition to have sin in our lives while we are trying to carry on the battle. We can never win it that way.

"Having shod your feet with the preparation of the gospel of peace." Shoes are necessary for standing. They speak of the foundation. We need a good, solid foundation, and preparation is foundational. I remember in hand-to-hand combat we were taught to make sure our feet were anchored. Are your feet anchored on the Rock? Christ is your foundation in this world. We are to put on Christ. Oh, how we need Him today as we face a gainsaying world and spiritual wickedness in the darkness of this world!

> *Above all, taking the shield of faith with which you will be able to quench all the fiery darts of the wicked one. And take the helmet of salvation, and the sword of the Spirit, which is the word of God; praying always with all prayer and supplication in the Spirit, being watchful to this end with all perseverance and supplication for all the saints.*
> (Ephesians 6:16-18)

The armor of the believer is a spiritual armor because we fight against a spiritual enemy. We are to stand in that armor, and that armor is Christ, the living Christ. Satan himself, in the Book of Job, describes how God protects His own. He said:

> *Have You not made a hedge around him [Job], around his*
> *household, and around all that he has on every side?*
> (Job 1:10)

God has provided protection for us today in the armor He supplies.

"Above all, [take] the shield of faith." The shield covered all of the armor. The shield referred to is a large shield the size of a door. It was the shield of Greece's heavy infantry. A soldier stood behind it and was fully protected. Christ is both the door to salvation and the door that protects the believer from the enemy without. This is the picture in John, chapter 10. Christ is both salvation and security.

Faith enables us to enter the door:

> *I am the door. If anyone enters by Me, he will be saved, and*
> *will go in and out and find pasture.*
> (John 10:9)

That is salvation. What about security? Faith places us securely in His hands. Faith also enables us to stand behind that shield which will quench all the fiery darts of the wicked one.

"The fiery darts of the wicked one." He is shooting them fast and furiously. I remember that when I was in college, I had a brilliant philosophy professor who had studied in Germany. I respected his intellect, although I did not realize at the time that he was intellectually dishonest. I looked up to him but, very frankly, he was taking my feet out from under me. I would try to answer him in class when I probably should have kept my mouth shut. But we became friends, and we used to walk together across the campus after class and discuss the questions I had raised. It became clear that his philosophies opposed the Word of truth. Discouraged, I came to the place where I went to the Lord in prayer and said, "Lord, if I can't believe Your Word, I don't want to go into the ministry." Then the Lord in a very miraculous way sent me to hear a man who was the most brilliant man, I think, I have ever heard. He gave me truthful answers to my questions. Then I began to learn that when a fiery dart comes my way and I do not have the answer, I am to put up the shield of faith. And this is what I have been doing ever since. I have found that the shield of faith has batted down the fiery darts of the wicked one.

The fiery darts come fast and furiously, and they are going to continue to come. The only thing that will bat them down is the shield of faith. It is like a big door. The hoplites, the heavily armed soldiers in the Greek infantry, could move with those tremendous shields, put them out in front of them, and stand protected shoulder to shoulder while the enemy shot everything they had at them. When the enemy was out of ammunition, the hoplites would move in, certain of victory. That is the way to stand against the fiery darts of the evil one.

"And take the helmet of salvation." The helmet protects the head, and God does appeal to the mind of man. I recognize that He appeals to the heart, but God also appeals to the intellect. Throughout the Scriptures God urges man to think, for example:

> *"Come now, and let us reason together,"*
> *Says the LORD,*
> *"Though your sins are like scarlet,*
> *They shall be as white as snow;*
> *Though they are red like crimson,*
> *They shall be as wool."*
> (Isaiah 1:18)

Paul mentions this helmet in connection with salvation again in another epistle.

> *But let us who are of the day be sober, putting on the breastplate of faith and love, and as a helmet the hope of salvation.*
> (1 Thessalonians 5:8)

All the parts of the armor mentioned so far have been for defense. Have you noticed that? Everything is for the front of the individual. There is no protection for his back; nothing is provided for retreat. Believe me, a retreating Christian is certainly open season for the enemy; the enemy can get through to him.

Now we have two weapons for offense. The first one is the Word of God, called "the sword of the Spirit." Christ is the living Word of God. He used the Word of God to meet Satan in the hour of His temptation. Out of His mouth goes a sharp, two-edged sword in the Battle of Armageddon (see Revelation 1:16 and 19:21). He gains the victory with that sword. What is it? It is the Word of God. We need that sharp sword going out of our mouths today. The Word of God is a powerful weapon of offense. You and I are to use it.

Our second weapon of offense is prayer—"praying always with all prayer and supplication in the Spirit." Praying in the Holy Spirit is not turning in a grocery list to God. It means that you and I recognize our enemy and that we lay hold of God for spiritual resources. We lay hold of God for that which is spiritual, that we might be filled with all the fullness of God. Paul here distinguishes between prayer and supplication. Prayer is general; supplication is specific. All effective prayer must be in the Spirit.

If you are able to stand firm in this world today, that's all God is asking you to do. He is not asking you to fight the devil. He is not asking you to do some great thing. He is only asking you to stand. Remember the prayer of our Lord in John 17:15, "I do not pray that You should take them out of the world, but that You should keep them from the evil one."

I never get through a day that I don't get home and get in bed and say, "Thank You, Lord, for getting me by the devil's trap again today." My friend, Satan is setting a trap for you and me all the time, and he's attempting to ensnare us. In this hour in which we live it is tragic to see many true believers being taken in by him in many subtle and unsuspecting ways. We ought not to be ignorant of his devices. We need to put on God's complete armor. We need to be on the alert, because Satan is loose in the world today.

> *Be sober, be vigilant; because your adversary the devil walks about like a roaring lion, seeking whom he may devour.*
> (1 Peter 5:8)

If you think Satan will show mercy to you, you are dead wrong. If he gets you in a corner, my friend, and if you leave off the armor of God, he'll destroy you in a minute. And he has destroyed many good men. He can ruin your testimony. He can absolutely ruin your life if you don't wear the whole armor of God so that you might be able to stand.

I'm afraid that Christians today take life a little too lightly and easily. You know, our forefathers thought life was serious. And they thought how they lived was very important. And, my friend, they did not crack up like we're cracking up today. What is it that's happening in this world right now? It's impossible to explain what is happening in every country right now, apart from this creature.

Thank God, Satan will be judged someday. God's going to get rid of him. God's going to destroy him. God's going to put him in the lake of fire. But in the meantime he is at this moment your greatest enemy, and he is my greatest enemy. He will do everything in the world to wreck and to ruin us. In this world we are in his system. He is running this world today. He's the one who is back of the nations of the world. He is the one who is bringing the misery and the heartbreak to this dark world today. And the interesting thing is, the world doesn't even believe he exists. Boy, is he smart! I take my hat off to his ability. I respect him, and I'm afraid of him.

I want to flee to the One who can *keep* me. The Epistle of James admonishes us:

> *Therefore submit to God. Resist the devil and he will flee from you.*
> (James 4:7)

You had better submit yourself to God *before* you start resisting the devil! I tell you, if you're not out and out for God today, Satan has *got* you. And that's the reason he catches so many cold and indifferent church members. Why do the cults send out their people to knock on doors on Sunday morning? Because they know that careless, indifferent church members are at home. And the devil knows they are the ones he can get, and he snares them—boy, does he snare them! Satan does not necessarily ask you to go out and get drunk. He asks you to become very religious—but don't come to Christ, and don't trust His death on the cross for your salvation, and don't even acknowledge that you *need* the Lord Jesus Christ! Just try to be a big old boy yourself—and are you in for a fall!

Oh, my friend, if we could only be wise enough to place our faith in what God says and use God's Word to guide us through this life!

So then faith comes by hearing, and hearing by the word of God.
(Romans 10:17)

CHAPTER 8

SALVATION: PART 1

When we come to the doctrine of salvation, a great many folk think that we've come to something very simple, something we know all about. May I say this, and I want to say it kindly, but I think it should be said: In Southern California where perhaps more gospel is preached than in any other area of the country today, there is *more* confusion and cloudy presentation of the gospel. One day I listened by radio to a lady preacher, and she used quite a few of the common Christian clichés that we all use, pious phrases which are acceptable to people, but in attempting to declare the gospel, this dear lady didn't even know what it was! She was entirely confused as to the gospel and to what salvation really is. Frankly, the gospel is something on which there is a great deal of confusion. How tragic that is!

We're going to center on some important words in this section for the simple reason that if we know the meaning of these words and can make a sharp distinction among them, then we will be able to understand something about salvation.

The thing that keeps a great many people from witnessing is not the method so much as it is not knowing what to say. That is, they do not know how to present the claims of Christ and to be clear on the gospel. Oh, my friend, this is one place we should be clear!

Following you will see a list of certain words, and no two of these words mean the same thing. Yet each one of them sets before us one of the facets of our wonderful salvation:

> Atonement
> Substitution
> Redemption
> Propitiation
> Reconciliation
> Regeneration
> Justification
> Faith
> Repentance
> Assurance
> Sanctification

Now, friend, if these words are new to you, don't shy away from them. By the time we finish this book, you will see how simple and how wonderful they really are.

Atonement

First of all, I want to deal with the word *atonement*. The Hebrew word for atonement is *kaphar*, and it only means "to cover." That's all in the world atonement means. I realize that there has been an attempt to simplify it by making a play on words, by calling atonement "at-one-ment." May I say that though that concept may be there, it is not the meaning of the word at all, because the word means "to cover." And it is strictly an Old Testament word.

You do not find the word *atonement* anywhere in the New Testament. Now, I'm sure that somebody's going to counter this statement and say, "Wait a minute! I remember reading it over in Romans 5:11: 'We also joy in God through our Lord Jesus Christ, by whom we have now received the atonement' [KJV]. You see, it's there."

Well, if that is how your Bible reads, the word *atonement* ought not to be there. If you check the original Greek, you will see that the correct translation is the word *reconciliation* and not *atonement* at all. *Atonement* is a word that does not occur in the New Testament because God could not forgive sin on the basis of animal sacrifices. He merely let the people bring the sacrifices previously because they were types or prefigures, pointing to Christ; and on their part it was an act of faith, and God accepted that and covered their sin. But there was never any merit in the sacrifice per se. When you get to the last book of the Old Testament, God says through Malachi, "Away with your sacrifices; I don't want them." In other words, God was saying, "Do you think I'm interested in your offering up an animal? I'm not interested because you've missed the value of it, you've missed the meaning of it, you've missed the intention of it. I intended it to teach you something."

We're definitely told that the sacrifices in the Old Testament never did take away sin:

> **For it is not possible that the blood of bulls and goats could take away sins.**
> (Hebrews 10:4)

That's a clear-cut statement, isn't it?

Back in the Old Testament, the blood of bulls and goats could not take away a person's sin. Every instructed Israelite knew and understood that the little sacrifice he was bringing was pointing on to Christ.

> **By that will we have been sanctified through the offering of the body of Jesus Christ once for all. And every priest stands ministering daily and offering repeatedly the same sacrifices, which can never take away sins. But this Man [the Lord Jesus],**

> *after He had offered one sacrifice for sins forever, sat down at*
> *the right hand of God.*
> (Hebrews 10:10-12)

The Lord Jesus Christ offered Himself, and every sacrifice in the Old Testament foreshadowed Him. And that's what Paul meant in Romans 3:25 when he wrote of Jesus:

> *. . . whom God set forth as a propitiation by His blood,*
> *through faith, to demonstrate His righteousness, because in His*
> *forbearance God had passed over the sins that were previously*
> *committed.*

What does he mean by the "passing over" or remission of sins that are past? Does he mean your past sins, my past sins? No. He has no reference to that. It's a chronological word meaning every sin committed before Christ's death on the cross. God forgave those people who brought the sacrifices in faith, when they realized that the sacrifice was prefiguring the Lamb of God who was going to take away the sin of the world, all the way down from the sins of Abel.

Now suppose you had met Abel as he was approaching the altar to offer that little lamb, and suppose you had stepped up to him and said, "Abel, do you really believe that the blood of that little animal is taking away your sin?"

Abel happened to be a very intelligent man. Remember, he was the son of Adam, and he had a higher I.Q. than any of us. I believe people were much more intelligent in the beginning than we are today. And this brilliant man Abel would have said, "No, I don't think the blood of the little animal takes away my sin."

"Then why are you doing it?"

"Well, God commanded me to do this temporarily, as this little animal is pointing down to the expiation, to the sacrifice that God will make in His own time. And I'm coming, merely by faith, offering this lamb—it's only a type of that which is going to come."

Those in the Old Testament understood that the blood of bulls and goats did not take away sin but pointed to the One who was going to take away sin. So when God forgave Abel, He forgave him on *credit*. When God forgave Abraham, He forgave him on credit. Sin wasn't paid for. He said, "I'll forgive you, Abraham, for doing this, but your sin has not been paid for." Christ came and died on the cross, Paul said,

> *to demonstrate His righteousness, because in His forbearance*
> *God had passed over the sins that were previously committed.*
> (Romans 3:25)

You see, when Christ died on the cross, He paid for all those sins of the past. All of them were paid for when our Lord was made sin for us. So back in the Old Testament the proper word is *atonement*, meaning "to cover." God merely covered them until Christ came, and He blotted them out so that today when you trust Christ your sins are washed away and remembered no more. God removes them. They've been paid for through the death of Christ upon the cross. So, friends, *atonement* is only an Old Testament word.

Unfortunately, there have been theologians who have used this term, and many do it today. Especially in these half-liberal seminaries they use this term to speak of all that Christ did, and they call it the atonement. And you'll find that there are many theories of the atonement. Let me mention several of them which are being preached today.

MARTYR THEORY

I listened to a liberal preacher here in Southern California as he preached on the death of Christ. He told about how He died on the cross, and someone said to me, "Dr. McGee, he preaches the Cross of Christ just like anyone who is fundamental in his doctrine." You see, this person wasn't able to make the distinction. What the preacher was actually saying was that Christ died as a martyr. He emphasized the point that He was poor and helpless and hopeless here and that He stood for a cause. And because He stood for what was right, He was put to death—and the preacher considered that to be the value of the death of Christ. There was no mention that He died as a substitute or that His death was necessary to satisfy the holiness and justice of God. That was not mentioned. It was only that His death was an awful thing—and it was! He depicted it in all of its gory detail so that many people said, "My, isn't he sound in the faith to talk about the death of Christ?" No, he was merely presenting Him as a martyr.

Now did Christ die a martyr's death? Absolutely not! That's one thing you cannot get from the Word of God. Will you notice several things: Jesus made basic doctrines very clear. For instance, He said that He was not a martyr:

> *No man takes it [My life] from Me, but I lay it down of Myself. I have power to lay it down, and I have power to take it again. This command I have received from My Father.*
> (John 10:18)

May I say, if you feel sorry for Him, don't do it. Remember that as Jesus was being led to His crucifixion, among the great multitude following Him were women mourning and lamenting Him. He turned and said:

> *Daughters of Jerusalem, do not weep for Me, but weep for yourselves and for your children.*
> (Luke 23:28)

The interesting thing is, He was in entire control at the time of His crucifixion. After all, He predicted it:

> *You know that after two days is the Passover, and the Son of Man will be delivered up to be crucified.*
> (Matthew 26:2)

And today the Lord Jesus Christ is still in control.

Now let's continue through verse 5 and see something very interesting here:

> *Then the chief priests, the scribes, and the elders of the people assembled at the palace of the high priest, who was called Caiaphas, and plotted to take Jesus by trickery and kill Him. But they said, "Not during the feast, lest there be an uproar among the people."*
> (Matthew 26:3-5)

In verse 2 Jesus tells His disciples that He is going to die. According to the record, this is the sixth time He has told them. Six months before this, beginning at Caesarea Philippi, He announced His impending death. And now He sets the *time* of His death. He tells them that He will die during the Passover. But the religious rulers had other plans—notice *they* said, "Not during the feast, lest there be an uproar among the people." The very ones who put Him to death said that they would *not* crucify Him during the Passover; *He* said that He would die during the Passover. When did He die? He died during the Passover. You see, Jesus, not His enemies, set the time of His execution. He is in command.

And to Judas that night, at the Last Supper, after he had been singled out as the betrayer, our Lord said, "What you do, do quickly." So Judas rushed out of the place and went directly to the religious leaders to inform them that Jesus was going to the Garden of Gethsemane, away from the crowds. Evidently he told them something like this: "If you want to take Him, you'd better take Him tonight. He's aware of our plot. He told me, 'What you do, do quickly.' He intends to leave. You'd better seize Him now." And that night they went out and arrested Him at midnight.

Now whose bidding were they doing? They were doing our Lord's bidding. He didn't die a martyr. I hope you don't have merely a sentimental feeling in your heart toward Jesus, as I'm afraid a great many people do. Jesus says, "Do not weep for Me." He did not die for that reason. He did not die as a martyr. In fact, I've heard the death of Christ likened unto a blood transfusion! It was not a blood transfusion. He didn't die for any such reason.

MORAL INFLUENCE THEORY

Another theory of atonement of which we should be aware is known as the "moral influence theory." This idea was started by a heretic named Sosinais, and the theory is called Sosinianism. It postulates that the Lord Jesus died in order that He might have an influence. He went to the cross and died for that which was right, and for truth, in order to influence us to say, "Well, if He did that, then I'm going to do better"—reformation. It's another type of liberalism that you still hear.

Oftentimes one of these preachers will say, "Now look here, Jesus died on a cross"—they don't mind saying that since it is a historical fact—"and when you see Him dying there, that ought to inspire you to want to live better. It ought to influence you to improve your lifestyle."

Oh, my friend, Jesus did not die for that reason at all. He didn't die to inspire anybody to do anything. He died as a forsaken Man on a cross who said, "My God, My God, why have You forsaken Me?" He wasn't a martyr, and there was nothing there to influence you. It was an awful, horrible thing. His death is unspeakable, and not one Gospel writer describes the crucifixion, not one. The Holy Spirit drew a veil and put it over that cross, as if to say, "That which happened here is too horrible for you to look at."

Therefore, His brutal death is not to inspire you to do anything. He died, the just for the unjust. He died, the innocent for the guilty. He died, the sinless One for the sinners. But our Lord did not die to influence you to reform your life.

GOVERNMENTAL THEORY

Now there's another theory that is actually called the "governmental theory." A Dutch theologian by the name of Grotius is the one who developed it. This theory holds that Christ died to show God's hatred of sin; that He did it to maintain the government of God. This is closer to the truth than any we've considered. He did die to satisfy the law of God. However, this theory becomes a brutal sort of thing. Jonathan Edwards held this theory, and this is the reason for his famous sermon, "Sinners in the Hands of an Angry God." It is said that when he preached that sermon—he was a tremendous orator—the people in his audience would hold onto the edges of their seats to keep from falling into hell. He made it really vivid! And one time when he preached that sermon the fire department went by, and in that day the engines were crude, smoking things, and there was absolute panic in the church where he was preaching.

May I say to you that the governmental theory does not reveal the love of God at all. And it is not what we believe the Scriptures teach. Actually this is not a theory of the atonement, although we list it as such. Rather, it is the *truth* of the atonement, if you want to call it atonement. Jesus Christ died as a satisfaction to God for the sins of man. And we're going to develop that truth as we move on because we believe that when He died on the cross there were some wonderful things that took place.

Substitution

There were a number of conspicuous accomplishments of Christ on the cross; a number of wonderful works were accomplished when Jesus Christ gave Himself up for us. The first wonderful accomplishment when He died on the cross was that He became a substitute for sinners. Back in the Old Testament God had already put down these great principles for His people. In Leviticus you'll find one of the axioms of God:

> *For the life of the flesh is in the blood, and I have given it to you upon the altar to make atonement for your souls; for it is the blood that makes atonement for the soul.*
> (Leviticus 17:11)

The life of the flesh is in the blood. It wasn't until the seventeenth century that William Harvey made the discovery that our blood circulates and that the life of the flesh *is* in the blood. And in our day we have institutions that maintain blood banks and send out pleas for donors. Why? Because the life of the flesh is in the blood. That's a great truth—and think of Moses putting down that axiom in his day when man had to wait several thousand years to make the scientific discovery that the life of the flesh is in the blood.

God said, "I have given it to you upon the altar to make an atonement for your souls." The blood of another had to be shed because it is a substitution for us. Therefore Isaiah could write:

> *But He was wounded for our transgressions,*
> *He was bruised for our iniquities;*
> *The chastisement for our peace was upon Him,*
> *And by His stripes we are healed.*
> (Isaiah 53:5)

When Peter quotes this, it's obvious that the healing is not physical. Peter makes it clear that Jesus Himself bore our sins in His own body:

> *. . . who Himself bore our sins in His own body on the tree,*
> *that we, having died to sins, might live for righteousness—by*
> *whose stripes you were healed.*
> (1 Peter 2:24)

"By whose stripes you were healed!" What from? Sin! Jesus died a substitutionary death on the cross. This is a truth that is so difficult to get over to the human family! Even today so many pastors do not preach that Christ died a substitute for sinners! Just think of it! They say that He died for some other reason—one of the theories we have just dealt with or another. There are others out there. I did not mention all of the theories, by any means.

But may I say to you that God was attempting to instruct His people, and He did it in many ways. The Passover was one of the ways.

> *Speak to all the congregation of Israel, saying: "On the tenth of this month every man shall take for himself a lamb, according to the house of his father, a lamb for a household. . . . Your lamb shall be without blemish, a male of the first year. . . . Then the whole assembly of the congregation of Israel shall kill it at twilight.*
>
> (Exodus 12:3, 5, 6)

Just look at how exact that language is. Each family was to have a lamb. But when God was telling them about the killing, He didn't say to kill *them*, He said to kill *it*, because the sacrifice spoke of One, even of Christ. The exactness carried through even in the grammar.

> *And they shall take some of the blood and put it on the two doorposts and on the lintel of the houses where they eat it. . . . For I will pass through the land of Egypt on that night, and will strike all the firstborn in the land of Egypt. . . . Now the blood shall be a sign for you on the houses where you are. And when I see the blood, I will pass over you. . . .*
>
> (Exodus 12:7, 12, 13)

This was the first great lesson that these people had when God took them out of slavery. They were in Egypt, a land given to idolatry and, friend, they were idolaters themselves. Israel was so tied into idolatry that when they reached Mount Sinai, from the minute they got into the wilderness and Moses was gone from them to get instructions from God, the people wanted a golden calf to worship! Why would people who had been so wonderfully delivered by God do such a thing? Well, my beloved, because they had lived in Egypt all of their lives and had been worshiping idols. They were brainwashed people. And so they wanted an idol:

> *Now when the people saw that Moses delayed coming down from the mountain, the people gathered together to Aaron, and*

> *said to him, "Come, make us gods that shall go before us; for as for this Moses, the man who brought us up out of the land of Egypt, we do not know what has become of him."*
> (Exodus 32:1)

They wanted something they could see, something they could bow down before. That was the custom under which they had been brought up in Egypt.

God is instructing these people concerning the way He's going to forgive their sins. So He says, "This night is going to mark the beginning of months, the first month of the year for you. This is the night I will take you out of the land of Egypt. Now I want it made clear to you, I'm not taking you out of the land of Egypt because you are superior to the Egyptians. You're not." Later, after forty years in the wilderness, Moses wrote in the Book of Deuteronomy that God had said, "I knew all the time you were a stiff-necked people. I didn't bring you out because of any merit in you." In Exodus 2:24 He gave Moses two reasons He came down to deliver them. He "heard their groaning," and He was moved with compassion toward them. The second thing was, He "remembered His covenant with Abraham, with Isaac, and with Jacob."

And, my friend, when God saves you and saves me, it's not because He sees any good in us at all. He sees only that we are sinners, ungodly and *lost*. Although He sees no merit in us whatever, He remembers His covenant with His Son; that is, if the Son would die in our stead, He would save those of us who would trust Him:

> *For God so loved the world that He gave His only begotten Son, that whoever believes in Him should not perish but have everlasting life.*
> (John 3:16)

In other words, God says, "That's the covenant I made. When you recognize your sinfulness and trust My Son to be your Savior, I will save you. On what basis? On your great need and to keep the covenant I have made with My Son." Jesus died to be your substitute, friend.

Likewise the people of Israel had to have a substitute. God didn't redeem them from Egyptian bondage because they had signed on the dotted line and promised to do a little bit better than they had been doing. Honestly, they did worse! They were bad in Egypt. They were terrible in the wilderness. He didn't deliver them because they had promised to reform. Instead God said, "This night is the first month of the year for you. You can mark this down—this is the Passover feast. Tonight you are to take a lamb, kill that lamb, take it to your home, roast it, feed on it, and share it. Then I want you to take the blood of that lamb outside your home, sprinkle it on the two doorposts and on the lintel above the door."

Then God said, "Tonight, I am coming to Egypt. And when I come to a house, I am not going to knock on the door and say, 'I'm wondering if you would like to be delivered, and if you will promise to serve Me if I will lead you out of Egypt.'" He didn't do that. The only basis on which God spared the firstborn of any family in the land of Egypt was this: "When I see the blood I'll pass over!" That little lamb died, and they were delivered, teaching that when Christ died, you and I are delivered just like the people of Israel were delivered that first Passover night. The lamb prefigured Jesus, the Lamb of God who takes away the sin of the world.

Christ's death is what redeemed them, and Christ's death is what redeems you and me. He died a substitution for sinners. When He went to the cross, He took my place. He took your place. The Lord Jesus Himself put it like this:

> *The Son of Man did not come to be served, but to serve, and to give His life a ransom for many.*
> (Matthew 20:28)

Over in the fifth chapter of Romans is the finest exposition of the love of God in the Bible. John 3:16 is not an exposition—rather, it's merely a declaration. But this is the exposition:

> *For when we were still without strength, in due time Christ died for the ungodly. For scarcely for a righteous man will one die; yet perhaps for a good man someone would even dare to die. But God demonstrates His own love toward us, in that while we were still sinners, Christ died for us.*
> (Romans 5:6-8)

My friend, when He died upon the cross, He was a substitute for you! And He was a substitute for me! What happened to Him at that time should have happened to us—we are guilty, He is innocent. That's important to see.

Don't feel sorry for Him. It was for the joy that was set before Him that He endured the Cross. He did it willingly and gladly. He doesn't want your sympathy, He wants your *faith*.

> *For He made Him who knew no sin to be sin for us, that we might become the righteousness of God in Him.*
> (2 Corinthians 5:21)

In other words, for you and me down here, Christ became sin in order that you and I might have His right in heaven! That's the only basis on which God receives sinners.

You see, mankind thinks too much of himself. Honestly, what could you contribute to heaven? May I say to you, I would dirty up the place if I got up there, and you would too. You wouldn't decorate heaven, and your talent is not needed up there. God doesn't have to have you. But you and I have to have Him.

He's saving us, my beloved, and He finds all the explanation in Himself. When Christ died, He died a substitutionary death so a holy God could reach down and save us. God gave the children of Israel a day of atonement, Yom Kippur. And again the blood of an animal sacrifice was taken into the Holy of Holies, and Israel was accepted for another year. But this Man—He didn't offer many sacrifices. He doesn't go in every year. Once, at the end of the age, He offered Himself. He went into the Holy of Holies for you and for me, and He is there for us at this hour.

My friend, I don't know about you, but the only thing I'm counting on is Christ. I am not counting on Vernon McGee's performance. Now maybe you thought I was. No, my friend, I am counting on Jesus Christ, my Lord. He is the substitution for sinners. That enables me to go to bed at night and sleep. I'll be honest with you, I don't care what happens—life or death. And I sometimes think, the way things are going, I'd like not to wake up here but to wake up in His presence. My hope is in Him. I am not trusting Vernon McGee for anything— not *anything*. Christ is my substitute.

Are you trusting Him today? Is He really a substitute for you? You don't need to feel sentimental about His death. He died for you. And you are the fellow to feel sorry for if you have never trusted Him. Because, my friend, what happened to Him will have to happen to you if you don't trust Him. But He died, the just for the unjust, the innocent for the guilty, the One who is holy for the unholy. He took my place. He took your place. That's a *wonderful* truth!

Redemption

Our Lord's death is not only a substitution for sinners, it is a redemption toward sin. The psalmist wrote:

> **[He] *redeems your life from destruction.***
> (Psalm 103:4)

That's what He came to do. He came to redeem us.

Now *redemption* is a Latin word. It actually means "to pay a price." Our Lord came, He said, for that purpose.

> *Jesus said to them, "My food is to do the will of Him who*
> *sent Me, and to finish His work."*
> (John 4:34)

Then He could say in His great high priestly prayer when He turned in His report to God shortly before His crucifixion:

> *I have finished the work which You have given Me to do.*
> (John 17:4)

On the cross He shouted, "It is finished!" What was finished? His work of redemption was finished forever. What is redemption? Redemption means to pay a price. It means that something has been sold and is either owned by another or it is in slavery and needs to be bought and brought back to the rightful owner. We have that pictured in the Book of Ruth, which is the reason, by the way, I wrote my book on Ruth, *Romance of Redemption*. I graduated from a Presbyterian seminary, and it was a good one, don't misunderstand me—some of the best scholars in America were teaching in that seminary, both liberals and conservatives. But during my years there I felt like the liberals were winning the day, because redemption was presented as a cold business transaction as though Christ paid with His blood, cash on the barrelhead, and that was it. Well, that is not it. Redemption is a love story, which is the reason the Book of Ruth is in the Bible.

Ruth was a poor widow. She was a foreigner. She was shut out, an outsider, and in her poverty she had to go out in the fields and glean. Then somebody she had not seen before came to the field one day, and he owned that field. His name was Boaz, and he fell in love with her. Immediately he wanted to redeem her according to the law of the kinsman-redeemer:

> *If . . . one of them dies and has no son, the widow . . . shall*
> *not be married to a stranger outside the family; her husband's*

brother shall . . . take her as his wife. . . . And it shall be that the firstborn son which she bears will succeed to the name of his dead brother. . . .
(Deuteronomy 25:5–6)

Ruth had lost the property that had belonged to her husband, and she herself was in danger of being sold into slavery. Because Boaz loved her, he set out to pay the price to redeem her and to redeem her property according to the law in Leviticus 25:25:

If one of your brethren becomes poor, and has sold some of his possession, and if his redeeming relative [kinsman-redeemer] comes to redeem it, then he may redeem what his brother sold.

Redemption is always toward sin. That is, you and I have been sold under sin. We today are as Romans 6:17 tells us, "slaves of sin." And the Lord Jesus said:

Most assuredly, I say to you, whoever commits sin is a slave of sin.
(John 8:34)

Now the Lord Jesus redeemed us, which means He paid a price. That price was His blood, in order that He might buy us, if you please, out from under the slavery of sin.

Therefore if the Son makes you free, you shall be free indeed.
(John 8:36)

He bought us to set us *free.* Therefore we have redemption in the blood of Christ. That was the price that was paid.

But when the fullness of the time had come, God sent forth His Son, born of a woman, born under the law, to redeem those who were under the law, that we might receive the adoption as sons.
(Galatians 4:4-5)

Any way that you take man, he is a slave. If you put him under the Mosaic Law he can't keep it, and he needs to be redeemed from under law. He needs to be redeemed from sin. And the Lord Jesus is the Kinsman-Redeemer. He came down here and took upon Himself our human flesh. On the cross He took our place, and He paid the price, which was His own precious blood.

Now here's a poor man who has lost his property, but he's got a rich uncle. He sees his rich uncle one day, and the rich uncle says, "How much will it cost to redeem it?" So he writes out the check and pays the price. It's wonderful to have a rich uncle when you've lost your property!

Not only that, but will you notice:

> *Now if a sojourner or stranger close to you becomes rich, and one of your brethren who dwells by him becomes poor, and sells himself to the stranger or sojourner close to you, or to a member of the stranger's family, after he is sold he may be redeemed again. One of his brothers may redeem him.*
> (Leviticus 25:47-48)

Suppose a man sold himself into slavery—he had lost everything, and that's all he could do. So he sold himself to his rich neighbor and he's a slave, expecting never to be free again. But then suppose one day he looks down the road and sees his rich uncle coming and taking out his checkbook to pay the price of his redemption!

May I say, friend, this is a fine illustration of our redemption. You and I live in a world that has been sold under sin. This creation today is groaning and travailing in pain; we have lost our property. Adam, you see, was given dominion over the earth, but he lost it. The human family has absolutely lost its inheritance. Not only that, we were sold in the slavery of sin. And when Christ came to this earth, He came to pay a price in order to redeem us, to buy us back.

There are several Greek words that are used. The *agora* was the ancient marketplace, and the word *agorazo* means "to go and buy in the marketplace." Another word, *exagorazo*, means to go and buy in the marketplace with the idea that you are taking it out of the market. Some folks may have a fruit stand, so they go to the wholesale market, buy there, and then take the fruit out to their market and up the price a little so they can make a profit, you see. They don't buy it because they love the stuff. They buy it to sell it.

Suppose a man goes down to the *agora*, and he sees an antique or something else that he likes very much, and he says, "I want to buy that for myself." Suppose he sees a slave, and he wants to buy that slave, not to sell him, not to make money, but to use him. May I say, *exagorazo* is also used for redemption.

Now here is another word altogether: *lutroo*, which means "to pay the ransomed price." In the Gospel of John we find still another word, *eleutheroo*, which means not only to go and buy and not expose for sale again, but to buy and set free. And that's the reason the Lord Jesus said:

> *Therefore if the Son makes you free, you shall be free indeed.*
> (John 8:36)

He did not buy us in order to make us His slaves. And that's one reason I don't like the song that says something like this, "I gave My life for you—what have you done for Me?" When He saves you, He puts you under no obligation. He saves you to set you free. Then if you are free, you have the freedom to go to Him as Paul did. In effect, Paul said, "I'm free from the law. I'm now a free man! But I went to Jesus Christ and I yielded to Him, and I said, 'I want to be Your slave.'" And Paul called himself the bondslave of Jesus Christ. Why? Because he did it voluntarily.

If you want to be a servant or slave of Christ, you will have to initiate it. When Christ saves you, He doesn't put you under any obligation—that's what grace is. If you are under obligation to pay Him back, then it is not grace, you see. God saves you by grace. And grace creates no debt whatsoever. When God saves you, you are free. And the glory of it is you can go in your freedom and yield to Him.

My friend, you'll never know what real joy is until you have yielded to Him. Just as we came to Him for salvation, I believe we can make this transaction: "Lord Jesus, I'm coming to yield to You. You made me free, but I want to be Your servant, Your slave forever."

In the state of Alabama years ago, before the Civil War, a beautiful Negro girl was being exposed on the slave block for sale, and a very brutal slave owner was bidding for her. Every time he made a bid she winced. Standing at the edge of the crowd was a wealthy plantation owner who was a Christian, and he saw what was going on. So when it looked as if the brutal slave owner might get this girl, the plantation owner stepped forward and raised the bid so the other man couldn't touch it. The plantation owner bought her, signed the necessary papers, and started to walk away, then noticed that she was following him. He turned around and asked, "Why in the world are you following me?"

She said, "Sir, you bought me."

"Oh, you don't understand. I didn't buy you for a slave, I bought you to set you free."

She stood there stunned for a few moments, then all of a sudden she just dropped to the ground and said, "I'll serve *you* forever!"

A service of love, you see, is the kind of service you and I can render to Christ. He won't have it any other way. He redeemed you to set you free. And now you can choose to yield yourself to Him. That's redemption. Redeemed—how I love to proclaim it!

_____

Propitiation

Now we are coming to another wonderful word: *propitiation*, and propitiation is toward God. It occurs seven times in the Greek text of the New Testament. The reason it may not occur all seven times in your Bible is because in several places it's not translated correctly into the same English word *propitiation*. For instance:

> *Therefore, in all things He had to be made like His brethren,*
> *that He might be a merciful and faithful High Priest in things*
> *pertaining to God, to make propitiation* [reconciliation in some
> English translations] *for the sins of the people.*
> (Hebrews 2:17)

It should be propitiation here, for it is that in the Greek.

First of all, let me say that the word *propitiation* is absolutely void
of any pagan meaning. If you have read any Greek mythology or read
anything concerning the pagan religions, or if you've read any of the
stories of the Greeks, you will recall that even Agamemnon had to
make a human sacrifice to appease the gods on Mount Olympus. They
were perceived to be angry, therefore a sacrifice had to be made, and
that was called a propitiation. In fact, the Greeks used it like that.

Well, may I say to you that the word as used in the Scripture does
not even hint of being used to appease a deity. It doesn't convey the
idea that God is angry and you've got to do something to win Him
over. It doesn't have that thought at all.

Therefore, I want to turn to several passages where this word
occurs, and let's look at them. First,

> *. . . being justified freely* [that is, without a cause] *by His*
> *grace through the redemption that is in Christ Jesus, whom God*
> *set forth as a propitiation by His blood, through faith, to*
> *demonstrate His righteousness, because in His forbearance God*
> *had passed over the sins that were previously committed.*
> (Romans 3:24-25)

The word *propitiation* actually means "*place* of propitiation." I want us
to see something in Hebrews, where we'll find again this word in the
Greek text. It is not translated *propitiation* here but with another word,
a very vivid word. I'll move back and quote a few verses before the
occurrence of this word since the writer to the Hebrews is describing
the tabernacle. He says:

> *. . . behind the second veil, the part of the tabernacle which is called the Holiest of All, which had the golden censer and the ark of the covenant overlaid on all sides with gold, in which were the golden pot that had the manna, Aaron's rod that budded, and the tablets of the covenant; and above it were the cherubim of glory overshadowing the mercy seat* [here is our word propitiation]. . . .
> (Hebrews 9:3-5)

Propitiation means "to be a mercy seat." That's the picture. Notice again the passage in Romans for just a moment:

> *. . . whom God set forth as a propitiation by His blood, through faith, to demonstrate His righteousness, because in His forbearance God had passed over the sins that were previously committed.*
> (Romans 3:25)

This is the tabernacle. Outside was the laver and also the brazen altar.

The Holy Place. The entrance faced east. Inside there was the golden lampstand on the left (south), and over on the right (north) the table of showbread, and then before the veil was the golden altar, which speaks of prayer.

The Golden Altar. It is interesting that the writer to the Hebrews puts the golden altar inside the Holiest of All. The Old Testament places it in front of the veil, so why did the writer to the Hebrews put it inside where the ark is? Because when we come to the New Testament the veil which represented the body of Christ is torn in two, opening the way into the presence of God, and Christ has gone up to heaven. This altar of prayer is where the priest went to pray. And that's where our Lord is now. He is in heaven, making intercession for us. Properly, the altar of prayer belongs there now.

The Holiest of All. Behind the veil was the ark. And inside the ark there were three things—the tables of stone on which the Ten Commandments were written, a pot of manna, and Aaron's rod that budded. On top of the ark, which was shaped like a box, there was this very highly ornamented cover with two cherubim of gold over-shadowing it. Once a year the high priest went inside, and we are told that the Shekinah Glory was there, indicating that God dwelt there. This is where they were to meet with Him, and the high priest went there once a year and sprinkled blood on the ark's cover between the cherubim. And this is the throne of God where the presence of the holy God is. Now it is a mercy seat. It's where God can extend mercy to His people. That which was a throne of judgment before has become a mercy seat now.

Let's refer again to Romans 3:25. The apostle Paul, speaking of Christ, wrote, "Whom God set forth as a propitiation [mercy seat]." Christ on the cross served as our mercy seat. We know that as He hung on the cross, blood was running down His face from that thorny crown, blood was coming from the nails in His hands and in His feet. It is John who mentions the propitiation, by the way. He and Paul are the only two writers who do that. John tells us at the time of the crucifixion:

> *One of the soldiers pierced His side with a spear, and immediately blood and water came out. And he who has seen has testified, and his testimony is true; and he knows that he is telling the truth, so that you may believe.*
> (John 19:34-35)

We know that this made a tremendous impression on John because, when he wrote his first epistle, he made this statement again. He didn't forget about this incident:

> *This is He who came by water and blood—Jesus Christ; not only by water, but by water and blood. And it is the Spirit who bears witness, because the Spirit is truth.*
> (1 John 5:6)

Without going into detail, we will skip verse 7 since it is not in our better manuscripts:

> *And there are three that bear witness on earth: the Spirit, the water, and the blood; and these three agree as one.*
> (1 John 5:8)

John was present at the crucifixion. Remember it was there at the cross that the Lord said to him, "Behold your mother!" In other words, "You take care of My mother," and John says, "When I was there I watched, and I was very close." It seems that at the trial of Jesus, John got in closer than anyone else. And he's also closer at the crucifixion than anyone else. He said in effect, "While I was watching, blood was coming from His head, blood was coming from His hands and His feet. Finally, this soldier came up to make sure He was dead, and he ran a spear into His side." John says, "Out of that side there came water and blood." May I say that John is going to tell us that our Lord was the propitiatory sacrifice for our sins. It was Christ, Paul says, "whom God set forth as a propitiation by His blood, through faith" (Romans 3:25). Jesus Christ on the cross shed His blood. I think that every drop of blood went out of His body and that His whole body was covered with His blood. That, my friend, is the mercy seat for you and me. Because He shed His blood, taking your place and my place, a holy God now is able to extend mercy to us. And that's the meaning of propitiation. It means simply that Christ is our mercy seat.

Now I want to follow through on what John has said. Let's look at that for just a moment:

> *And He Himself* [Jesus Christ] *is the propitiation for our sins.*
> (1 John 2:2)

John is the one who says, "I was there and I saw that soldier put the spear in His side, and there came out blood and water." And he adds,

"These three bear witness on earth and they agree." The Spirit and the water and the blood—and that blood speaks of the fact that He shed His blood that He might be the propitiation for your sins and my sins. This is tremendous! "He Himself is the propitiation for our sins, and not for ours only but also for the whole world."

Notice something here which is very important: John said this: "My little children, these things I write to you, so that you may not sin." Well, John, I wish I could say I didn't sin, but I do. Now what shall I do?

> *And if anyone sins, we have an Advocate with the Father, Jesus Christ the righteous.*
> (1 John 2:1)

And after all, John says, "He Himself is the propitiation for our sins," referring to our sins as Christians. I need a mercy seat every day, don't you? I don't want justice from God. I don't want Him to treat me on the basis of legality because I would come off a loser. I want *mercy* from God. That's the thing I want from Him—mercy. And that is the thing both you and I need. He is the propitiation for our sins.

John doesn't stop there:

> *. . . and not for ours only but also for the whole world.*
> (1 John 2:2)

There is a mercy seat today for every person on topside of this earth. And people are not lost because of the fact they are so bad and cannot do enough to gain God's forgiveness. That's not the reason. They are lost because they won't go to the mercy seat. There's mercy for *every* person. God is *merciful* today. And the reason He is merciful is not because He's just bighearted and sort of sentimental. No, He is not that. God is holy and righteous. And He *loves*. God loved long before He did anything about it—but God is not only love, God is holy. And though He might love a sinner, He cannot take the sin into heaven. But then Christ died and was covered with blood. So He is the mercy seat. A holy God now can extend mercy because Christ paid the ultimate penalty for our sin.

And that's not all. He wants to mention it again to us: "In this is love, not that we loved God, but that He loved us." He loved us, and what did He do? Did He fling open the door of heaven and say, "Everybody, come in"? No, He cannot do that because He is holy.

> *In this is love, not that we loved God, but that He loved us and sent His Son to be the propitiation* [to be the mercy seat] *for our sins.*
> (1 John 4:10)

And so today a holy God is prepared to extend mercy down here to lost men and lost women.

> *For I will be merciful to their unrighteousness, and their sins and their lawless deeds I will remember no more.*
> (Hebrews 8:12)

God says, "I will be merciful to their unrighteousness." How can a holy God do that? Because there is Christ on the cross, covered with blood, His precious blood is poured out, and there is a mercy seat. The throne of God, where a holy God would judge you and judge me—that very throne at this moment extends mercy to us.

Oh, my friend, God is not a police officer waiting around the corner to give you a ticket or to find fault with your conduct. God is not demanding. He is saying to the world tonight, "I have My arms outstretched toward you, and I am prepared to extend mercy to you because Christ died. There is a mercy seat for you."

Now let's see that in action. Turn with me to the eighteenth chapter of Luke's Gospel, starting with verse 9, our Lord

> *spoke this parable to some who trusted in themselves that they were righteous, and despised others: "Two men went up to the*

temple to pray, one a Pharisee, and the other a tax collector [a
publican]. The Pharisee stood and prayed thus with him-
self. . . ."

It's sort of like Hamlet's soliloquy. In Shakespeare's play, Hamlet goes
out and talks to no one but himself:

> To be, or not to be, that is the question:
> Whether 'tis nobler in the mind to suffer
> The slings and arrows of outrageous fortune,
> Or to take arms against a sea of troubles,
> And by opposing, end them? To die, to sleep—
> No more, and by a sleep to say we end
> The heart-ache and the thousand natural shocks
> That flesh is heir to; 'tis a consummation
> Devoutly to be wish'd. To die, to sleep—
> To sleep, perchance to dream—ay, there's the rub,
> For in that sleep of death what dreams may come. . . .

And so on. He's just talking to himself. And when a soliloquy is done
by a fine actor, with expression, it's tremendous! But may I say that
the Pharisee's prayer was a soliloquy. Our Lord says, "He prayed thus
with himself." He didn't pray it to God. He had a big time patting
himself on the back and, in essence, said, "What a fine actor I am!"
And an actor was what he was.

> **The Pharisee stood and prayed thus with himself, "God**
> **[although he addresses God, he is not really talking to Him],**
> **I thank You that I am not like other men—extortioners, unjust,**
> **adulterers, or even as this tax collector. I fast twice a week; I**
> **give tithes of all that I possess."**
> (Luke 18:11-12)

Now that's what a lot of people brag about today. But, you see, that
kind of talk didn't get anywhere, didn't get out of the rafters, and it

did not get to God. My friend, you never get to God when you go to Him and tell Him how good you are and all that you're doing for others. No one gets to our holy God that way.

Then will you notice, a publican, a despised tax collector, was there.

> **And the tax collector, standing afar off, would not so much as raise his eyes to heaven, but beat his breast, saying, "God, be merciful to me a sinner!"**
> (Luke 18:13)

The only thing is, he didn't actually say, "God, be merciful to me a sinner." Literally, he said, "O God, if there was only a mercy seat for me to go to!" You see, the Pharisee was the fundamentalist of that day, and he was quite separated. Well, listen to him, and know that everything he said was true. He said, "I do this," and he did do it, friend. And he said, "I'm not like this publican," and he wasn't. But he sure was proud, and he was depending on his works. He was depending on himself, not recognizing he needed to have mercy from God. As you know, most people—your neighbors and my neighbors—don't think they need mercy from God. Oh, my friend, we all need mercy from Him. He is the propitiation for our sins. For those of us who are Christians, He is the mercy seat for *our* sins. And He is the mercy seat for the sins of the whole world.

But this publican stands way off and he beats his breast. He won't even look up. He says, "God, I'm a poor publican. I have no access to that mercy seat yonder in the temple. If there was only a mercy seat for me to go to!" Why did he say that? Because when he became a publican he denied his people. When he denied his people, he denied his God and his religion, and he no longer had any access to the mercy seat in the temple of that day. Therefore when he went to the temple to pray, he couldn't claim mercy there. He was pleading, "O God, if there was only a mercy seat for a publican to go to." And the Lord Jesus Christ said, "That fellow went down justified." Why? Because the Lord Jesus right there and then was on His way to make a mercy seat for him.

And our Lord has made a mercy seat for you and me. Today we don't need to ask God to be merciful. My friend, He is already merciful! What can *you* do to make Him merciful? Do you think you can shed a few little tears and win Him over? Do you think you could promise to do some good little thing to persuade Him? My friend, what do you want Him to do? He gave His Son to die for you. Don't you know that when Christ died on the cross He paid the penalty for your sins? You can't add anything to that. He is holding out His arms to you. Don't *ask* God to be merciful—claim it, my friend! Claim it!

That's the way I stay in fellowship with Him. Bad as I am, I have to go to Him constantly and say, "Lord, I need mercy. Oh, I need mercy." He hasn't run out of it yet, and He has enough for you. In fact, He has enough for the whole world. Jesus Christ is the mercy seat for the sins of the whole world. Oh, how we need to get to that mercy seat! Have you been there recently?

Reconciliation

We have seen that propitiation is toward God. Now we'll see that reconciliation is toward man. *Katallasso* is the Greek word, and that means "to change thoroughly" or "to change completely." In the classical Greek it meant to change from enmity to friendship.

Reconciliation is strictly a New Testament doctrine. Back in the Old Testament, the word is always *atonement*, which does not even have the connotation that reconciliation does in the New Testament. Nowhere in Scripture does it say that God is reconciled. That is, God is not changed completely. You see, God is immutable—God never changes.

That's the error of the wicked. A great many people would like to believe today that the Hebrews had a crude idea of God, that according to the Old Testament concept He was a God of judgment, but that now in the New Testament era He is not a God of judgment. May I say this: The God of the Old Testament is the God of the New

Testament, and He is the God of the present hour. God has never changed. He doesn't have to change. He never makes mistakes. He doesn't learn things. He didn't learn something today that He did not know at the beginning—He is immutable. He never changes.

So this idea that you can change God is a delusion, friend. Reconciliation does not apply to God, it applies to man, but God brings it to pass.

This is the thing I want you to understand:

> *For if when we were enemies we were reconciled to God through the death of His Son, much more, having been reconciled, we shall be saved by His life.*
> (Romans 5:10)

Let me repeat, nowhere does it say that God is reconciled. It says that God has reconciled the world. That is, God through the death of Christ has changed the world in reference to Himself. No longer is God looking at the world as being a place that He must move against in judgment immediately. That's the reason He doesn't move in today. God's attitude toward the world now is that He has reconciled the world to Himself. He has not changed, but He, by the death of His Son, has changed the world to Himself so that today He can reach down and save.

Look at this again. "For if when we were enemies we were reconciled to God through the death of His Son, much more, having been reconciled, we shall be saved by His life." In other words, Paul is saying that when we were enemies God gave His Son to die for us, and instead of judging us, Christ bore the penalty. Now God wants to deal with us on a different basis altogether. He says to us, "I am reconciled to you." That's what Christ's vicarious death accomplished. That is the reason a holy God doesn't strike out today and judge this world.

Somebody asks the question, "Why doesn't God do something today? It seems like He would do something about the frightful conditions in the world." Well, the reason is simply this: God is reconciled to the world, and He is not willing that any should perish. His arms are outstretched to the world, and He's saying to it, "I'm not demanding anything, I'm not asking anything. I am reconciled to you. I would like for you to be reconciled to Me." And reconciliation is always toward man.

Let's look at 2 Corinthians 5, for this is the great passage on reconciliation:

> *Now all things are of God, who has reconciled us to Himself through Jesus Christ, and has given us the ministry of reconciliation, that is, that God was in Christ reconciling the world to Himself, not imputing their trespasses to them, and has committed to us the word of reconciliation. Now then, we are ambassadors for Christ, as though God were pleading through us: we implore you on Christ's behalf, be reconciled to God.*
> (2 Corinthians 5:18-20)

Friend, this is what the gospel is and the gospel is *nothing else* but this. The gospel is not God asking you to *do* something. He is not asking you to jump through a hoop or to come up to His standard or to do this or to do that. God is now saying to a lost world, "When Christ died, I reconciled the world to Myself through the death of My Son. My message to you is the gospel that was preached to you. And that's what you believed. And that's the way you were saved."

> *Moreover, brethren, I declare to you the gospel which I preached to you, which also you received and in which you stand, by which also you are saved. . . . For I delivered to you first of all that which I also received: that Christ died for our sins according to the Scriptures, and that He was buried, and that He rose again the third day according to the Scriptures.*
> (1 Corinthians 15:1-4)

That, my friend, is the gospel.

Lewis Sperry Chafer, founder and first president of Dallas Theo-logical Seminary, speaking to a class of seminary students, used to put it like this: "You never preach the gospel, young men, until you give people something to believe. The gospel is something to believe, not something to do."

When man sinned back in the Garden of Eden, that wonderful fellowship which God had enjoyed with man was broken; broken in two ways. God, because He is a holy God, had to turn away from this disobedient child of His, this rebellious one. And man in his rebellion turned away and ran from God. They were separated. Then what happened? When Christ died on the cross, God turned around to the world. He brought the world around and put it in a different relation-ship. Now He is saying to man, "Be reconciled to Me. I'm satisfied with what Christ did for you on the cross. Are you satisfied? Will you accept it? Will you be reconciled to Me?"

Today those who have accepted it declare, as Paul the apostle says, "We are ambassadors." Ambassadors? Yes. An ambassador is kept in a country as long as that nation is maintaining relationships. God has not called His ambassadors home. "We are ambassadors for Christ, as though God were pleading through us: we implore you on Christ's behalf, be reconciled to God." The gospel is not your getting God to do something, or promising God you will do something, nor your doing something for God. The gospel is what God did when He gave Christ to die, and you are reconciled when you agree with God that what He did was right.

You see, the death of Christ satisfies God. Does it satisfy you? When God and man meet at that place, there is fellowship again. We meet about the person of Christ, and now God says, "This is My beloved Son." And you come and say, "Yes, He's my Savior." You and God have met now, and there's fellowship, there's agreement, and through Christ you are brought back into a relationship with Almighty God.

May I say, that's the only way you can come to God. You can build your own little altar, your own little system, and you can say, "Well,

I like to do it this way," and you can do it that way. But, friend, the Cross of Christ is the only place where God says that He will meet any of us. That's the reason the Lord Jesus, when He was here, said:

I am the way, the truth, and the life. No one comes to the Father except through Me.
(John 14:6)

In other words, "I'm the way. God has reconciled the world to Himself through Me, and He wants you to be reconciled."

The other night I couldn't sleep, so I read a review of a new book on psychiatry—not that I thought I needed it, but I felt maybe I ought to read it. In it the writer confesses that he's a layman and knows very little of theology, but he admits that the great difficulty with the human family is guilt. And this psychiatrist writes that because man has sinned, he has a guilt complex. The doctor admits he knows little about the Bible but then says he doesn't believe in a cheap salvation, one without some sort of works—this thing of just coming to Jesus. He suggests that to appease our consciences we should perform some flagellation of the flesh or make some sacrifice.

Oh, what little he knows about what Christ did on the cross! And when you know that, you do not consider it a "cheap" salvation. It cost God *everything*. It's an expensive salvation! It's His precious blood He shed in order that there might be a mercy seat to come to. And when we come there, we find out He is reconciled. You don't have to do something to win Him over. You don't have to do something to make Him favorable toward you. Christ did that. And you and I, we just come as sinners—like that poor publican described by our Lord in Luke 18—recognizing that we are sinners. And we do not even have to say what he said, "God, provide a mercy seat for me. I cannot go to the mercy seat in the temple. I am shut out." Thank God, no one is shut out today. Not one of us is shut out.

I do not know who the worst man in the world is, but let me say this to you: he could come today to God and find mercy and find that

God is reconciled to him—but he must come. Because otherwise there is only judgment. Judgment is coming, but today God is reconciled. And He is

> *not willing that any should perish but that all should come to repentance.*
> (2 Peter 3:9)

God is longsuffering. He is patient. I do not think He will strike out of the heavens today. He might, but I don't think He will. He is infinitely patient because He wants people everywhere to be reconciled to Him.

We have a wonderful Savior, do we not? We have a wonderful salvation, do we not? How wonderful to know today that God is not angry. He is not finding fault. He is not hard to please. He is saying, "Just be reconciled to Me. I gave My Son to die for you in order that you might be saved."

You can come, there is mercy with the Lord.

CHAPTER 9

SALVATION: PART 2

Up to this point, the doctrines concerning salvation have had to do largely with the work of Christ upon the cross. We dealt with atonement, substitution, redemption, propitiation, and reconciliation. All of them had to do with the work of Christ on His side.

Now we are dealing with something else: first, regeneration, and following this we will cover the tremendous subjects of justification, faith, and repentance. These four doctrines are very important for us to know. They are closely related, yet there is a sharp distinction among them that must be made in order to understand our salvation. All four of them are involved, and not one of them will stand alone.

Will you notice this distinction here at the beginning: Regeneration is subjective; it has to do with the interior person. Justification is objective; it is without cause—a judicial act of God. You and I are dead in trespasses and sins. Therefore we need a new nature. We need life, if you please, life from God, which is regeneration.

But we need something else—justification—because by nature and conduct we are guilty. That is, we are guilty sinners before God, and justification is that work or act of God whereby He deals with this fact of guilt. He removes the guilt from the sinner.

And then faith is the instrument. It is that which you and I exercise in order that we might stand justified before God. And repentance is included in saving faith. It's important. In fact, it's essential.

We will go into detail as we come to these doctrines. I've made this distinction, and yet mention them together, so that you might see that they are related, although each one of them is a separate doctrine.

Regeneration

First let's consider regeneration. This word does not occur many times, actually only twice in the New Testament, and the Greek word is *palingenesia*, which actually means "to recreate." It means "the new birth," and that is the word we associate with it. It is that which is essential because of the fact that you and I are dead in trespasses and sins.

Notice something for just a moment back in the first chapter of Genesis:

> **Then God said, "Let Us make man in Our image, according to Our likeness; let them have dominion over the fish of the sea, over the birds of the air, and over the cattle, over all the earth and over every creeping thing that creeps on the earth.**
> (Genesis 1:26)

In other words, God said, "I intend to make man, make him after Our image, and this is what I will do for him: I'll give him dominion."

In the second chapter of the Book of Genesis you find the detailed account of the creation of man, and in verse 7 we are told:

> **And the LORD God formed man of the dust of the ground, and breathed into his nostrils the breath of life; and man became a living being.**
> (Genesis 2:7)

This means that the creature God created had been taken out of the dirt, if you please. On the physical side we are dirt. "For dust you are, and to dust you shall return" (Genesis 3:19). That speaks of our physical being.

But God breathed into this man. And He breathed into him the breath of life, and man became a living being. That is, man now is able to commune and have fellowship with his Creator. But you see, man sinned. God had told him:

> *Of every tree of the garden you may freely eat; but of the tree of the knowledge of good and evil you shall not eat, for in the day that you eat of it you shall surely die.*
> (Genesis 2:16-17)

Man didn't die physically that day. It was almost a millennium after that before Adam and Eve died. But they did die spiritually that day. That is, they were dead to God. The apostle Paul confirmed that. When he was writing to the Gentiles, to you and to me, he said:

> *And you He made alive, who were dead in trespasses and sins.*
> (Ephesians 2:1)

That's the reason you and I must be born again. Because of Adam's sin, we were dead to God, dead to the things of God. We had no relationship to Him at all.

The human family demonstrates this in a very emphatic manner. Look into the land of India today, and look into China, and look into any other nation of the world. In fact, look into our own nation today. How many people are actually in a right relationship with God and are having fellowship with Him? Very few. Well, what's the explanation? Men and women are dead in trespasses and sins. The reason the new birth is so essential is because, first of all, we are dead.

We see something of the necessity and the nature of the new birth when we come to our Lord's first recorded interview, which He had with a religious man. This was *not* an accident. You see, if this had been Zacchaeus, there would have been folks who would have stepped up and said, "Of course Zacchaeus needs to be born again. He's a publican, a rotten sinner." Or suppose that the man Jesus spoke to had been from over in Gadara, the country of the Gadarenes. People would have said, "Well, I can understand. That fellow was demon-possessed. Of course *he* needed to be born again."

But Nicodemus was a Pharisee, a leader of the Pharisees, religious to his fingertips. He was following the Old Testament precisely. And yet our Lord said to that man:

> **Most assuredly, I say to you, unless one is born again, he cannot see the kingdom of God.**
> (John 3:3)

May I say that the expression He used is very interesting. It is *genosthe anothen*. It means "to be born from above." If you want it literally, "to be born from the top." You've been born down here physically, but you are dead to God. Now you need to be born in the spiritual sense. You need to have life, and that's *regeneration*.

A man told me about taking his son, whom he thought was color-blind, to the doctor. He was put through all the tests at the clinic, and it was determined that the boy was indeed color-blind. The parents seemed to be distressed over it, for the father told me, "I said to the doctor, 'Is there any cure for this at all? Is there any way in the world that we can change this?'" And the doctor made this strange statement, "The only thing in the world you could do for him is to have him born all over again."

Well now, isn't that what the Lord Jesus said to this man Nicodemus when he came to Him, wanting to talk about the Kingdom of God? Our Lord says, "You can't see. Unless one is born again, he cannot see the Kingdom of God." In other words, "You do not have eyes to see the Kingdom of God. You can't understand about the Kingdom of God because your brain is dead as far as the things of God are concerned."

My friend, this fact is being more and more impressed on my mind. I'm not invited as often as I was formerly to speak to groups like the Rotary Club and the Lions' Club. But I've detected the few times I have gone that it's becoming increasingly difficult to present the gospel to unsaved men—actually, to intelligent men. When I was in the East I spoke in a little town to a group of men who represented the top businessmen of the community. It was amazing. They were sharp men. Certainly they were not dummies, and yet they were the densest men spiritually that I had ever addressed! I recognized that I was speaking to a bunch of dead men sitting there.

May I say, that's the thing which disturbs and rather frightens me today. Oh, the spiritual deadness that there is! Men are dead in trespasses and sins. And our Lord said to this man Nicodemus, "Unless one is born again, he cannot see the Kingdom of God."

There are those who will interject here, "Our Lord also said, 'Most assuredly, I say to you, unless one is born of water and the Spirit, he cannot enter the kingdom of God'" (John 3:5). Some folks interpret "born of water and the Spirit" to mean that you have to be baptized by water before you can be saved. It's hard to believe, but there are two denominations which are built on the assumption that you must be baptized by water before you can be saved. Consider what God's Word means when it says here:

> *Jesus answered, "Most assuredly, I say to you, unless one is born of water and the Spirit, he cannot enter the kingdom of God. That which is born of the flesh is flesh, and that which is born of the Spirit is spirit."*
> (John 3:5-6)

Notice that He dropped the word *water* in verse 6, but He did mention it in verse 5. What did He mean? May I say to you that water speaks of the Word of God. Anywhere you turn in the Scriptures, you find that water, when used in a symbolic sense, refers to the Word of God.

For instance, Paul, writing to the Ephesians concerning the husband and wife relationship, said:

> *Husbands, love your wives, just as Christ also loved the church and gave Himself for her, that He might sanctify and cleanse her with the washing of water by the word.*
> (Ephesians 5:25-26)

The Word of God is the water that he's talking about.

The Lord Jesus, talking to His own yonder in the Upper Room, said:

> *You are already clean because of the word which I have spoken to you.*
> (John 15:3)

James, in his epistle, wrote:

> *Of His own will He brought us forth by the word of truth, that we might be a kind of firstfruits of His creatures.*
> (James 1:18)

You'll also find that Peter wrote about this:

> *. . . having been born again, not of corruptible seed but incorruptible, through the word of God which lives and abides forever.*
> (1 Peter 1:23)

And you'll find in the Book of Acts that

> *many of those who heard the word believed; and the number of the men came to be about five thousand.*
> (Acts 4:4)

Our Lord is certainly emphasizing the importance of the Word of God for the new birth. I personally take the position—and I think I can substantiate it—that never is there a genuine conversion apart from the Word of God. We have to use the Word of God. There is no substitute.

This is the reason that all of the good courses in evangelistic work tell you never to argue. You never win people by arguing. You may win the argument, but you will lose the person. It's the Word of God only that can convict people. It's the Word of God only that can cleanse. It's the Word of God only that can be used in regeneration, because

> *faith comes by hearing, and hearing by the word of God.*
> (Romans 10:17)

Unless they hear the Word of God they cannot receive it, they cannot believe, and they cannot be born again. The Word must be used.

When I was a student at Dallas Seminary, some of us fellows used to go down to the mission on Ackard Street. A gray-haired lady known to everyone as Mother Moore lived right there and ran that mission on skid row, and many times she did it alone. My, what a witness that woman was!

One day when I was there I heard a testimony from a man who was a graduate of either Yale or the Massachusetts Institute of Technology. He was a top engineer. He had worked on Boulder Dam but was finally discharged from the job, not because he didn't have ability, but because he stayed drunk all the time. And when he was thrown off that job it was difficult for him to get another, so he began just bumming around—and he stayed under the influence of liquor. When he got to Dallas, he did what a lot of these bums do, he headed for the mission, knowing that he would at least have one or two nights there.

Mother Moore always talked to the men when they first came in, and so she wanted to talk to this engineer—but not in the manner he anticipated. He had been through that ritual before elsewhere, so he knew what was coming when she said, "Now after you get cleaned up, you come down before dinner. I want to talk to you." He went upstairs to the showers with a feeling of self-satisfaction. *That poor old woman down there, when she starts trying to convert me, will I tie her up intellectually! I will make her look very foolish!* This highly educated engineer could see that she was not what you'd call a member of the intelligentsia.

When he went downstairs, he saw it was the same old routine he had been through before, and he knew all the answers. Mother Moore began to present to him the plan of salvation. Now he had been able to tie up many of the smart boys, because they would argue with him. But she didn't argue. He'd say, "Well now, I don't believe this because of this." But she'd say, "Well, but the Bible says . . ." and she would turn to another verse. Then he'd say, "Wait a minute." And she'd say, "Yes, but the Bible says. . . ." He'd say, "Yes, I know, but I want to put in this," and he would insert a contradiction, and she would say, "Yes, but the Bible says. . . ."

Later in his testimony he said, "You know, I never could get that old woman away from the Bible. If I had for one minute, I would have tied her up, but she wouldn't let go of it." Then he said, "That's what finally got me. I found out I couldn't answer it. All of a sudden, I discovered that the Bible was answering me! It was giving me the answers, and if I was honest at all, I would have to accept what it said."

That man came to Christ by the use of the Word of God. And I do not believe that our clever books nor our clever tracts, and certainly not our clever arguments, win people to Christ. Nothing does but the Word of God. Unless one is born of water and the Spirit, he cannot be born again! Born of water, yes, the Word of God. But don't bring H_2O into this verse! The Bible is the water that our Lord is talking about; it's the Word of God.

There are three outstanding conversions in Acts: the conversion of the Ethiopian eunuch, the conversion of Saul of Tarsus, and the conversion of Cornelius. In the conversion of all three of these men the Word of God was used. Always the Word of God is used, or there can never be a conversion. And that is exactly what our Lord was talking about to Nicodemus.

Now let me present that which to me is conclusive, and I do not believe there is a rebuttal to this at all. I turn to Paul's first letter to the Corinthian believers. The Corinthians were babes in Christ, carnal believers, and they were arguing over who was their greatest instructor. Each was saying, "I am of Paul" or "I am of Apollos" or "I am of Cephas" or "I am of Christ."

Notice this very carefully—if Paul thought baptism by water meant salvation, he sure slipped up here!

> *For though you might have ten thousand instructors in Christ, yet you do not have many fathers; for in Christ Jesus I have begotten you through the gospel.*
> (1 Corinthians 4:15)

Their contentions were causing divisions among them, you see. And Paul says, "Listen, you may have many instructors, but you have only one father—I am your father. The way I begot you was through the gospel. All of you believers there in Corinth are my children because of the Word of God I used. That was what brought you to a saving knowledge of Christ and made you children of God." But wait a minute. Paul had already told them back in chapter 1, verse 14, "I thank God that I baptized none of you except Crispus and Gaius"— then he was reminded of another—"the household of Stephanas" (verse 16). But their new birth came when he preached the gospel. Apparently the water of baptism was not essential to salvation, because Paul said he was thankful that he had baptized only a very few. "And if there were any others, I have even forgotten about it. But I do know this, I preached the gospel to all of you, and you were saved." Baptism was not essential for salvation, you see.

Let me emphasize that regeneration, *palingenesia*, means "the new birth," "born from above," if you please. This is God's work. Do you remember what was said in the Epistle of James?

> *Of His own will He brought us forth by the word of truth,*
> *that we might be a kind of firstfruits of His creatures.*
> (James 1:18)

May I say this to you today, and would you pay careful attention, because we hear a great many wild-eyed ideas about witnessing: The work of conversion is the work of the Holy Spirit. The work of regeneration is the work of the Holy Spirit! Look carefully again at what James says here: "Of His own will He brought us forth." The Holy Spirit is sovereign in this matter. You don't tell the Holy Spirit whom to convert; He will tell you.

I get so many letters from folks who write, "I witnessed to So-and-so and he didn't accept Christ. What's wrong?" If this is your question, you ask God—He's running it, not I. You ask Him. He is sovereign in this matter. "Of His own will He brought us forth." And you and I need to remember that He is the One who is leading the parade. We are following.

Oh, how we need to follow the Holy Spirit in this matter! That's the reason I believe we need more prayer for doing evangelistic work than for anything else we do. You need to pray, really pray about it, and ask the Lord to open up the door for you. Maybe you have a neighbor next door to whom you witnessed, but she slammed the door in your face! Well, did you pray about it before? Did the Holy Spirit lead you to do that?

"No, I wanted to witness."

Well, I know, but you are to let the Holy Spirit lead you in this matter. "Of His own will He brought us forth." And, my friend, that just happens to be very important. "Born of the Spirit" is His work. He is God, and you and I need to follow along in this matter and trust the Holy Spirit to do the converting.

I'd like to give you a personal illustration of this. When I was a young preacher in Nashville, there was a young man whom I was determined to lead to the Lord. I went after him, and I really antagonized him and drove him away. Months went by, and one night he knocked at my door and asked me, "Would you explain to me the plan of salvation?" After I had quit, given up, there were other people praying for this man, and there came the day when the Holy Spirit could take over and get rid of some of us who wanted to run ahead of God in the matter. What a thrill it was when that man knocked on my door and *asked* to hear the plan of salvation! I got a big piece of paper and put it down on the living room floor. He wanted to know about the dispensations, and since I like to explain those too, I had him down on the floor with me. I charted them out, explaining how God saves us today by grace.

May I say to you, let's quit trying to take the place of the Holy Spirit. Regeneration is God's work, and when we are born again, it opens up a new world, a brand-new world.

> *Therefore, if anyone is in Christ, he is a new creation; old things have passed away; behold, all things have become new. Now all things are of God. . . .*
> (2 Corinthians 5:17-18)

A new world opens before us. And when it says that old things are passed away, it means relationships—not little habits, but relationships. We no longer are joined to Adam; we're now joined to Christ. This world becomes a new world to us. When you are born again you become *a child of God*. We are joined to Christ, and we are *in* Christ, if you please. We have a new life, and that new life is a very wonderful thing. I want to give you two Scriptures in this connection.

> *Whoever has been born of God does not sin, for His seed remains in him; and he cannot sin, because he has been born of God.*
> (1 John 3:9)

> *We know that whoever is born of God does not sin; but he who has been born of God keeps himself, and the wicked one does not touch him.*
> (1 John 5:18)

When we are born again we are given a new nature, and that new nature can never sin. That may be the reason some Christians are having such a hard time—including this preacher. Do you know why? It is because when we were born again we were given a nature that cannot sin and won't sin. And when you and I lapse back to living in the flesh and in sin, the very fact that we are having trouble is probably the proof we are children of God. The man in the world can get by with sin, but if you are God's child, you can't get by with it for long. Your new nature won't let you, because that new nature is of God and knows your life is wrong.

That may be the reason you toss and turn in your bed and cannot sleep. And this is the reason you said, "Oh, why did I do that thing? I'll never do that again." That new nature won't sin. It's when you drop back into the flesh and live in it, committing sin, that you can expect to have problems and difficulties. And that's the reason you're not satisfied with your life.

My friend, you can see that regeneration is a tremendous word!

Justification

We have come now to the most important word of all. Have you noticed that some of the words we have considered are used very seldom in Scripture? You find very little concerning *reconciliation*, *propitiation*, and *regeneration*. But *justification* is a word that you'll find again and again and again. The fact of the matter is, it occurs about 229 times in the Bible, and in one epistle, the Epistle to the Romans, it occurs 92 times! To be justified before God simply means to be right before God.

We are hearing today what I first heard in college when the sociology teacher and the psychologist asked the question, "What is right?" How do you know what's right? One person says this is right, somebody else says another thing is right. How do you know what is right? My friend, that which is right is what God says is right. And if anyone is to be righteous, he or she has to be right with God. Now you may disagree with God's standard, and you may not like some of the things that He likes, but to be right with God is to agree with His standard and to meet it. You and I cannot be accepted until we have done this.

May I say that to be justified before God never means to be made righteous. God never *makes* a sinner righteous because the word *justified* means "to be declared righteous." It's a legal term. For instance, you are arrested and brought up before a judge, and the charge is read against you. The judge hears the evidence and the judge says, "Not guilty." That doesn't change you, but it does change your standing before the law. You may have been guilty before you were arrested. Now you have been declared "not guilty," and you are turned loose. That is what being justified or declared righteous is.

And that's also what it meant back in the Old Testament. I have been reading a most profound book, *The Apostolic Preaching of the Cross* by Leon Morris, an Englishman. It is one of the finest books I've read, and he has two chapters on justification. I have been greatly blessed by reading what he has to say concerning this. He points out that justification carries this same thought even back in the Old Testament. Abraham had it. When God told him He was going to destroy Sodom and Gomorrah, this is what Abraham said: "Shall not the Judge of all the earth do right?" (Genesis 18:25). It's an Old Testament concept, you see, this matter of being right and doing right.

Notice Deuteronomy 25:1, which concerns a legal matter:

> *If there is a dispute between men, and they come to court,*
> *that the judges may judge them, and they justify the righteous*
> *and condemn the wicked. . . .*

You see, it's a legal term. When two men are at odds, one is right and one is wrong. They are to come before the judge, and the judge is to declare one of them righteous and the other one wrong.

Now, friend, God exercises that prerogative. He must judge you and me as guilty sinners; there is no other alternative for Him. He has done that. He says that you and I do not meet His standard; we have never kept His law; we are in rebellion against Him; we are sinners and are guilty before Him. And He says that the penalty is death: "The soul who sins shall die" (Ezekiel 18:4). God goes on to say this, "You are guilty, the penalty must be paid, and I cannot be lenient with you."

Oh, if we could only see that! God, when He forgives you, my friend, is not being lenient with you. It's not that He's letting down the bars. It means this: Christ bore the penalty. So now God can justify a guilty sinner and declare the guilty sinner "not guilty," because the penalty has been paid by Another. We are now right before God because God has declared that we are righteous in His sight. Jesus our Lord

> *was delivered up because of our offenses, and was raised because of our justification.*
> (Romans 4:25)

The picture is of a courtroom. The Judge (God the Father) looks down at mankind and He says to us, "You are guilty. The penalty is death—eternal separation from Me." But, you see, the Judge (God in the person of His Son) leaves the bench, and He comes down to where the prisoner is. He says to the prisoner, "Move over." He then looks back at the Judge on the bench and says, "I will pay the penalty."

The Judge says, "That's satisfactory to Me. You can take the penalty. You are worthy and You are able." So God the Son takes the penalty. The Lord Jesus bears the crushing load of our sin in His own body on the tree—delivered for our offenses and raised for our justification. Now a holy God can look down on a sinner, and He can declare that sinner righteous, not because of anything within the sinner, not because of anything that he has done.

> *Therefore we conclude that a man is justified by faith apart from the deeds of the law.*
> (Romans 3:28)

God now can look down at a lost sinner, and He can say to that sinner, "You are no longer guilty. I make over to you the righteousness of Christ so that you can stand in My presence, and there can be no charge brought against you."

Who shall bring a charge against God's elect? It is God who justifies.
(Romans 8:33)

So today a sinner stands in God's presence saved! Not because of some compromise that's been worked out in the back room, or because God has somehow or another opened the back door and slipped us in. That's not the way we get to heaven. We come in the front door. We come in like Christ comes in! We stand complete and accepted in Him.

Now you have the same right in heaven as Christ has or you don't have any right there at all. You are in Him completely, 100 percent saved, or you are lost, out of Christ, 100 percent lost, and it doesn't make any difference how many merits you are trying to earn. We are not saved by our character.

For by one offering He has perfected forever those who are being sanctified.
(Hebrews 10:14)

Jesus Christ, by the offering of Himself, has made us 100 percent acceptable to God, so nothing else is added to that.

Faith

The only thing that God asks of you and me is faith. Faith is more than intellectual assent. It includes that, but it is also personal trust in God. Faith does, however, rest upon knowledge.

So then faith comes by hearing, and hearing by the word of God.
(Romans 10:17)

The only condition of salvation is faith—it's to believe God. It rests upon one foundation: the integrity of God. We believe Him. We take Him at His word; we believe in God.

> *He who comes to God must believe that He is, and that He is a rewarder of those who diligently seek Him.*
> (Hebrews 11:6)

It's the same old illustration we have everywhere that "saving faith" is mentioned. It is always used with a preposition, either the preposition *eis*, "into," or the preposition *epi*, which means "upon." To be saved means to put your trust either "into" or "upon" Christ. You can stand by a chair from now until judgment day and say, "I believe this chair will hold me up," but faith is not exercised until you sit in it, trust your whole weight to it—believe *into* it, if you please, or believe *upon* it—and when you do that, then the chair is holding you up.

At this moment you say you believe in Christ. But *how* do you believe in Christ?

> *You believe that there is one God. You do well. Even the demons believe—and tremble!*
> (James 2:19)

The demons believe and tremble, but they are not saved. Is this faith? And among some Bible-believing folks in our day it has become just sort of a little intellectual assent to something. Oh, friend, that's not salvation. It's not until you and I come and trust ourselves to Jesus Christ that we are 100 percent saved.

Repentance

Faith alone saves. Somebody says, "What about repentance? Don't we need to repent?" Well, the word for *repent*, *metanoeo*, means "to change your mind." And all the repentance God asks for is in the word *believe*. You see, in the New Testament, salvation is made a matter of believing.

> *For God so loved the world that He gave His only begotten Son, that whoever believes in Him should not perish but have everlasting life.*
> (John 3:16)

Paul and Silas said to that Philippian jailer:

> *Believe on the Lord Jesus Christ, and you will be saved.*
> (Acts 16:31)

There are 150 passages in the New Testament that make salvation dependent on believing and believing alone. In the Gospel of John and in the Epistle to the Romans, it is faith and faith alone. Repentance is not there.

"But," somebody says, "isn't repentance necessary?" Yes, it is. But it is included in saving faith. Paul, when he was writing to the Thessalonian believers, said:

> *For they themselves declare concerning us what manner of entry we had to you, and how you turned to God from idols to serve the living and true God.*
> (1 Thessalonians 1:9)

Obviously, Paul, when he came to Thessalonica, found the people worshiping idols. He probably said to them the same thing which he later said in Athens. Let me paraphrase, "When I came, I found an idol to the 'unknown God.' You worship every kind of god here, and you're afraid you'll miss one of them, so you put up an idol to an unknown god. Well, I'm going to tell you about an unknown God. And that One is the living and the true God." And then these people heard about Christ. They heard that He would save them from sin, and they turned to God. But when they turned to God, they turned from idols. And when they turned from idols, that was repentance. *Metanoeo* means "change of mind," and that's in faith. You could not turn to Jesus Christ in faith without turning from something.

For this reason I keep repeating that these people today whose lives have not been changed, although they say they trust Christ, are deceiving themselves. The apostle James makes it very clear:

> **Show me your faith without your works, and I will show you my faith by my works.**
> (James 2:18)

In other words, "I want to see something," James says. He is not talking to them now about being saved by works. He is saying that you are saved by faith, but the faith which turns to Christ turns *from* something, so repentance is there. And we need lots more of it today.

Repentance is not just shedding tears nor just being sorry. Repentance means a change of mind. It means right-about-face and turning to God. When we turn to God, my beloved, we certainly turn from something. Believe me, people will know when you have been converted because your manner of life changes. And if it doesn't change, there is something radically wrong.

May I say that repentance is a word that's primarily in the New Testament, and it's used for believers. When our Lord wrote to the seven churches of Asia Minor (Revelation, chapters 2 and 3), He used the word *repent* frequently. And that's His message to every church in our day: "Repent." That's His message to every believer: "Repent." This is something that we as believers need to do a great deal more of, since repentance is changing our minds and our direction about sin and indifference. How many of us are really convicted about being cold and indifferent? I don't find many.

Are you satisfied to keep going along in an indifferent way? Are you satisfied to be a nominal Christian in these difficult days? Are you satisfied doing nothing for God? Well, what our Lord says is, "Turn around, and start in the other direction."

"Remember," He says, "and repent." That was His message to the church in Ephesus. "Remember." Do you remember when you were converted? Do you? Do you remember what a thrill it was? I never shall forget that Christmas holiday conference in Memphis, Tennessee, when Dr. Harry Ironside and Dr. Louis Sperry Chafer spoke. I had never heard anything like that before, and I would get down to the church before they even opened the doors. The caretaker said to me, "You're a funny fellow, coming this early!" I said, "I don't want to miss a thing."

Remember? I even go back to God today and say, "Oh, restore unto me those days. And give me the thrill I had at that time." Remember, and repent. Start in the other direction.

Oh, may I say, there needs to be repentance for the sinner, but there is repentance for the believer also. The believer needs to do a great deal of repenting. We need to see more tears in church than we are seeing today. We need to see more of these cold hearts of believers stirred and sorry and turning to God with a full purpose of, and an endeavor after, a new obedience to Him. Beloved, how we need to repent!

CHAPTER 10

ETERNAL SECURITY AND ASSURANCE

Many of you will remember the definition of eternal security in your catechism as "the perseverance of the saints," although actually they do not persevere very much. But the concept, the eternal security of the saints, is one of the great doctrines of the Word of God.

Now the doctrine of election is the broad doctrine, and there is a close relationship between election and eternal security. Eternal security rests upon election and the grace of God.

There is also a sharp difference between eternal security and assurance. Nevertheless they are two sides of the same subject. It's like two sides of a door. Eternal security is the exterior—that's the outside of the door. Assurance is the inside of the door, and that's internal. Eternal security is objective—it depends on that which is on the outside of us. It doesn't depend on anything inside of us. Assurance depends on the inside. It is subjective. Eternal security is not an experience at all. Assurance *is* experienced. And eternal security is theological, while assurance is psychological.

Every believer is eternally secure. But it is possible for a person to be saved and not have the assurance of it. May I say that a believer who is saved and does not have assurance is a subnormal or an unnatural believer. Certainly he can be a believer, but God does want us to have the assurance of our salvation.

Eternal Security

To clarify this, we need to look at this great doctrine of eternal security and the perseverance of the saints. Actually, the perseverance of the saints is not their perseverance at all, as we shall see.

May I make some distinctions now, and they are rather sharp. I'd like for you to follow them very carefully. There is actually no difference between salvation and security. Will you notice this? The only *salvation* God is offering is *eternal* salvation. He's not offering any other kind. The kind of life that God is offering is *eternal* life. This is quite simple, and yet it is so important to see. We could select, as you know, a dozen Scriptures to illustrate, but let's use the most familiar:

> **He who believes in the Son has everlasting life.**
> (John 3:36)

Now if a believer loses that life in ten years, it was not everlasting life that he had, was it? It was ten-year life—sort of like a ten-year life insurance policy. But it was not the kind of life God gives to us.

When you say to me, "I knew somebody who for ten years was a very active Baptist deacon, and then he went off into sin. What about his eternal security?" Well, it simply means either the fellow is a prodigal son and will eventually return to the Father or that he had a ten-year, make-believe life and never did have eternal or everlasting life. The one peculiarity about everlasting life or eternal life is that it is everlasting and eternal. And if it's anything short of that, then it's not that kind of life.

The only kind of salvation God is offering today is eternal salvation. So if you get saved, you get eternal life. And if you get eternal life, then it's going to last. And if it doesn't last, you've got something else. You did not have eternal life, my beloved.

> *He who believes in the Son has everlasting life; and he who does not believe the Son shall not see life, but the wrath of God abides on him.*
> (John 3:36)

Jesus says, "He who believes in the Son has"—what kind of life? *Everlasting* life. You see, there is actually no difference between salvation and the security of the believer, because the only kind of salvation God is offering and has ever offered is an eternal salvation.

Now will you notice something over in John 17, the great high priestly prayer of our Lord. Jesus is praying to His Father:

> *You have given Him authority over all flesh, that He should give eternal life to as many as You have given Him.*
> (John 17:2)

What kind of life? *Eternal* life.

Listen to what He says in this prayer. Because He knew that you and I would be considering it, He gave an explanation of eternal life:

> *And this is eternal life, that they may know You, the only true God, and Jesus Christ whom You have sent.*
> (John 17:3)

What kind of life is it? It's eternal. This is eternal life. My friend, if the believer is not secure, then this matter of eternal life means nothing at all. It may have other aspects, but we know there is one thing that is true: God is giving only eternal life to those who are saved.

Now I recognize that there are objections, and I'm going to consider them in just a moment, but I think I ought to take another Scripture that is very familiar to you. It is found in John's Gospel, where our Lord is answering the religious rulers, His enemies. They had challenged Him when they said, "If You are the Christ, tell us plainly."

> *Jesus answered them, "I told you, and you do not believe. The works that I do in My Father's name, they bear witness of Me. But you do not believe, because you are not of My sheep, as I said to you. My sheep hear My voice, and I know them, and they follow Me. And I give them eternal life, and they shall never perish."*
> (John 10:25-28)

Now if they perished, our Lord was wrong.

> *Neither shall anyone snatch them out of My hand. My Father, who has given them to Me, is greater than all; and no one is able to snatch them out of My Father's hand. I and My Father are one.*
> (John 10:28-30)

The picture is this: Both are hands of Deity. Christ says, "No created thing can take them out of My hand, no created thing can take them out of My Father's hand." These are the two hands of Deity. You can't get to the sheep that are in those hands. You just can't!

"I give them eternal life. They shall never perish. Nothing can snatch them out of My hand." That's a tremendous statement, is it not? It's an audacious statement!

Foreknown and Foreordained

Now let's go over to the eighth chapter of the Epistle to the Romans.

> *For whom He foreknew, He also predestined to be conformed to the image of His Son, that He might be the firstborn among*

> *many brethren. Moreover whom He predestined, these He also*
> *called; whom He called, these He also justified; and whom He*
> *justified, these He also glorified.*
> (Romans 8:29-30)

It's very important to see what is being said here. Four things occur: People are *predestined* first, then *called*, and those called are *justified*, and those who are justified are *glorified*! Those are the four steps.

You see, it begins with predestination. People say, "That's an awful doctrine, it means you are predestined to be lost!" May I say to you, beloved, nowhere in the Word of God is predestination ever used in connection with the lost. *Nowhere!* Then what does *predestination* mean? It simply means, as stated here, whom He predestines He calls, whom He calls He justifies, and whom He justifies He's going to glorify. It means that when God starts out with a sinner whom He saves, He's going to take that person all the way home to glory. That's all in the world *predestination* means. In other words, God is going to see him through, and these are the steps.

Let's put it like this: He predestines one hundred sheep. How many sheep does He call? One hundred. How many sheep does He justify? One hundred. How many sheep will He glorify? Ninety-nine? Well now, He gave a parable, didn't He? Let's look at it. A shepherd had a hundred sheep, and one of the little sheep got lost. Pretty good percentage, don't you think? When He starts down here with a hundred sinners, and He gets to heaven with ninety-nine, isn't that pretty good? Ask these sheepmen who begin on the range with the sheep and start to the market in Chicago with them. If they start out with a hundred and get through with ninety-nine, they say it's excellent. In fact, they would be delighted to be able to get through with that many.

But what about this Shepherd in the parable? One of His little sheep got lost. Don't miss that—he got *lost*. One little sheep didn't make it. What did the Shepherd do? He went out and looked for that sheep until He found it, then He put it on His shoulder, the place of strength, and He brought it to the fold. And when He brought it into the fold, He had one hundred sheep. He started out with a hundred; He got through with a hundred.

All predestination means is that God is able to get them through to glory. And He's been in the business now for about two thousand years, calling out the sheep.

> **All we like sheep have gone astray;**
> **We have turned, every one, to his own way;**
> **And the LORD has laid on Him the iniquity of us all.**
> (Isaiah 53:6)

Remember that the Shepherd calls. Do you remember when you were called, when you heard the gospel and believed it? What did God do? He justified you. Then He is going to glorify you.

Somebody says, "Oooh, from here to there is a big, big leap! It's too far for me." God knows that.

Someone else says, "I may get lost." You probably will, but it won't depend on how far and how high the sheep can jump. The question is, will the Shepherd be able to get each of the sheep into the fold? My friend, the real question is what kind of Shepherd you have, not what kind of sheep you are. He has already said that you are a sheep, which means you're dumb and stupid and weak. That's what a sheep is, and it's what He calls us. I think He smiles when He says that. He starts out with a hundred. He gets through to heaven with a hundred. That's the picture before us here, and that's all that is before us.

Don't say predestination is a terrible doctrine. It's a comforting doctrine for me because, honestly, there have been times when I've wondered about Vernon McGee. And I've always felt I would be that little sheep that got lost. Well, thank God, He will go out and look for the sheep until He finds him, and He won't stop until He has a hundred in the fold. What a Shepherd! I praise the Shepherd. There is no praise to the sheep, friend—no use to brag on the sheep. Let's brag on the wonderful Shepherd they have.

Enduring to the End

Now there are those who do not accept this truth, as you well know. And they have certain Scriptures on which they base their objections. We will deal with key verses, because we want to be very fair with these dear folks. The verses are merely samples of certain classifications. In other words, there are certain Scriptures which all can be answered by a single explanation—this one, for example:

> *But he who endures to the end shall be saved.*
> (Matthew 24:13)

Many folks say, "Oh, I don't think I'll be able to endure to the end!" You won't. "Well, it says then I won't be saved!"

Friend, let's look at this verse in context. It has application to the Great Tribulation period. It has no application to us who live before the Tribulation. Matthew 24 was given by Jesus as He was teaching on the Mount of Olives. It is part of what we know as the Olivet Discourse, which has reference only to the Great Tribulation period and the Kingdom that will follow. It will be a brief period.

Our Lord said in Matthew 24:22:

> *And unless those days were shortened, no flesh would be saved [that is, nobody would survive]; but for the elect's sake those days will be shortened.*

He will be able to keep His own, His elect. But how will He keep them? In Ephesians 4:30 we're told that believers are sealed by the Holy Spirit for the day of redemption, so that they are eternally secure in God's hand. In fact, in Revelation 7 we are introduced to a great multitude which no one could number of all nations, tribes, peoples, and languages, standing before the throne of God, whose faith endured during this awful period of the Great Tribulation. And they will endure, not because they are wonderful but because He has put His seal upon them. He is the One who will enable them to endure to the end.

This explanation will answer any number of questions that have to do with Matthew 24 and have application to the Great Tribulation period. Be alert to the fact that there are other passages of Scripture that also have applications which are dispensational and do not refer to conditions today at all. You have to put these verses back in their context to make an accurate application.

The Fallen Are the False

In 1 Timothy 4:1-3 the apostle Paul refers to false teachers, and they are the ones he is talking about:

> *Now the Spirit expressly says that in latter times some will depart from the faith, giving heed to deceiving spirits and doctrines of demons, speaking lies in hypocrisy, having their own conscience seared with a hot iron.*
> (1 Timothy 4:1-2)

Somebody says, "Well, they will depart from the faith, which means that there are some believers who are going to fall by the wayside." No, all of that has to do with false teachers. And may I say that the false teachers are those who have never been saved at all.

You may remember that many years ago word got around that Dr. Harry Emerson Fosdick, an influential crusader for liberal theology, had become what we would call today a conservative, Bible-believing Christian. And it's on record that he got up and denied it—oh, he was vitriolic in his denunciation of it. This man, who had been brought up under sound biblical theology, said that he never did believe it. You see the point.

The Word of God warns us that there will be those who are false teachers, and their numbers have increased dramatically in the twentieth century until they dominate most seminary faculties in our day. They are men and women who have never accepted the truth, although they may profess to believe it. In Dr. Fosdick's day he had to profess to accept it to become a Baptist preacher, and that's what Dr. Fosdick was. He was tried by the presbytery of New York also because he was a Presbyterian for a while. May I say that these men and women who come in under the category of false teachers are people who actually have never been saved at all. Yet they pastor churches and use their pulpits to propagate other ideologies.

I'm convinced that there are many men in the ministry today because Mama and Papa put their hands on their heads and persuaded them to go in that direction. In fact, I was in seminary with several boys who have since fallen by the wayside. Each one of those boys was studying for the ministry to please his parents.

There is one, by the way, living in Southern California, and I've had lunch with him on a couple of occasions. He was a "mama's boy," and she made two or three trips down to the seminary to make sure he was still studying for the ministry. But he very candidly told me that he never believed the Bible was the Word of God nor what was being taught at the seminary, and he doesn't believe any of it today.

So you see that this passage in 1 Timothy 4:1-3 is one which has application to false teachers. It has no application to a believer who has backslidden or fallen away, none at all.

Faulty Translations

Let's come now to another category which has to do with a faulty translation. In English, as in other languages, the meaning of certain words changes just a little over the years. I suppose that I've heard 1 Corinthians 9:27 quoted to refute eternal security as much as any other verse. Let's first read it in the 1611 King James translation: "But I keep under my body, and bring it into subjection: lest that by any means, when I have preached to others, I myself should be a castaway."

This verse is used to prove that even this great apostle Paul was afraid that he would become a castaway, that is, lose his salvation. Well, unfortunately, the word *castaway* means something today it didn't mean at the time of the 1611 translation. The word in the Greek is *adokimos*, and it simply means "disapproved" or "disqualified." This problem has to do with translation, which is clarified when we see it in context:

> *And everyone who competes for the prize is temperate in all things. Now they do it to obtain a perishable crown, but we for an imperishable crown. Therefore I run thus: not with uncertainty. Thus I fight: not as one who beats the air.*
> (1 Corinthians 9:25-26)

Let's continue reading the passage in question from the New King James Version in which the word *castaway* has been properly changed to *disqualified*:

> *But I discipline my body and bring it into subjection, lest, when I have preached to others, I myself should become disqualified.*
> (1 Corinthians 9:27)

Paul is not talking about salvation; he's talking about working for a crown, a reward. In other words he says, "I do not want to come into the presence of Christ and hear Him say to me, 'I'm sorry, Paul, you do not get the blue ribbon for being first, because you didn't finish your course.'"

Paul said that he wanted to so live that when he came into God's presence he would receive the blue ribbon, the crown, for being first in the race. And, friend, when Paul came to the end of his life he could say, "I have finished my course—I made it, I'm coming in first!"

Obviously, he is not talking about salvation, but he's talking about receiving the crown.

Rewards are one subject and salvation is another. After we're saved we run our race for rewards, which come as a result of good works. But salvation is a gift, and you cannot work for that at all.

Reformed Versus Regenerated

May I say that Scripture does say a great deal about our lives. Here is an example:

> *When an unclean spirit goes out of a man, he goes through dry places, seeking rest; and finding none, he says, "I will return to my house from which I came." And when he comes, he finds it swept and put in order. Then he goes and takes with him seven other spirits more wicked than himself, and they enter and dwell there; and the last state of that man is worse than the first.*
> (Luke 11:24-26)

This parable is easy to explain. Our Lord gave this parable about a demon possessing a man, and the demon went out of the man, then the man was swept clean and put in order. Meanwhile the demon wandered around dry places but couldn't find a place to land, so he came back to his original launching pad, and he brought seven of his friends with him. Our Lord's comment is, "The last state of that man is worse than the first." The thing our Lord is talking about here is moral reformation. This man was not regenerated. It is not suggested that he ever became a son of God. He only got cleaned up. He was nothing but an empty, vacant house. He never was indwelt by the Holy Spirit of God. He was just a cleaned-up house. And a great many people today think that's what it means to be a Christian.

By the way, I heard a man make that statement on television the other night. He had lived a clean, moral life, and he considered himself a Christian. Well, he wasn't, according to the Bible's standard. The devil could move in with seven demons anytime he wanted to and take over that man. For some reason he hasn't done it. But a great many of these folks will fall, as you well know, when all they have is moral reformation. And that's what Jesus is referring to.

Proof of Profession

There's also another set of Scriptures where the Word of God talks about our profession of faith being proven by our fruits. John 15:6 is an example. Today the demonstration that you and I are genuine believers is by the fruit of the Spirit—that is, love, joy, peace, and so on—which can be seen in our lives. That's the way the world is going to know our faith is genuine. The Lord Jesus said:

> *If anyone does not abide in Me, he is cast out as a branch and is withered; and they gather them and throw them into the fire, and they are burned.*
> (John 15:6)

May I say, that has to do with fruit. It hasn't anything in the world to do with a person's salvation, but it has to do with the production of fruit that's in his life. And fruit is to be tested. Our Lord said, "By their fruits you will know them" (Matthew 7:20). Our lives, you see, are to be tested.

James is talking about faith when he writes:

> *Show me your faith without your works, and I will show you my faith by my works.*
> (James 2:18)

That is, "I'll show you that my faith is a living faith because a living faith produces works." Seeing fruit is the only way you and I can know that another person's profession is genuine. "By their fruits you will know them." James is saying that a genuine, saving faith will produce good works. And it has to, my beloved. But that has nothing in the world to do with the eternal security of a true believer. It will show only that a great many people do not have genuine fruit.

As you know, we're living in a day when folks can produce flowers and fruit that look more real than the real article. I see artificial flowers being made today, and they're better looking than the flowers I grow. I told my wife, "No use my bringing in flowers anymore. You can buy them." They're not genuine, though. I am told that some of this man-made fruit looks so real the birds come and pick at it. But it's not real. And a great many professing believers today look like believers, but they are not. They are not producing fruit. Genuine fruit will be in the life of a true believer, one who is really saved.

What Do We Have to Lose?

Paul did talk about the fact that we can lose our reward, but losing our reward doesn't mean that we can lose our salvation. Will you notice what Paul says in 1 Corinthians 3:10-15 as he talks about having one foundation and then building on it. The foundation is Christ—He is the only foundation you and I can build on. Now you can put up a great big straw stack, but what happens? Every man's work is to be tested by fire. Well, a straw stack goes up like all these homes did out here in Bel Air. They immediately went up in smoke, and nothing was left.

But you can also build on the foundation with gold and silver. It was interesting to see that quite a few of those people who lost their homes searched through the ashes to see what they could recover. And I noticed one of the movie actors had found a gold plaque which he had received years before. The fire hadn't touched it, but it had touched everything else. It will burn up the straw, but gold will stand the fire. Every man's work is to be tested by fire.

However, this has nothing to do with salvation, as verse 15 makes clear:

> *If anyone's work is burned, he will suffer loss; but he himself will be saved, yet so as through fire.*
> (1 Corinthians 3:15)

As we have said many times, there are going to be folks in heaven who will smell like they were bought at a fire sale—and they were! They will be in heaven because they are saved, and they are on the foundation. But everything they put on that foundation was nothing in the world but a straw stack. And it will not stand the white light of Christ's presence, the One whose eyes are like a flame of fire, because He will ferret it all out. Everything we did for self and everything we did for show and everything we did because of pride will be revealed at that time. Only what we have done for our Lord will be rewarded.

This passage, you see, has to do with rewards. It has nothing in the world to do with a person's salvation. In fact, we have just read that though all our works may be burned up, we ourselves will be saved. The straw stack will go up in smoke, but you will be saved through the fire. You are saved! Thank God for His mercy!

Grace Is Greater

Now there's only one other passage of Scripture we are going to consider. I've taken up, as far as I know, an example of every other objection to eternal security that I've ever heard. Of course, there are many other Scriptures we could have cited, but they fall under one of these classifications. The last one is Galatians 5:4:

> *You have become estranged from Christ, you who attempt to be justified by law; you have fallen from grace.*

Paul speaks of falling from grace. What does it mean to fall from grace? Paul, speaking to the believers in Galatia, is saying they were at one time under the Mosaic Law, but now no longer are they under Law. Instead they have been brought to a higher plane, and that's the plane of grace. To paraphrase, Paul says, "Now that you have been saved by grace, you are to keep on living by grace. If you attempt to come down to the lower plane of living by the Law, you are falling from grace." He does not say you are losing your salvation, but he is saying that you are going down to live on a lower plane than God intended.

THE FATHER'S WORK OF GRACE

May I say to you, eternal security rests upon something very real. First, it rests upon the Word and work of God the Father: *The sovereign purpose of God* is expressed in this familiar verse:

> *For God so loved the world that He gave His only begotten Son, that whoever believes in Him should not perish but have everlasting life.*
> (John 3:16)

This is the covenant He made. It is His purpose for our lives.

Second, eternal security rests on *the power of God.* (My book on Romans goes into much more detail.)

> *What then shall we say to these things? If God is for us, who can be against us?*
> (Romans 8:31)

Friend, if God is for you, who could be against you? Who could? No one, no created thing at all, could be against you.

Third is *the love of God.*

> *For scarcely for a righteous man will one die; yet perhaps for a good man someone would even dare to die. But God demon-*

*strates His own love toward us, in that while we were still
sinners, Christ died for us.*
(Romans 5:7-8)

Do you think, if God gave His Son to die for you when you were a
rebellious sinner, that having saved you and put into your heart a
desire for Him, He would ever let you go now? No, my friend, He
would never let you go. Since God loved you enough to give His Son,
why would you doubt the love of God?

Then the fourth is, *the Father hears the prayer of the Son.* If you
doubt your salvation, take time to read the entire Lord's prayer—I
mean John 17—and listen to the Lord Jesus as He prays to the
Father:

> *I pray for them. I do not pray for the world but for those whom
> You have given Me, for they are Yours. And all Mine are Yours,
> and Yours are Mine, and I am glorified in them. Now I am no
> longer in the world, but these are in the world, and I come to
> You. Holy Father, keep through Your name those whom You
> have given Me, that they may be one as We are. . . . I do not
> pray that You should take them out of the world, but that You
> should keep them from the evil one.*
> (John 17:9-15)

Do you think Christ has a prayer that has never been answered?
His prayer is that God the Father will keep you. Do you think that
prayer is not being answered? He is praying, "Those whom You have
given Me, those who have believed on Me, I pray You will keep them."
God will keep you because Christ has asked for you.

THE SON'S WORK OF GRACE

Notice what God the Son did. First was His *substitutionary death.*
We turn to Romans 8:34 to get all of this in one verse of Scripture,
though there are other verses we could quote:

Who is he who condemns? It is Christ who died, and further-more is also risen, who is even at the right hand of God, who also makes intercession for us.

God the Son died a substitutionary death for us. And He was raised from the dead.

He is our *advocate in heaven,* He is our intercessor. He died down here to save us; He lives up there to keep us saved. You see, our salvation doesn't rest only on a work He did some two thousand years ago with no continuing involvement. He has not gone off and left us. He is keeping His own who are in the world. He has prayed that the Father would keep them, and He is there to make intercession for His little born-again ones. I think that's the most wonderful thing imaginable. What a comfort that ought to be in these difficult days.

Friend, I've got an Intercessor up there who is going to take care of me, and that doesn't mean that I won't be blown up by a bomb or a nuclear explosion. But if I go that route, it will be because that's the way God wanted me to go. And I'm not going to worry too much about that.

THE HOLY SPIRIT'S WORK OF GRACE

Now God the Holy Spirit does a number of things to make sure that you are saved. First He *regenerates* you (Titus 3:5); then He *indwells* you (1 Corinthians 6:19-20); He *baptizes* you (1 Corinthians 12:13); and He *seals* you until the day of redemption (Ephesians 4:30). When is the day of redemption? When He presents you to Christ at the Rapture. May I say, friend, you are saved for sure up to the moment the Holy Spirit presents you to Christ up yonder. You are sealed until the day of redemption. Certainly the Lord Jesus will be able to take over from then on and will be able to keep you after He gets you to heaven.

Assurance

We come now to the doctrine of assurance. Assurance rests upon an intelligent and spiritual comprehension of the Word of God. That's one reason we do not believe you can have the assurance of your salvation and be ignorant of the Word of God. In fact, that is one of the reasons many Christians do not have the assurance of their salvation. They simply do not know what the Bible really says. Paul longed for the Colossians,

> *that their hearts may be encouraged, being knit together in love, and attaining to all riches of the full assurance of understanding, to the knowledge of the mystery of God, both of the Father and of Christ, in whom are hidden all the treasures of wisdom and knowledge.*
> (Colossians 2:2-3)

Here Paul talks about the full assurance of understanding and knowledge, which means, again, that we should have an intelligent and spiritual comprehension of the Word of God.

It is also a recognition of what God has done for us, which we enter into by faith. Isaiah has said it well:

> *The work of righteousness will be peace,*
> *And the effect of righteousness,*
> *quietness and assurance forever.*
> (Isaiah 32:17)

The child of God who has entered into this wonderful doctrine of justification by faith knows that the righteousness of Christ has been made over to him! That person, Isaiah says, can have quietness and assurance. It's an assurance that only the Holy Spirit can give to us. The believer—each and every one of us—ought to be able to say with Paul, without boasting or pride and without any presumption:

> *For I know whom I have believed and am persuaded that He is able to keep what I have committed to Him until that Day.*
> (2 Timothy 1:12)

"I know whom I have believed" is something that God wants His children to be able to say. He wants us to be saved; He wants us to know that we are saved, that we might have joy and assurance of salvation.

That's the reason John wrote his Gospel. He said:

> *And truly Jesus did many other signs in the presence of His disciples, which are not written in this book; but these are written that you may believe that Jesus is the Christ, the Son of God, and that believing you may have life in His name.*
> (John 20:30-31)

The apostle John wrote his gospel record that we might be saved. He wrote his first epistle so we might know that we are saved:

> *These things I have written to you who believe in the name of the Son of God, that you may know that you have eternal life, and that you may continue to believe in the name of the Son of God.*
> (1 John 5:13)

God wants you to *know* that you have eternal life.

There are many reasons why some believers do not have the assurance of their salvation. First let me say that if you are a carnal believer who is governed by your human nature rather than by the Holy Spirit and yet you do have assurance, it is merely presumption on your part. God has never made any arrangement for a carnal believer to have assurance, as 1 John makes clear.

There are certain bases that cause a great many people today to lack assurance of salvation, and I'm going to mention them briefly.

First, some people have the gospel presented to them only partially. And this is the reason that I myself have to say I do not know whether or not I was saved when I went down to that altar underneath a brush arbor behind a Methodist church in southern Oklahoma. Nobody explained anything to me. I was only a little towheaded boy, ignorant as I could be of spiritual things. I didn't know anything about the Bible. And yet, as I think back, the preacher that night spoke on the prodigal son, and he told about how the father loved that boy like God loves sinners. And my heart went out to this God who loved bad boys like me. But nobody explained to me what it all meant, and before many months had gone by my chum and I were caught stealing peaches. He and I had both gone down to that altar, and we both were caught stealing together. When I got him alone I said, "Do you reckon we are saved?" And he said, "I don't know." And we guessed we'd lost it. The gospel had not been presented to us thoroughly at all.

That's one reason when I give an invitation to receive Christ, a counselor is provided to sit down with those who respond. We want to make sure that they not only have accepted Christ, but that they know what they've done. And, friend, God wants us to know.

Notice how the apostle Paul felt about this when he had been in Thessalonica less than a month:

> *For our gospel did not come to you in word only, but also in power, and in the Holy Spirit and in much assurance.*
> (1 Thessalonians 1:5)

Paul says that when he preached the gospel over there, he made it clear. And when they came to Christ, the Word came to them in power and much assurance.

My personal experience has been that a great many people who think they get the assurance of their salvation really get saved. A couple came to me one Wednesday night when I was a pastor in Pasadena. They were newcomers, and they were just glowing. They said, "We got the assurance of our salvation tonight." I congratulated them, and the next Wednesday night they came up to me and said, "Correction, please. We didn't get the assurance of our salvation last Wednesday night. When we got home and talked it over, we realized that we had never really been saved before."

Friend, if you do not have assurance, maybe you aren't saved. Honestly, I mean that. The gospel is to come to you in power and in much assurance. You see, our Lord offers only one kind of salvation— eternal salvation. So you must have gotten another kind if you don't have assurance.

Sometimes justification by faith is not presented in its fullness and so people don't have assurance. But God wants them to have assurance. I thank God for the pastor who, when I was a teenager, talked to me about justification by faith and about how you could have peace, the peace of God.

Sitting on the porch swing one day, Dr. Albert Allen said, "Vernon, do you know how God justifies a sinner?" I did not know what he was talking about. I didn't even know what "justify" meant, but I knew it was what I needed. And Dr. Allen led me to Christ.

> *Therefore, having been justified by faith, we have peace with God through our Lord Jesus Christ.*
> (Romans 5:1)

Oh, I never shall forget that. It was the most wonderful thing I had ever heard. You could have *peace* with God, being justified by faith.

The second reason for lack of assurance is that some people are psychologically fearful and uncertain, and a lot of things enter in— heredity, environment, or any number of religious backgrounds. My background was Methodist. When I was a boy the only people in west Texas and Oklahoma who were preaching the gospel were the Methodists. That is not true today, but it was true then. And I thank God for them. But there was no assurance taught. And that's the reason I didn't get it in those days, you see.

Many people have a similar background. But God wants us to enjoy our salvation and to be assured of it.

May I use an old and familiar illustration: As you may know, I don't like to fly. I just don't enjoy it at all. But when I do fly, I sit there miserable for the entire flight. During the first years of Youth For Christ when the planes didn't go over 10,000 feet up, I flew often over to Phoenix for Youth For Christ rallies. One morning we all started talking to each other because the turbulence got so rough. One man said to me, "I've flown around the world, and this is the roughest trip I've ever taken!"

I thought the plane was hitting bottom several times. Somebody tried to tell me that planes don't fall. That one fell! I don't know how far it went down, but it went way down, and I was frightened. I held onto the seat in front of me—I just grabbed it and held onto it with an iron grip! That was crazy, because the seat in front of me was falling just like the one I was sitting in, but it felt good to hold onto it.

Sitting across from us was a fellow sleeping! We finally woke him up. He said he was a pilot and had flown fifty-seven missions over Germany. That explained why he had been dozing during the entire trip. The turbulence never bothered him a bit. He thought we were silly to be even uneasy about it.

May I say to you, that plane offered me as much security as it offered him. If that plane went down he would go down just like I would. If that plane landed safely, which it did, I would land just as safely as he would. The difference was, he had assurance and I didn't. There are a lot of people today who are saved, but because of their backgrounds or because of their psychological makeup they just don't have the assurance of their salvation. But God wants all of His children to have it.

There are also believers who are out of the will of God. I do not think you can have the assurance of your salvation if you are out of the will of God. Unconfessed sin in the life of a believer cancels out whatever assurance was there. And, friend, if you have unconfessed sin, you *know* that robs you of assurance of salvation.

And then there are those today who are anticipating some great emotional experience. A man in my church in Pasadena has never had assurance to this good day. He is an old man now, ready to pass over. He's saved, but he doesn't know whether he is or not. I have gone over this ground with him a hundred times, and he says, "Well, it looks to me like I'd have a great emotional experience." Then he says, "Now that man Paul on the Damascus Road—look what happened to him. And nothing has happened to me. You just presented Christ and I accepted Him, and nothing has happened. I've had no great emotional upheaval."

That's what he has been looking for, and he is still looking for it. He has never had it, and he never will. But when he goes into God's presence, I think he will get one then, because he sure doesn't think he's going there! But he will. I tried to tell him, "Sure, Paul had a great emotional experience, but what about the Ethiopian eunuch? He had none whatsoever. All he did was pick up a hitchhiker, and the hitchhiker presented Christ to him and he got saved, that's all it was."

You may be saying, "Well, I've never had any great emotional experience either." My friend, it all rests upon the Word of God, what God says, and whether you can take God at His word.

Then there are those who say, "Well, I don't want to say that I'm saved. That seems to me to be a lack of proper humility to say that we're saved and we know it." Oh, my beloved, it is merely taking God at His word:

> *He who has the Son has life; he who does not have the Son of God does not have life.*
> (1 John 5:12)

Do you believe God? God says if you have His Son you have life. Do you trust His Son? Then you have life. On what basis? Your feelings? Your experience? No, sir. Our rest is upon exactly what God said. Can you believe God? You honor God when you believe Him. You dishonor Him when you do not believe Him. You glorify God when you tell Him you accept His Son and that you're resting only upon that.

Now suppose a telegram is handed to me, and the telegram is from Mr. Gotrocks. He says, "I understand that you have been talking about me, and I want to show you my goodwill. If you will meet me tonight at midnight in the lobby of the Biltmore Hotel, I will give you a check for your missionary program for ten thousand dollars." Well, why not make it one hundred thousand as long as we're dreaming?

Let's suppose he sent a telegram with that message. Now look, where would I be tonight at twelve o'clock? Home in bed? Well, you're wrong. I would be down at the Biltmore Hotel at 11:30—I wouldn't want to miss him! I would be there waiting. I would take him at his word, believing what he said.

But suppose I did go home and go to bed, and he called me up at 12:30 and said, "Did you get my telegram?"

"Yes."

"Well, why aren't you down here?"

"I'm sorry, but I didn't believe you."

I wouldn't honor him, you see, and I don't think I'd get the one hundred thousand dollars.

Oh, my friend, we honor God when we take Him at His word. And He says if we trust Christ, we have eternal life. And He wants you to have that assurance.

CHAPTER 11

SANCTIFICATION

T he subject we want now to consider is sanctification. Let me give you a definition of sanctification as it is described in the Westminster Confession of Faith:

> Sanctification is the work of God's free grace, whereby we are renewed, in the whole man after the image of God, and are enabled more and more to die unto sin, and to live unto righteousness.

That may seem to you to be a rather long and elaborate definition. But I consider it a very fine definition of what sanctification really is.

There is more difference of opinion relative to sanctification than probably any other subject. I do believe that up to this chapter every person who is considered conservative would have agreed with every doctrine I have dealt with, except possibly in a few minor points.

On the doctrine of sanctification, however, you may disagree with me. And certainly you could disagree with me and still be sound in the faith, I can assure you of that. But I do believe that what I am presenting here is the correct and the scriptural position on sanctification.

What Sanctification Is

There are two words for sanctification. In the Old Testament the Hebrew word is *gadas*; and in the New Testament the Greek word is *hagiazo*. These two words mean the same thing. And they both have two meanings: "separation" and "to set apart." So in sanctification there are two aspects, the negative part, which is separation from evil, and the positive side, which is dedication to God.

Unfortunately today we have certain groups that will emphasize the negative, and that's all. But there is also danger in talking only about the positive and not even mentioning the negative. It takes both of these concepts to give a full-orbed view of exactly what sanctification is. It is separation from evil, and it is also dedication to God.

I want to look at a passage of Scripture that will illustrate both of these. Turn with me to Colossians 3:5. Your Bible may read "Mortify," "Put to death," or "Put out of operation," or even closer to the meaning than any other, "Put out of gear." Let's substitute that one:

[Put out of gear] *your members which are on the earth.*

This instruction is needful because, when you are saved and receive from God a new nature, you still retain your old nature, and that old nature wants to dominate you. It still wants to run your life, but you are to put it out of gear. As you know, even if you have your motor running, your car won't move if it's out of gear. And that is exactly what the believer is to do relative to the old nature. You are to put out of gear your members which are upon the earth.

Now let's be specific. These are the things you are to put out of gear:

. . . fornication, uncleanness, passion, evil desire, and covetousness, which is idolatry.
(Colossians 3:5)

This is all negative. These are the things that you are to get rid of as a believer.

> *Because of these things the wrath of God is coming upon the sons of disobedience.*
> (Colossians 3:6)

God will judge the unsaved for these things. Do you think that He will let a believer, one of His own, get by with doing these things? He will not. He will judge that believer.

Notice what Paul says next:

> *. . . in which you yourselves once walked when you lived in them.*
> (Colossians 3:7)

That is, before you were saved, those things were in your life, "But now you yourselves are to put off all these. . . ."

Here are some more negative things that you are to get rid of. Look at your Bible very carefully, because it is well for you to know the correct translation here. We as believers tend to make our own lists of superficial things which we consider unacceptable behavior if we are to be a separated Christian. "But now ye also put off using makeup, jewelry, dancing, going to movies"—aren't those in your Bible? May I say that they're not in my Bible either. I was just making them up, because that's what a lot of people tell me it means to be separated. And yet you can refrain from doing all those things and still be the meanest little stinker there is in your town.

But here is what God says you are to put off:

> *But now you yourselves are to put off all these: anger, wrath, malice, blasphemy, filthy language out of your mouth. Do not lie to one another, since you have put off the old man with his deeds.*
> (Colossians 3:8-9)

Do you tell the truth? "Well," you say, "every now and then I stretch a point." May I say, and I say it from the Word of God, you are not a separated Christian.

Now don't misunderstand me. I am not approving or disapproving some of these other things, like dancing or going to movies. I'm just saying that we tend to emphasize the wrong set of things, and we do not emphasize the things God does. As a result, we have more satisfied little believers running around who think that they're separated, and they are not separated. They have mean tempers, they will gossip, they will misrepresent—they will do all of these things and yet consider themselves separated. Paul says they are not, and I'm just agreeing with him. Let's go by the Word of God, friends, not by the new standard of conduct that people have today.

You see, this is the negative side of separation, separation from evil, and I've stated here the evil that Paul identifies.

We come now to the positive side. To be a sanctified believer means you are not to be just negative, putting off certain things, but you are also to live a positive lifestyle, since you

> *have put on the new man who is renewed in knowledge according to the image of Him who created him.*
> (Colossians 3:10)

Then continue with verse 12:

> *Therefore, as the elect of God, holy and beloved, put on tender mercies. . . .*

Your Bible may read "bowels of mercies," which is an accurate translation from the Greek, indicating that the viscera, the internal organs, are the seat of our emotions. I think that even psychology is moving to the view that not much emotion happens in the head, but a whole lot happens down lower. I have noticed that when I am in a very stressful situation I don't hurt in my mind—I hurt in my tummy.

And it is down in the viscera area where you and I are to be merciful. The point is that mercy is the thing that the believer is to exercise.

Now notice that the next word in verse 12 is "kindness." That's a positive thing. Are you known as a believer who is kind? Are you kind to everyone?

> *. . . kindness, humility, meekness, longsuffering; bearing with one another, and forgiving one another, if anyone has a complaint against another; even as Christ forgave you, so you also must do. But above all these things put on love, which is the bond of perfection.*
> (Colossians 3:12-14)

"Perfection" is completeness or real sanctification, by the way.

> *And let the peace of God rule in your hearts, to which also you were called in one body; and be thankful.*
> (Colossians 3:15)

This was the truth that brought John Wesley to conviction and eventually to saving faith in Christ. John Wesley was a fine young man and practicing Christian. In fact, at Oxford he and his brother organized a society for spiritual improvement known as the "Holy Club." These men had rigid rules, and they refrained from doing certain things. John Wesley thought he was a believer. He was the son of a preacher, he had a godly mother, and he even came to America as a missionary to the Indians and colonists.

But on the way over here the ship got into a terrific storm. Wesley, although it wasn't visible, was terror stricken. As he watched the German Moravians on board he saw that they had the peace of God in their hearts, something that he did not have. It brought John Wesley under such conviction that when he got to this country, according to the account, he never did any mission work. He was a failure here. His record in Georgia was nil; he did nothing at all.

His cry was this when he returned to England: "I went to America to convert the Indians, but who shall convert John Wesley?" He knew that he didn't have anything on the inside. He thought he was sanctified, but in truth he was not even saved. It's not what is on the outside, but what is inside.

You see, friend, sanctification is like taking off an old garment and putting on a new garment. And this figure of speech in the Scripture is a good figure. It is actually a picture of a habit—we speak of a riding habit or a walking habit or another kind of habit that we wear. It is laying aside this old garment, which is the negative aspect. But then it is putting on a new garment, and it's this new garment which is such an important part of sanctification, you see.

What we are trying to do is get to the meaning of sanctification. It means to take off and it means to put on. This is the goal for a believer as found in Colossians. It spells out things which you and I are to put on.

Now I'm confident that we who are believers, as we read down through the negative list—anger, malice, blasphemy, lying, and so on—we recognize that there are certain things there that we have not put off. Right? Also there are certain things on the positive list—tender mercies, kindness, humility, meekness, longsuffering, and bearing with one another—that we have not put on. Oh, my friend, for this reason sanctification ought to mean a great deal to us. None of us, regardless of who we are, has reached perfection. Now I know there are some folks who think they have, but they have not arrived at all.

Let me make only one other point by way of trying to isolate and identify this. Justification, which we dealt with in a previous chapter, is our standing before God. We are guilty, lost sinners in our natural state, but when we come and trust Christ, our standing before God changes. God, who had to pronounce us guilty, now says that we are not guilty, that we are accepted in the Beloved, accepted in Christ our Savior. Our standing is changed by justification. Regeneration, which we looked at in a previous chapter, means that God has not only done an exterior job of decorating, but He has also done an interior job. We are regenerated. We have been given a new nature on the inside if we are children of God.

Sanctification has to do with the character and the conduct of the believer. Justification is an *act*; it happens one time. Sanctification is a *work*. Justification is what God does *for* us; sanctification is what God does *in* us. And they go together. May I say that having justified us, God wants to sanctify us. He wants to improve us. He wants to develop us.

But there are three dangers to which we must be alert. First of all, there is a danger that we interpret our sanctification by our experience. A great many people do this today. And, I say this kindly, this is the difficulty with some of our more charismatic friends. They attempt to interpret sanctification by an experience. And if they have had some great, overwhelming experience, they feel that they have been sanctified.

Oh, my friend, this is the rule that we should follow: The Bible interprets our experience, but our experience does not interpret the Bible. It's so easy for us to have an experience and use that experience to interpret the Word of God. But the Word of God must interpret the experience that you and I have. There's danger in getting the cart before the horse.

The second great danger is in thinking sanctification means sinlessness, that is, to reach the place where you do not sin. No, beloved, that is not sanctification. You will find, for instance, that Paul said to the Corinthians that they were sanctified; then he turned right around and told them what a bunch of carnal believers they were. Yet they were sanctified. You see, sanctification does not mean sinlessness under any circumstances.

The third danger is thinking sanctification is an act. It is not a single act but a continuous work. It is without cessation. As long as you and I are in this world, God wants continually to improve us. And you and I, in this life and this frail flesh, will never reach the day when we can say, "Well, I've arrived. I don't need to go on." Now I have a feeling that there are believers today who think that they have already arrived. But, honestly, to believe that is a matter of ignorance. You and I will never reach the place where we don't need to progress in our Christian walk.

Three Aspects of Sanctification

Now I've come to the subject at last! Here are the three aspects of sanctification.

POSITIONAL SANCTIFICATION

The first is positional sanctification:

> *To the church of God which is at Corinth, to those who are sanctified in Christ Jesus, called to be saints. . . .*
> (1 Corinthians 1:2)

Notice in your Bible that "to be" is in italics, which means it is not in the original. The fact is, the word *saint* means "sanctified," and every believer is positionally sanctified. Paul addressed the Corinthians: "to those who are sanctified in Christ Jesus, called saints," if you please, not "to be" saints. Will you notice also another verse here in the first chapter:

> *But of Him you are in Christ Jesus, who became for us wisdom from God—and righteousness and sanctification and redemption.*
> (1 Corinthians 1:30)

Let's look at this for a moment. The Lord Jesus Christ is our sanctification, and all that He is has been made over to us. The moment you trust Christ, you are made accepted in the Beloved. And you have as much right in heaven as He has because you have *His* right—all of His worth, all of His merit is made over to you! That is the *position* you and I have.

Let me remind you that God through Paul is giving this marvelous information even to the Corinthians. A little later he is going to be rough on them. He is going to tell them they are carnal; he's going to scold them for having divisions among them, running after teachers who please them. They are nothing in the world but a bunch of little babes in Christ. And yet to them Paul says, "Christ has been made unto you sanctification." He is your sanctification, and you are accepted in Him. You cannot improve on that! Keep in mind that this is your *position*. This is what you occupy up yonder in heaven.

PRACTICAL SANCTIFICATION

However, down here on earth where you and I live, we have *practical sanctification*. And this, by the way, is progressive, it's experiential, and it's what most people have in mind when they talk about sanctification. It is where we all live and move and have our being, the place where there is latitude for growth, for development, for improvement.

God has provided for you and me the means for us to grow and develop into the kind of Christian He intends us to be. And I want you to look with me at these provisions God has made for you and me to be sanctified. I am going to give you five means that God has provided, and I am bold enough to say that you and I can never be sanctified in this life on earth, we can never grow in grace, and we can never develop unless we use the means which God has provided for us.

The Word of God is the first provision, and that is very clear. The Lord Jesus, during His final days on the earth, prayed for us: "Sanctify them by Your truth. Your word is truth" (John 17:17). I want to make a statement that may seem strange to you. This Book, the Bible, is a miracle cleaner. The media has a great deal to say about the right kind of miracle powder to put into your washing machine, and every one of the manufacturers claims to have a secret formula and that if you don't use his, those clothes will come out tattletale gray, or they won't be as you'd like for them to be. So you must use their miracle cleaner. Well, the public falls for that type of thing today!

But, friend, I want to talk to you now about a real miracle cleaner. This Book I hold in my hand, the Word of God, is the best bar of soap for a believer that you'll find anywhere. This is the miracle bar of soap. This Word has the power which prompted our Lord to pray:

> *Sanctify them* [make them holy] *by Your truth. Your word is truth.*
> (John 17:17)

I do not believe that any child of God can grow and develop and be sanctified—that is, be made holy unto God—apart from the Word of God. God has no other method except this.

Now this is the reason that all of this business of experience we hear in our day is not worth a snap of the fingers when the experience is divorced from the Word of God. This Book has the power to cleanse you. It has the power to clean up your life! It has the power to transform your life!

Let me share with you some of the experiences of folks whose lives God has absolutely transformed by the simple teaching of the Word of God on radio. In the early days of teaching the Bible by radio, I would be by myself in my studio, and when I would turn around after the thirty minutes were over, I would sometimes wonder if anybody had listened and if anything had happened.

Let me tell you a couple of things that encouraged me during those first years. There was a young man who was sitting down on the wharf in San Diego. He was as vile as a man could possibly be. He had such a tongue that, when he started using it, even those roughnecks on the docks would move back because he knew how to blaspheme.

Somebody else down there brought a radio with him and tuned in our program. The young man told me later that the first thing he said was, "Turn off that [blankety-blank] preacher. I don't want to hear him!" But the fellow left the preacher on, and God in His great mercy brought the blasphemer under conviction. He started listening to the Word. He listened to the simple teaching of the Word for six months. I met him at the First Baptist Church in La Mesa, and I want to tell you, that young man has been transformed! He's one of the sweetest fellows I have ever met. You know what did it? This Book, the Word of God. It has power today to transform.

I can tell you about a family out in the San Fernando Valley who had come from the East. They were not saved, although they were churchgoing folks. But when they came to California they went to Disneyland one Sunday, and the next Sunday they went to the beach, the next Sunday somewhere else. They got away from God. Neighbors invited them in to have cocktails. That was new to them, but they tried it, and they liked it. First thing you know, they were in trouble.

Then, occasionally, they began listening to our broadcast. They got to the place where one morning they realized that they had made a shipwreck of their lives, their marriage, their home, and everything. The wife actually said, "I'm packing up and going back home."

But instead, that couple started coming to church for our Thursday night Bible study. I had never even talked with them, only greeted them out in the foyer. The Word of God is responsible for putting them back together again.

I believe I hold in my hand the only miracle cleanser there is! This Book is the only thing that has power to sanctify you, my friend.

Now honestly, how much time do you really spend in it? I say to you, this Book has the power to transform a person's life. I could give you illustration after illustration from people all over this world of what this Book can do. I have great confidence in the Book, the Word of God. In fact, it's the only thing I do have confidence in today. It is a miracle cleanser!

The Holy Spirit is the second provision that sanctifies. Would you look with me at 2 Thessalonians 2:13:

> *But we are bound to give thanks to God always for you, brethren beloved by the Lord, because God from the beginning chose you for salvation through sanctification by the Spirit and belief in the truth.*

You see, the Holy Spirit using the Word of God is the way it works. The Holy Spirit sanctifies also. And may I say, and I won't take time to develop this point, when sanctification is mentioned in connection with the person of Christ, in practically every instance it is positional sanctification. When it's mentioned in reference to the Holy Spirit, it is practical sanctification.

The body and the blood of Christ, my beloved, is a third means that God uses to sanctify us. And I want you to look at several Scriptures which have to do with the blood and the body of Christ.

> *Therefore Jesus also, that He might sanctify the people with His own blood, suffered outside the gate.*
> (Hebrews 13:12)

And will you notice this in particular:

> *The blood of Jesus Christ His Son cleanses us from all sin.*
> (1 John 1:7)

This is present tense: The blood of Jesus Christ, God's Son, just *keeps on cleansing* us from all sin.

The reason I dwell so much on the Cross and the blood of Christ is that I believe there is personal value in our talking about the blood and body of Christ. I believe that the elements taken at the Lord's Supper are more than symbols. I hear people say, "Well, the bread is just a symbol, and the fruit of the vine is just a symbol." It's true that the juice is only juice, and the bread we serve is only unleavened bread. And honestly, there's no value in those elements. But if partaking of them directs us to the body and blood of Christ, there is a sanctifying value in that!

In too many churches today, especially Bible-teaching churches, we take the Lord's Supper as if it is only a form, a ritual, to go through. But, my friend, there is a spiritual value in it. Are you getting it? Does it sanctify your own heart and your own life? Is it developing you? It ought to, because that's the purpose of it.

Now notice two other Scriptures:

> *By that will we have been sanctified through the offering of*
> *the body of Jesus Christ once for all.*
> (Hebrews 10:10)

> *But God forbid that I should boast except in the cross of our*
> *Lord Jesus Christ, by whom the world has been crucified to me,*
> *and I to the world.*
> (Galatians 6:14)

May I say to you that the body and blood of Christ is a means that God uses to sanctify us.

Yielding to God is the fourth means of sanctification, and this is the one that some people consider to be all that is necessary. But I believe that all of the other three should be in our lives before we come to this matter of yielding to God.

> *But now having been set free from sin, and having become*
> *slaves of God, you have your fruit to holiness, and the end,*
> *everlasting life.*
> (Romans 6:22)

You've been made free from sin. You've become now the servants of God. And that's what Paul means when he says in Romans 12:1:

> *I beseech you therefore, brethren, by the mercies of God, that*
> *you present your bodies a living sacrifice.*

We have to yield to God if we're to be sanctified and if we are to grow in grace.

I want to say something now that is sure to sound strange to you. I don't want you to misunderstand this because it is important. Someone asked Dr. C. I. Scofield, the editor of the Scofield Reference Bible, if it were possible for a person to live without sin. And Dr. Scofield's reply was this: "God has made an arrangement whereby you can live without sin, but I never met a Christian who had reached that place."

May I say to you, I do not believe in sinless perfection. But I do believe that God has made a perfect arrangement for you to live for Him.

Read this carefully:

> **My little children [my little born ones]**, *these things I write* *to you, so that you may not sin.*
> (1 John 2:1)

Isn't that wonderful! This ought to be the goal of every believer. And you and I ought not to be satisfied. We can have peace in our hearts and all that sort of thing, but we ought never to be satisfied, never content, as long as there is sin in our lives. This means simply, as I've already said, that we can never in this life, as far as I can see, get to the place where we have arrived.

"But," you say, "God has made an arrangement." Yes, but I've never met anybody that entered into it perfectly. God has made a perfect arrangement, and that's the challenge today, it's always the challenge for a child of God. I wish we could get the challenge back into Christian living.

I watched these boys out here at USC several years ago on the track jumping over the little cane pole. Since I used to high jump, I watched them with a great deal of interest. I saw that they never were satisfied with their jumps. They kept moving that bamboo pole up, inching it up. Why? Well, they wanted to go just as high as they could go.

God has made a perfect arrangement for you and me to achieve in our Christian life. But a lot of us, with the pole way up there, are satisfied with mediocrity in our Christian experience. We wonder what's the use of trying, which is the other extreme from thinking we've arrived. However, God has made a perfect arrangement: "My little children, these things I write to you, so that you may not sin" (1 John 2:1). Wouldn't you like to get to that place? Are you tired of failure in your life? Well, if your answer is yes, there's hope for you. If you said no, there's no hope for you. But, friend, can you say with me, "I want to live for God; I want to live on the higher plane; I want to be a better Christian"? Listen again to the apostle John: "My little children, these things I write to you, so that you may not sin"—God has made a perfect arrangement, and I want to go to Him and say, "O Lord, help me to enter more perfectly into this arrangement You have made."

Now if our Lord had stopped there, I would have to go to Him every night and say, "Lord, I failed. You'll have to count me out. There is no use my trying to get over that bar anymore."

But we have an Advocate! He said this to me:

And if anyone sins, we have an Advocate with the Father, Jesus Christ the righteous.
(1 John 2:1)

So at the end of this day I'm going to have to go to Him, as I've been going to Him for years, and say, "Lord, I didn't clear the pole today. I didn't go over it where You put it. I failed You!" But, thank God, I have an Advocate. He's on my side; He will plead my case. Do you know what He tells me? He says, "McGee, you get up tomorrow morning and I'll put the pole up and we'll try again." He has been saying that every day, and as long as He will put the pole up, I'm going to jump. I sincerely want to live for Him, and I think you do too. Oh, may God help us.

FINAL SANCTIFICATION

We must move on now. We've got one more point under the subject of sanctification: perfect, or final, sanctification. You may remember that in the epistle Paul wrote to the Ephesian believers, he said that the church is the bride of Christ:

> *Husbands, love your wives, just as Christ also loved the church and gave Himself for her, that He might sanctify and cleanse her with the washing of water by the word, that He might present her to Himself a glorious church, not having spot or wrinkle or any such thing, but that she should be holy and without blemish.*
> (Ephesians 5:25-27)

What kind of church? Perfect. When we are presented to Him someday, we will be *perfect*. That's final sanctification.

> *Beloved, now we are children of God; and it has not yet been revealed what we shall be, but we know that when He is revealed, we shall be like Him, for we shall see Him as He is.*
> (1 John 3:2)

Although I keep falling down in this life, I do hope I'm getting a little higher on the pole each day. But though I'll never be able to clear it at the height my Lord has put it, one of these days I am going to be presented to Him and I will be perfect! You may not recognize me. And I may not recognize you either, since we will be perfect. We will be presented to Him without spot, without blemish. Then our sanctification will be complete. But you and I now are in training down here.

I believe God uses many means today to sanctify us. Do you know one of the greatest means that He uses? Discipline. He not only disciplines us, God actually sends us trouble, and He uses it like sandpaper to get the rough edges off our lives. God is doing all of that to develop us, and I'm convinced of this (although I have to pause many times and ask God why He's permitting a certain thing to happen). This week I've had occasion to ask Him that question, and

I do not know the answer. But I am persuaded of this: God will not let anything come into the life of a believer which will not aid in his sanctification. My friend, everything God sends to you He sends into your life to sanctify you.

God wants to produce fruit in your life, the fruit of the Spirit. He wants your life to be improved. We are saved by faith, but God is not satisfied to leave us in sin. So we cannot live in sin if we have been saved. We must, my friend, be pressing on.

A dear brother, a retired Methodist preacher, used to visit the church where I served, and one day he said to me, "McGee, there's only one thing wrong with the holiness movement, and that is it lacks holiness." And this, my friend, is the thing needed today in our own lives. We're a little afraid of the word. When we mention holiness, we say, "Oh my, no, that means a fanatical group." No, it's a good Bible term. God wants to create holiness in your life and in my life. That is, He wants to develop us. He wants to sanctify us. He wants to bring us up to maturation, make us full-grown children of His, living for Him and bringing honor and glory to His name.

My, what a challenge is held out today to the child of God. None of us could ever be satisfied, and yet none of us, even the weakest, needs to despair because we have a wonderful, wonderful heavenly Father who every day will begin with us again. Though intent on developing us, He will be patient with us as He leads us on.

CHAPTER 12

HEAVEN AND HELL

Let me ask a question or two of you now: What do you know about heaven and hell? How much of what you know is scriptural, and how much of your thinking about heaven and hell is due to speculation? How much is due to mythology, to the Middle Ages, to the writings of Dante, or Goethe the German, or Milton the Englishman? How much of what you know is really the Word of God?

May I say that the accretions of men's imaginations and the impressations of time have largely shaped our thinking on both of these subjects. And one of the reasons is that Scripture has very little to say about either of them. Actually, more is said about hell than about heaven, but very little has been said about either one. However, that which has been said is both specific and it's unmistakable. You cannot misunderstand the language. You may not believe it, but you can certainly understand what's being said.

Our subject is not as simple as it may appear. For example, we need to distinguish between the intermediate state and the eternal state after death—there is an intermediate state for both the saved and the lost. Then there are different classes of creatures. There are angels, and they are divided into the fallen and the unfallen. There are the Jews, and they're divided between the remnant and those who are lost. There are Gentiles, and they are divided into the saved and the lost. And then there is the church. So when you talk about heaven and hell you have to think of these different classes and different groups.

Also we must know the meaning of certain words in Scripture pertaining to heaven and hell. One is *sheol*, another is *hades*, and then there are *gehenna*, *tartarus*, and hell; also heaven, the kingdom of heaven, and the heavenlies. May I say, we need to be able to distinguish and know these different areas we're talking about.

Hell

Now I want to preface what I have to say with this remark: There is nothing more repulsive to the natural man than the subject of hell. There is no subject that causes him to rebel more than this one. It's very interesting. I have noticed that on the radio I can speak on any subject under the sun and find a certain amount of agreement. But the minute I touch on the subject of hell, that changes.

I spoke on it the other day, and it triggered several letters; someone wrote me a poem; someone else called me at home. In fact, they said things like, "You belong to the Middle Ages; you're not up to date. Apparently you haven't done any thinking recently. Don't you know that no intelligent person today speaks of hell, that it is absolutely a figment of the imagination?"

These kinds of reactions don't disturb me anymore, because if they reacted any differently I'd know there was something wrong. The natural man must inevitably rebel against this. He'll see red when you begin to talk on this subject. May I say that if you are reading this today and you're not a child of God, you'll not like what I'm going to say right now, I can assure you. The fact of the matter is that inside you will be rebelling against it.

What we are talking about is the subject of divine retribution, not punishment. When you talk about hell being a place of divine punishment, it gives the idea of discipline and that hell is a place where people are being disciplined. That is not true. It's divine retribution. It is a place of judgment, and it's not a place of discipline in any sense.

Actually, the more refined, cultured, and genteel people are, the more likely they'll rebel against this subject. That is the reason some lovely, refined folk who move so evenly on other subjects, at the mention of hell, respond so vehemently. For the unsaved person, it is a natural reaction—it couldn't be otherwise. Their argument will go something like this: "I believe in a God of love, and a God of love would never have a place like hell." May I say that if that were all that could be said about God, it would be true. But they forget that God is holy. They forget that God is righteous. They forget that God is enraged against sin. They forget that God cannot tolerate sin at all.

I've heard this kind of argument many times—generally coming from some soft-spoken person, but, oh, they get exercised over this subject! They say, "Do you think that I'd take one of *my* children and put *my* child in hell? Don't you know God would never do a thing like that!" That's the type of reasoning we hear. The answer, of course, is very simple. When a person says, "I would not put my child there," the answer is, "You are not God, and you do not know what is involved."

Friend, there is no other topic where a person reveals what a small comprehension he has of God and His infinite holiness. And he has no comprehension of the exceeding sinfulness of sin. As a result, the human family rebels against this and is not willing to leave matters like this in the hands of a God who has revealed to us certain great facts concerning hell.

Let me draw to your attention a verse of Scripture which Moses wrote:

The secret things belong to the LORD our God, but those things which are revealed belong to us and to our children forever, that we may do all the words of this law.
(Deuteronomy 29:29)

The secret things belong to God. And there are many things that God has not taken time or seen fit to reveal to us at all. It's in these areas that He expects us to trust Him implicitly. In fact, here's where we reveal faith, and here is where the lost reveal rebellion against God.

When Satan began to attack Job, and when God commended this man, one of the things He said concerning Job was that he had not charged God foolishly. Job never got to the place where he said, "God is being unfair to me. God is being unjust. God is not doing right." Job did get to the place where he said, "I don't understand what's happening to me, and I don't understand why God is permitting it." But Job said this: "Though He slay me, yet will I trust Him! I have confidence in Him" (Job 13:15). You see, that man is right with God. Job did not rebel; he did not charge God foolishly.

May I say to you, Christian friend, you need to be very careful in your conversation, especially with the lost man. He can detect immediately the rebellion that's in your heart because it's in his heart also. And if we have that rebellion in our hearts, when we say, "Why did God let this happen to me?" we are charging God foolishly, you see. We are not trusting Him.

Now there are some basics that we need to nail down. The first one is, God is holy. The second is, God permitted sin. And the third is, God gave Christ to die. Those are three great facts that we have to face. Ours is the holy God, and God did permit sin, and God gave Christ to pay the penalty for us. And if God today can let one person escape divine retribution, then the Cross of Christ was a blunder. God made a big mistake in letting His Son die on the cross if there is some other way even one person could slip into heaven without turning to Christ and accepting His gift of salvation.

ANYTHING BUT HELL

In the presence of this awful reality of hell and of the Bible revelation concerning it, many people have offered certain theories to offset the scriptural doctrine, and I'm going to suggest several of them to you. There is no Bible basis for any of these. They are pure speculation, and there is not a scintilla of fact for them.

The first theory is *annihilation*, and there are those today who say that they believe in utter annihilation; that is, that death is the cessation of existence, that man dies just like an animal dies. There are multitudes of folks who are living like animals and would like to believe it is true that death would end it all. But may I say to you, as far as the Word of God is concerned, there is no support for that sort of theory at all.

Another viewpoint is *transmigration* of the soul; that is, at death the soul passes into another body. When I brought a message on this subject several years ago, I was surprised to find the number of people in Southern California, members of Protestant churches, who believe in this. May I say, it's paganism and it's Buddhism. It is said by some scholars who know Buddhism from beginning to end that this matter of transmigration is not in the Vedic scriptures at all, nor do you find it anywhere in Buddha's writings. It is something that has grown up as a tradition. It has led, of course, to this other explanation of nirvana—that you keep moving, and when you die your soul will go into an animal. This is the reason they don't kill a cow in India—it could be your mother-in-law, so you have to be careful about those things.

Then it is believed that after each death the soul moves on again, and finally it just ends up in nirvana, that is, total extinction. This is the reason that a great many people right here in the United States will stand on their heads in the morning and practice yoga. That is where they learn to just think, to contemplate, to spend time in meditation. The teaching is that if you just keep meditating and keep thinking, preparing yourself, one of these days you will meditate out into nothing. This, of course, has no scriptural basis; it's paganism from beginning to end, and it's amazing to me.

I talked to a young man who has practiced yoga, and he believes in transmigration. He approached me after the message I had brought on it, and he wanted to talk about it. And I said to him, "On what basis?"

"I reject the Bible doctrine of hell."

"You do?"

"Yes, I reject the Bible doctrine of hell."

"All right. Now then, would you give me the facts for what you do believe? What is the basis of your belief?"

And he had none!

It's amazing to me that intelligent people will reject the Word of God—a document that you can have confidence in—and they will turn their backs on truth and pick up an absolutely baseless theory. Why? Because the natural man hates the idea of hell and will believe anything in order not to believe in a hell. If a person believes in a literal hell, he is open to hear the gospel. A man said to me: "If I believed in hell as you believe in hell, of course I would turn to Christ. But I don't believe in it." That's the natural man.

Conditional immortality is another explanation that bypasses the reality of hell. It teaches that the grave is hell for the lost. You are acquainted with a cult that promulgates this—they probably knocked on your door last Saturday morning. Their belief that the grave is hell for the lost has no scriptural basis. It is almost asinine to use the Scriptures they point out in Proverbs and Ecclesiastes. As I was talking to one of those folks, I said, "Can't you find something better than that? It's obvious when you turn to the Books of Ecclesiastes and Proverbs that you are quoting from a writer who says he is talking about life under the sun. He's talking about this life, this physical life. So with that understanding, when you say that death ends it all, it is true as far as this life is concerned. You won't be able to come back and do it over, brother, but the very minute you leave this life, you are going to move on to somewhere else, and that's your problem."

That is the difficulty these people face, and they would like to think that death ends it. Oh, my friend, these folks are in deep darkness or they would see the abundance of Scriptures that contradicts them. That, by the way, is the theory of conditional immortality.

Then there is *universalism*, a doctrine that says all men will eventually be saved. That is, Christ died for all, therefore all are saved, and they will live happily ever after. A great many theological liberals actually take that position. To them the matter of this life and of Christianity is just a jolly nice thing, you know, and we don't want to talk about hell, it's an ugly, repulsive subject.

I was very much interested in talking with a family in a church in Fullerton where I was holding meetings. They were telling me that they had been in a certain denominational church in which they were hearing strange teaching from the pulpit. So they went to this pastor because they suspected he was even teaching Marxist propaganda. They asked him about some things, and one of their questions was, "Do you believe in heaven and hell?"

His answer is quite interesting. He said, "I do not believe in heaven and hell, either one. I believe in putting the emphasis on here and now."

Then he added, "If you want to hear about heaven and hell, go down to the Church of the Open Door and hear that fellow McGee. He preaches on that."

Well, they took his advice. In due time they received Christ as Savior and later became members of that fine church in Fullerton where I met them. They didn't miss a service during the four nights I was there.

May I say to you that universalism, which was founded in the eighteenth century to uphold belief in universal salvation, fails to teach Bible truth. It is a very nice sort of optimistic way of life; the only thing that's wrong with it is it's not true! There is no basis for it anywhere except in their imaginations. You couldn't ground it in fact anywhere.

There is abroad also a theory called *restitutionalism*, which holds that eventually all mankind, all angels, and even Satan will finally be reconciled to God. Right here in Southern California, a proponent of this contacted me after reading my published message, "Will Everybody Ultimately Go to Heaven?" Someone had sent him the booklet. I've had some correspondence with that man, and he has been quite exercised about the subject, but he admits that he and his father made the statement on radio that both Satan and Judas would walk arm-in-arm down the streets of the New Jerusalem someday. I asked him for his Scripture for that one, and although he hasn't given it to me yet, restitutionalists generally do use Scripture to support their theory. This is their favorite verse:

> *. . . until the times of restoration of all things, which God has spoken by the mouth of all His holy prophets since the world began.*
> (Acts 3:21)

They say, "Here you can see exactly what Peter said. He said there is to be the 'restoration of all things.'" They need to look at Acts 3:21 again. It is "the restoration of all things, which God has spoken by the mouth of all His holy prophets since the world began." All things that the prophets said would be restored are going to be restored.

Paul clarifies this by using the same expression in another matter. Look at Philippians 3:8 where he wrote: "I have suffered the loss of all things." What did he mean? Did Paul own the world? No. Well, what was it Paul lost? He suffered the loss of all the things that he had to lose—that's all! He couldn't lose what he didn't have.

Likewise, Acts 3:21 speaks of the restoration of all things that the prophets prophesied would be restored. These will be restored. Nothing else will. And nowhere does any prophet say that the lost are ultimately to be restored. May I say to you that the very verse of Scripture used by the restitutionalists, instead of carrying out their thought, confirms the opposite.

Restitutionalists also rely heavily on another passage.

> *. . . that at the name of Jesus every knee should bow, of those in heaven, and of those on earth, and of those under the earth, and that every tongue should confess that Jesus Christ is Lord, to the glory of God the Father.*
> (Philippians 2:10-11)

The restitutionalists say, "You see that every knee must bow to Him in heaven, in earth, and under the earth, so that the lost ultimately are going to come to Him." May I say again, that is false reasoning, which is made evident by Colossians 1:20:

> *. . . and by Him to reconcile all things to Himself, by Him, whether things on earth or things in heaven, having made peace through the blood of His cross.*

When Paul is talking about reconciliation through the blood of Christ, it is things in heaven and things on the earth, but not things under the earth. When he talks about how every knee must bow and acknowledge the lordship of Jesus, he includes the lost. And I say to you that the devil and his angels and all the lost are going to have to bow and acknowledge the lordship of Jesus, but that does not mean they are saved. That does not mean they are reconciled with God. In fact, these two verses of Scripture make it quite obvious that Paul never taught that the lost would be restored.

May I say to you, restitutionalism is purely a figment of the imagination. Isn't it amazing what folks will believe when they don't want to believe the Word of God? That's the natural man, and that's the natural mind. It will do anything rather than believe God!

There is a sixth theory used to offset the scriptural doctrine of hell, and that is *purgatory*. It teaches that purgatory is a place you go when you die, and there you will suffer for the sins you committed after you were baptized. This theory says that Christ's death covered your sins before baptism but not after you were baptized. You must suffer for those sins yourself in purgatory until you are fit for heaven. For some people that could take a long time. However, if you are smart, you will wait until you get on your deathbed before you are baptized so you can't commit any sins before you die, and therefore you will miss purgatory altogether.

Purgatory is nowhere mentioned in the Scriptures, but it appears in one of the apocryphal books. It's been, of course, developed through the years and has led to this matter of praying for the dead, because prayer is made for the release of those who are in purgatory. May I say to you that there is no scriptural basis for purgatory whatsoever, but you can see how it has softened the viewpoint concerning hell.

Those are six of the major detours folks will take in order to avoid the clear and explicit teaching of the Word of God on the subject of hell.

Let me add this: I do not believe that any saved person can take any delight in the reality of hell, and certainly we ought not to handle it in that way. It was said of Dwight L. Moody that he was the only man who had the right to preach on hell. Friends, it is a solemn, heartrending subject, and Moody preached it that way.

WHAT THE BIBLE SAYS ABOUT HELL

You may reject the Word of God, but you cannot reject the fact that the Word of God has some very clear statements on hell.

First, hell is a prepared place. May I add this right now, and this is the language of the Lord Jesus:

> *Then He will also say to those on the left hand, "Depart from Me, you cursed, into the everlasting fire prepared for the devil and his angels."*
> (Matthew 25:41)

The two individuals in the Scriptures who taught more on the subject of hell than any others were the Lord Jesus Christ and John, the apostle of love. In fact, if you take out of the Bible what they had to say, you will have practically nothing left on the subject of hell. They are the two who emphasized it, and when people talk today about the "gentle Jesus" and about following His teaching, what do they mean by "following His teaching"? It will lead you then to believe, and to know, that hell is a reality, my beloved.

The second fact concerning hell is that it is not only a prepared place, but it is also eternal:

> *And these will go away into everlasting punishment, but the righteous into eternal life.*
> (Matthew 25:46)

And John wrote this about the last days:

> *The devil, who deceived them, was cast into the lake of fire and brimstone where the beast and the false prophet are. And they will be tormented day and night forever and ever*
> (Revelation 20:10)

Now, my beloved, there's no way in the world of toning that down and trying to make it temporary. These verses mean exactly what they say.

Not only is hell a prepared place, and not only is it an eternal place, but it is a place of retribution. Let me give you some of the statements that are used concerning it. In Luke 16:28 it's called a "place of torment." In Matthew 25:41 it's called "everlasting fire." In Mark 9:44 it's "where the worm does not die, and the fire is not quenched"; in Revelation 21:8, "the lake which burns with fire and brimstone"; Revelation 9:2, "the bottomless pit"; Matthew 8:12, "outer darkness," a place of "weeping and gnashing of teeth"; Luke 3:17, "unquenchable fire"; Matthew 13:42, "furnace of fire"; Jude 13, "blackness of darkness"; and Revelation 14:11, "the smoke of their torment ascends forever and ever; and they have no rest day or night." May I say that this is solemn language indeed! Hell is a place of retribution.

FOUR DIFFERENT WORDS

Now let's consider these four Bible words: *sheol, hades, gehenna,* and *tartarus*. These four words we need to know because they explain a great deal as far as the subject of hell is concerned. First of all, let me say that *sheol* is the Hebrew word and *hades* is the Greek word, and unfortunately both are translated *hell* in many places. But although they mean the same thing, they do not mean hell as we think of it today.

I want you to note that they do mean the same thing. The psalmist in his prayer has written:

> *For You will not leave my soul in Sheol,*
> *Nor will You allow Your Holy One to see corruption.*
> (Psalm 16:10)

When that same verse is quoted by Peter, it is:

> *For You will not leave my soul in Hades,*
> *Nor will You allow Your Holy One to see corruption.*
> (Acts 2:27)

Sheol and *hades* are used synonymously. And they are used sometimes, if you please, to refer to the grave; that is, where the body is placed. I could give you at least fifteen examples, but let me give you just two. First,

> *But he [Jacob] said, "My son shall not go down with you, for his brother is dead, and he is left alone. If any calamity should befall him along the way in which you go, then you would bring down my gray hair with sorrow to the grave [sheol]."*
> (Genesis 42:38)

For in death there is no remembrance of You;
In the grave who will give You thanks?
(Psalm 6:5)

By the way, the second is one of the verses that Jehovah's Witnesses use for their doctrine of extinction, that the grave ends it all.[1] May I say that the reference, of course, is only to the body in this particular passage. A corpse is incapable of giving thanks.

In addition to the grave where the body is placed, *sheol* is also used to describe the place where the lost go, and a great deal is said about that. I could give you at least twenty-five verses, but I don't want to weary you:

The wicked shall be turned into hell [sheol],
And all the nations that forget God.
(Psalm 9:17)

The sorrows of Sheol [hell] surrounded me;
The snares of death confronted me.
(Psalm 18:5)

Now sheol is the place where the dead go, and it's divided into two compartments.

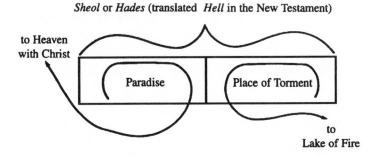

Sheol or *Hades* (translated *Hell* in the New Testament)

You are, I'm sure, familiar with the record our Lord gave about two men who died, a rich man and a man by the name of Lazarus who was a beggar. It is found in Luke 16:19-31. Jesus said that when these two men died, this is what happened: One of them, the rich man, went to a place of torment. The other, Lazarus, went to Abraham's bosom, which is also called paradise. The unseen world (*hades* in the Greek language and *sheol* in Hebrew) refers to both compartments. Half of sheol or hades is called "a place of torment," and this is where the rich man is. This is not hell, my beloved, but it is where the lost go today. They do not go directly to hell at all.

Now may I mention briefly the other two words for hell that we have in Scripture. *Gehenna* is a place of burning. It was in the Valley of Hinnom, a narrow ravine outside Jerusalem where city refuse, including bodies of beggars, was dumped and burned. Our Lord used it to picture hell.

Tartarus is found only once in the Scripture, and that time it was used by Simon Peter:

> *God did not spare the angels who sinned, but cast them down to hell [tartarus] and delivered them into chains of darkness, to be reserved for judgment.*
> (2 Peter 2:4)

The Old Testament saints were taken to paradise, called Abraham's bosom. They will not be raised bodily until Christ comes to establish His Kingdom. Then they will be raised from the dead. Since Christ's ascension into heaven, no believer has ever had to go to *sheol*. The Word of God says concerning believers today that they are

> *absent from the body . . . present with the Lord.*
> (2 Corinthians 5:8)

The following passage has caused some folks confusion, giving the impression that when Jesus died, He descended into the place we think of as hell.

> *Therefore He says:*
> *"When He ascended on high,*

He led captivity captive,
And gave gifts to men."
(Now this, "He ascended"—what does it mean but that He
also first descended into the lower parts of the earth?)
(Ephesians 4:8-9)

"When He ascended on high" refers to the ascension of Christ. He did not go into hell as we think of it. Rather, as He told the thief on the cross (see Luke 23:43), He descended into paradise, that section of hades where the saved were, to announce to them the deliverance that He had wrought for them, and at His ascension He led them "captivity captive" into God's presence.

But the lost who are in the place of torment today, we are told in Revelation 20:11-15, are to be judged at the Great White Throne, and then they are to be cast into the lake of fire.

> *The sea gave up the dead who were in it, and Death and Hades delivered up the dead who were in them. And they were judged, each one according to his works. Then Death and Hades were cast into the lake of fire. This is the second death. And anyone not found written in the Book of Life was cast into the lake of fire.*
> (Revelation 20:13-15)

The lake of fire is eternal.

Beloved, it is tragic beyond imagination to fail to receive Christ as your *Savior!*

——

Heaven

There are many who are willing to accept the fact of heaven while rejecting the fact of hell. Let me say again, Christ and the apostle John said more about hell than any others in Scripture. Yet neither said very much about heaven.

Apparently there is an intermediate state of the saved. I'm not sure that I know what Paul meant when he wrote 2 Corinthians 5; but I want us to consider carefully what he has written, and let's see if we might arrive at some sort of conclusion.

> **For we know that if our earthly house, this tent [*skenos* in the Greek, which refers to the body, the flesh], is destroyed, we have a building from God, a house not made with hands, eternal in the heavens.**
> (2 Corinthians 5:1)

There has always been a question here. In these days in which you and I live, what happens when a believer dies and goes into God's presence? Is he a spirit or is he given a temporary body? Apparently his body is not to be raised until the total church is caught up to meet the Lord in the air. Then he gets his new body. But does he have a temporary body in the meantime? I can't give you God's answer because all I know is what is said here, and 2 Corinthians 5:1 is the only Scripture on it.

Here is one view: Just consider this with me for a moment. I personally hope that, when I leave this earth and go into His presence, I get a body. I'm sure going to feel undressed without it. I can't conceive of Vernon McGee being a spirit. I'd feel like I was in a spiritual nudist colony if I didn't have a body. That's the way I express myself, that's the way you express yourself, so it's possible that we will have a temporary body until that day comes. After all, what is this body? It's only a house you live in.

Now here is the second view: I have never been too dogmatic about either interpretation of it. But I have now come to the conviction that what Paul is talking about here is *not* a temporary body. For many years I thought that God would have sort of a temporary body for us when we got to heaven. It would be like taking your car to the garage for repair work and having a loaner to drive until it is fixed. I thought that the Lord would give us a temporary body until our new body was given to us. I never liked that idea, but it seemed to be what Paul was saying. Now I don't believe he is referring to a temporary body, because he says it is "eternal in the heavens." He is talking about that new body that we are going to get.

WHAT THE SCRIPTURES SAY ABOUT HEAVEN

I want you to look at what the Scripture has to say about heaven itself. There are three heavens actually. Paul says in 2 Corinthians 12:2 he was "caught up to the third heaven," and I take it if he was caught up to the third heaven there must be a heaven number one and a heaven number two. The first heaven is presented in Scripture as earth's sphere. Actually it's a little bit more, I think, than the air spaces. Our Lord referred to "the stars of heaven" and "the birds of heaven." Well, the birds of heaven would use the air spaces, but you may recall (in Acts 1:10-11) that two men in white clothing appeared when our Lord ascended, and they asked the disciples why they were standing gazing up into *heaven*. Since they were looking up through the atmosphere, we know that was the first heaven.

You will also find air spaces mentioned in the very first chapter of Genesis, verses 6-8. Verse 6 says:

> *Then God said, "Let there be a firmament in the midst of the waters, and let it divide the waters from the waters."*

And there is water up there today, according to the weatherman. In fact, there is as much water up there as there is in any river in Los Angeles! And it will come down, you see. That's what God did—He divided the waters below from those above. Thus God made the firmament and divided the *raqia*, these air spaces, by dividing the waters which were under the firmament from the waters which were above the firmament.

> *And God called the firmament Heaven.*
> (Genesis 1:8)

That's the first heaven. And I think it reaches out even beyond our air spaces. Also note this very interesting verse:

> *The heaven, even the heavens, are the LORD's;*
> *But the earth He has given to the children of men.*
> (Psalm 115:16)

God has not given the heavens, these outer spaces, to mankind. He hasn't made our bodies for it.

Then there is the second heaven, and that is the heaven up yonder in the galactic systems of this universe, out beyond our solar system.

And beyond that there is the third heaven, and that is the place to which Paul said he was caught up. Evidently the throne of God is there. Paul said he saw things that he could not speak about. This third heaven is the abode of God.

Here are two Scriptures on that:

> *The LORD looks down from heaven upon the children of men,*
> *To see if there are any who understand, who seek God.*
> (Psalm 14:2)

> *He who sits in the heavens shall laugh;*
> *The LORD shall hold them in derision.*
> (Psalm 2:4)

This makes it clear that heaven is the abode of God.

Now here is something I'd like for you to note. The earth will be the eternal abode of Israel—that is, saved Israelites. And it will be heaven, as far as they are concerned. When we as children of God say, "I want to go to heaven," we are going to a prepared place. But it is not for the nation Israel. The Old Testament believer, for instance Abraham, never had any idea he would leave this earth. He had no expectation or hope above this earth. God never told him, "I go to prepare a place for *you*."

> *And the LORD said to Abram [Abraham], after Lot had separated from him: "Lift your eyes now and look from the place where you are—northward, southward, eastward, and westward; for all the land which you see I give to you and your descendants forever. . . . Arise, walk in the land through its length and its width, for I give it to you."*
> (Genesis 13:14-15, 17)

In other words, God said to Abraham, "Look about you. This is the land I have given to you for an eternal possession. This is your land."

And when God made the covenant with David that there would be One on this earth to sit on his throne, David said, "That is my salvation. That's my hope for the future." They had no hope above this earth at all. And saved Israel, including the Tribulation saints, will be here on this earth. And after God makes it a new heaven and a new earth, this is going to be a pretty nice place to live. And then I think you and I would enjoy it here also, but this won't be our place.

The New Jerusalem, which will come down from God out of heaven, will be our home. Apparently this New Jerusalem will become the center of this vast universe because God is going to be there.

SO YOU WANT TO GO TO HEAVEN

My friend, you say that you want to go to heaven. First of all, God says that heaven is a prepared place for prepared people. You and I have to be prepared for heaven. God cannot take us there the way we are now. If today God lifted up your church to heaven just as it is on a Sunday morning, what would you have? Heaven? No, you would have your church, and that's not heaven. Consider this:

> *We also who have the firstfruits of the Spirit, even we*
> *ourselves groan within ourselves, eagerly waiting for the adop-*
> *tion, the redemption of our body.*
> (Romans 8:23)

We have to be prepared for heaven.

As someone has well said, we are going to get our space suits and take off. I think that is a very appropriate figure of speech, because these bodies that we have now are adjusted for only this earth, you see. They are set for us to go at this speed down here. But the body we shall get in the future will be a body prepared for the New Jerusalem.

Also, within ourselves we have to be prepared:

> *Beloved, now we are children of God; and it has not yet been*
> *revealed what we shall be, but we know that when He is*
> *revealed, we shall be like Him, for we shall see Him as He is.*
> (1 John 3:2)

Have you ever stopped to think of your position in heaven? Not only do the people in heaven have to be prepared, but also their position in heaven must be determined. Remember that our Lord Jesus is going to give rewards. One of the last things He said was: "And behold, I am coming quickly, and My reward is with Me" (Revelation 22:12). Will you get a reward? Not everyone will. But He will give rewards to those who have earned them.

There will be no idleness in heaven. There will be rest, but rest and idleness are not the same. We are going to rest, but actually, what is it that disturbs us and wearies us mostly today? Isn't it all our frustrations and our irritations down here? Up there we'll be free from those and have a new body! My beloved, I don't believe there will be any idleness at all.

There will be recognition of others. Our faculties will be sharpened.

> *Now I know in part, but then I shall know just as I also am known.*
> (1 Corinthians 13:12)

That is when we will reach the place of supreme fulfillment.

I was talking to some friends in Santa Ana the other night, and I made this statement, "I wouldn't want to live my life over, but honestly, I would like to go back and make some corrections."

Wouldn't you? Would you like to go back and make a few corrections? May I say, it is going to be wonderful to get to a place where there will be no frustrations, but there will be the supreme fulfillment of life.

And heaven is going to be a place of love. To me the wonder of that is that everybody is going to love *me* in heaven! That's going to be wonderful, friend. And everybody will love you. Love is going to make heaven a very wonderful place. And everything will be there to delight the person. As I said, there will be no irritation. Nothing there to trouble you. No worries, no bother. Everything there will be for your delight and for your enjoyment.

And to top it all, Christ is there—what a glorious reality!

> *And thus we shall always be with the Lord.*
> (1 Thessalonians 4:17)

I would like to close this message on heaven and hell by reminding you that you are going somewhere when you die. I know a lot of people who like to think that death ends it all. But, my friend, if you are banking on that and then find out you were wrong, you'll be awfully wrong, won't you? It's a terrible thing to be lost and not know your way in this world today. But it is tragic beyond imagination to be eternally lost.

CHAPTER 13

ESCHATOLOGY

To conclude this book, I would like to chat with you on the subject of eschatology. What is eschatology? That's a fifty-cent word, by the way, but actually it's very simple when you break it down: The Greek word *eschatos* means "last," and *logy* means "doctrine." Since it is the doctrine of last things, it means the things that are yet in the future. The common colloquialism is "prophetic study" or "future things." It means "prophecy," so I think we had better use that familiar term.

Now in Southern California where I live, prophecy has often been brought into disrepute because there has been so much unreliable teaching. There have always been sensation-mongers who used prophecy for promotion rather than for imparting the Word of God that we might come to know Him better. I personally believe that these folks are just as much apostates as the liberals are. I think Jude was speaking of them when he wrote:

> *These are grumblers, complainers, walking according to their own lusts; and they mouth great swelling words, flattering people to gain advantage.*
> (Jude 16)

Although Jude is speaking of apostates, not all apostates are liberals. They can pose and pass as Bible-believing Christians and yet be attempting to use prophecy for some personal advantage—not always money, but some can be bought with a doctor's degree or by giving them some other honor or preferment. Anyone, you see, can become an apostate in that direction.

Also, there can be an overemphasis on prophecy. Because of this and the sensational character of prophecy, a great many folk have turned away from it. And yet, friend, prophecy is one of the great subjects of the Word of God. Did you know that at least one-fifth (some say one-fourth) of the Scripture, when it was written, was prophetic; that is, it announced things that would take place in the future? Just think of that for one moment. Before me right now is a Bible of 1,300 pages. That means about 260 pages of this Bible contain predictive prophecy.

That brings me to say that prophecy can be divided in many different ways. I think that probably the more obvious division is between that which is fulfilled and that which is unfulfilled. The Book of Revelation, which is the great prophetic book of the New Testament, was written about 1,900 years go. If you go back even further, you'll find that the earliest prophecy was written over 3,500 years ago. In the interval between the time they were written and where we stand, many things have come to pass, and I'm told that about one-third of predicted prophecy has already been fulfilled. Any intelligent person can take up these passages and see that when they were given, the projection was way out in the future, and in the meantime they have come to pass—so that what was given as prophecy is now a record of history. This to my mind is one of the greatest proofs that the Bible is the Word of God.

Why and How Prophecy Was Given

Now let's talk a little about why God has given prophecy to us.

BECAUSE OF GOD'S DESIRE

One of the most interesting things is that God seems to delight in revealing the future to His own. God likes to talk to us who belong to Him. Remember, He came down in the cool of the day to talk with Adam in the Garden of Eden. And you find God coming down to Enoch.

> *And Enoch walked with God; and he was not, for God took him.*
> (Genesis 5:24)

God enjoyed Enoch's fellowship so much that one day He just took him home, out of this earthly scene. Then there is Noah, the only man in his day who was found walking righteously with God. God likes folks to walk with Him and talk with Him, and He likes to have fellowship.

Oh, how many believers are robbing themselves of one of the most wonderful experiences they can have! We sing the song, "He walks with me, and He talks with me." Well, does He? He will if you'll let Him, but He's not going to walk and talk with you somewhere away from His Word. God speaks only in His Word, my friend, and there are a lot of saints who are very far from the Word today.

Again, God likes to reveal Himself, and He likes to reveal the future to those who are His children. To illustrate, let's look at a familiar incident in the life of Abraham. God was going to destroy Sodom and Gomorrah, which was God's business, although many people have made it their own business and say, "Why did God do this?" You may think that He is wrong, but He is right and you are wrong. Oh, my friend, let's not criticize God for doing this or that. Instead let's say, "I know God is right and I'm wrong, but I wish I could see it His way." Our problem is we always want to blame God. But God is not accountable to any one of us.

Well, when God was preparing to destroy Sodom and Gomorrah, He came down to visit with Abraham. And just as God was about ready to leave him, He did something that to my judgment gives us one of the most amazing passages in the Word of God:

> *And the LORD said, "Shall I hide from Abraham what I am doing?"*
> (Genesis 18:17)

Just think of that! He says in effect, "Hadn't I better stay around a little longer and tell Abraham what I'm going to do?" And, you know, God decided He would tell him, and this is what happened:

> *. . . since Abraham shall surely become a great and mighty nation, and all the nations of the earth shall be blessed in him? For I have known him, in order that he may command his children and his household after him, that they keep the way of the LORD, to do righteousness and justice, that the LORD may bring to Abraham what He has spoken to him.*
> (Genesis 18:18-19)

In other words, God said, "I'm going to tell him. I want Abraham to understand it because he is going to tell his children and I'm going to make him a blessing to the world, and I don't want Abraham saying that God is unjust. If I don't tell him, Abraham might not understand."

And you know, friend, it's a good thing God told Abraham what He was going to do because Abraham is like you and like me—Abraham misunderstood. Abraham thought God was doing wrong. Oh, if we could only get into our thinking that nothing God does is wrong, but it's so hard for us to do that.

> *And the LORD said, "Because the outcry against Sodom and Gomorrah is great, and because their sin is very grave, I will go down now and see whether they have done altogether according to the outcry against it that has come to Me; and if not, I will know." Then the men turned away from there and went toward Sodom, but Abraham still stood before the LORD.*
> (Genesis 18:20-22)

Abraham was amazed. These messengers from God gave the word, and Abraham just stood there before the Lord and worshiped, but he didn't understand. I suppose he was thinking, *God called me out of idolatry and all which was not right. I knew I was following a high and holy God, and I thought He was just and right in all He did, but now He tells me He is going to destroy Sodom and Gomorrah!* With these thoughts in mind, do you know what Abraham did?

> **And Abraham came near and said, "Would You also destroy the righteous with the wicked?"**
> (Genesis 18:23)

Oh, isn't it a good thing God told him? Because Abraham did misunderstand. Abraham would have always thought that God was unjust to destroy the righteous with the wicked in Sodom and Gomorrah. So Abraham said, "If there were fifty righteous there, would You save the city?" And God said:

> **If I find in Sodom fifty righteous within the city, then I will spare all the place for their sakes.**
> (Genesis 18:26)

Then Abraham brought God's promise down from fifty to forty, to thirty, to twenty, and even down to ten. And God said:

> **I will not destroy it for the sake of ten.**
> (Genesis 18:32)

Why didn't Abraham go below ten? Well, I believe he got cold feet. He came to the conclusion there was no one righteous in Sodom and Gomorrah. And I think when he reached that conclusion, his dark thoughts were that Lot, his nephew, had become an apostate, that he had turned his back on God. But Lot had not. Although Lot lived in Sodom we learn from the New Testament that he

tormented his righteous soul from day to day by seeing and
hearing their lawless deeds [in that city].
(2 Peter 2:8)

You can be sure of one thing, Lot had not turned his back on God, and God got him out of the city before He destroyed it. Of course, Mrs. Lot, she apparently was not one of the righteous. She got outside the city physically, but her heart was in Sodom, and when she looked back, she turned to a pillar of salt.

However, the important thing is that Abraham then understood something more about God. "Shall I hide from Abraham that which I do?" God says, "No, I want to tell him." And in our day God wants to tell us what is coming in the future.

But there are some things that are veiled even to this day. In the study of the Books of Daniel and Revelation, I want to let you in on something, and I hope you won't tell anybody this because some folks think I know all the answers to those two books on prophecy. I want to tell you right here and now, there are many things that I don't know about them. They are wonderful books, and it disturbs me when I meet somebody who thinks he has all the answers. But when I read the works of these men or listen to them, I find they don't have the answers either, although they think they do. God hasn't told us all things, and that's the way it should be.

BY THE HOLY SPIRIT

Let's turn to the Gospel of John at the point where our Lord is talking to His own disciples yonder in the Upper Room. This is what He said to them:

I still have many things to say to you, but you cannot bear
them now.
(John 16:12)

You see, God wants to tell you today a lot of things, but do you know what the trouble is? You're not ready for them. God wants to tell me many things, but I'm not ready for them. Many of us are not prepared or ready for God to speak to us and give us new truth. Oh, how we need to stay in a position to receive new truths from God!

Our Lord continues speaking:

> *However, when He, the Spirit of truth, has come, He will guide you into all truth.*
> (John 16:13)

Only the Spirit of God can guide you into truth today. That's the reason the Lord Jesus sent Him into the world—that He might be the One to teach you.

Many folks write to thank me for my teaching. Well, if they have gotten anything helpful from my speaking or writing, the Holy Spirit has been the teacher. He alone can open up the great truths of the Word of God. He is the only teacher in the world today who can teach us the Word of God. We are absolutely dependent upon Him.

As the Lord Jesus was preparing His disciples for His leaving them, He said:

> *Nevertheless I tell you the truth. It is to your advantage that I go away; for if I do not go away, the Helper will not come to you; but if I depart, I will send Him to you. . . . I still have many things to say to you, but you cannot bear them now. However, when He, the Spirit of truth, has come, He will guide you into all truth; for He will not speak on His own authority, but whatever He hears He will speak; and He will tell you things to come.*
> (John 16:7, 12-13)

Will you especially notice this: "And He will tell you things to come." In my opinion that is our authority for studying prophecy. It is God's delight, friend, to tell you some things He is going to do.

Although our Lord, when He was preparing to go back to heaven, told His disciples that the Holy Spirit would guide them into all truth and He would show them things to come, they still weren't prepared to receive some things. For instance, they didn't believe Jesus was going to die. He didn't reveal that to the disciples until six months before He went to Jerusalem to be crucified. He had told Nicodemus:

> *And as Moses lifted up the serpent in the wilderness, even so must the Son of Man be lifted up.*
> (John 3:14)

But it must have been more than two years later that He first revealed His impending crucifixion to His disciples. And they didn't understand even then.

Simon Peter said, "Far be that from You, Lord," and our Lord just had to tell him that it was satanic to say a thing like that. My, how far Simon Peter was from the truth! He didn't have any notion what was really going to happen. Our Lord, as He traveled with His disciples all the way from Caesarea Philippi to Jerusalem, reiterated to them again and again that He was going to Jerusalem to die.

Well, He died; He was buried; He was raised from the dead; He was with them forty days (Acts 1:3); then He ascended into heaven and, as He promised, He sent the Holy Spirit to lead and guide them into all truth. And in the third chapter of Acts, listen to Simon Peter—he doesn't even sound like the same fellow. He and John were at the temple; a crowd had gathered around them, amazed and wondering at the healing of the lame man, so Peter stood up and preached Jesus to them:

> *But those things which God foretold by the mouth of all His prophets, that the Christ would suffer, He has thus fulfilled.*
> (Acts 3:18)

Simon Peter didn't see that before—you remember he didn't. He had said, "Far be that from You, Lord," but now that the Spirit of God had come and led him into all truth, Simon Peter says, "The prophets told all about this!"

My friend, the only way you and I can understand prophecy is by the Spirit of God. You see, He must take these things of Christ and show them to us, and our Lord said that "He will tell you things to come" (John 16:13).

FOR OUR EDIFICATION

Now why and how does the Holy Spirit do that? Does He reveal these things in order to satisfy our curiosity, to entertain us for the evening perhaps? No. Prophecy is to affect our hearts and lives. That's what John, who wrote the Book of Revelation, meant. God says:

> *Everyone who has this hope in Him purifies himself, just as He is pure.*
> (1 John 3:3)

And if prophecy doesn't make you live a better life, if it doesn't lead you to the place of separation to God, it is not fulfilling its purpose.

When I say "separation," I do not mean some little man-made separation. I mean that you have presented yourself a living sacrifice to God. That is real separation, and that's what the study of prophecy should produce, friend. If it doesn't help you in your daily living, it is of no value. What difference does it make to know how many bowls of wrath are going to be poured out in judgment during the Great Tribulation unless it has some effect on your living here and now?

You will also find out that the Book of Daniel is a wonderful book for Christian living. You may be amazed at that statement, but it's true. Did you know it's one of the greatest books on separation that's ever been written? And it's one of the greatest books on prayer that's ever been written.

Somebody might say, "I thought it was prophecy." Oh, it is! But, you see, the purpose of prophecy is that "everyone who has this hope in Him purifies himself." Simon Peter is an example, as I've already pointed out. Before the Cross and before the Day of Pentecost, he was rebuking Christ for saying He was going to Jerusalem to die, but a short time later he was telling these religious rulers, "The prophets spoke about this." Where did he find that out? "The Holy Spirit will show you things to come," our Lord had told him.

TO EXPLAIN COMING KINGDOM

And then there was something else. You remember, before the Day of Pentecost these apostles had asked Jesus about the coming Kingdom.

> *Therefore, when they had come together, they asked Him, saying, "Lord, will You at this time restore the kingdom to Israel?" And He said to them, "It is not for you to know times or seasons which the Father has put in His own authority."*
> (Acts 1:6-7)

Believe me, the commentators have had a field day with that. They have put these apostles in the ring and really punched them for asking that question. You'd think they made the biggest mistake in the world by asking such a thing. But our Lord didn't tell them they had made a mistake. They asked a very sensible question. Our Lord gave them a very sensible answer. He told them it wasn't for them to know the times or the seasons when it would be, which means that it would not be established in their lifetime so it wouldn't concern them.

And actually, it doesn't concern us today either. After two thousand years, we still don't know when the Kingdom will be established. We only know it has not been established yet. Oh, I know a lot of churches today are "building the Kingdom." I used to go to denominational meetings, and always some brother was "building the Kingdom." About the best thing they had to offer was a good-sized chicken coop which was a disgrace to any architect! But they're still busy building it. The kingdom that I hear these folks talking about is not much of a kingdom, is it? Well, the reason we don't know anything about it is because the Kingdom does not concern us at all.

"It is not for you to know times or seasons," our Lord said. He will build it, and when He builds it, it's going to be a good job. In fact, it's going to be a wonderful job. And He hasn't let out the contract to any church to build it. He still holds the contract. The Lord Jesus is the author of it, and He's going to be the finisher of it. He is the One who drew the blueprints, and He is the One who is going to put the last shingle on the top. He's not going to ask anybody down here to do it for Him. He is going to establish His own Kingdom.

Now you and I have another job to do which, of course, is to preach the gospel. But if statistics are correct, we're not getting very far, are we? We're sort of like the proverbial cat that climbed up the pole three feet during the daytime but slipped back three feet at night. He didn't get up the pole very fast like that. And apparently we are not making any progress today in preaching the gospel. We ought to!

In the first chapter of Acts the apostles did not know much about the Kingdom, you see. But a little later they got an entirely different conception of it. Simon Peter said, speaking to the amazed crowd who had seen the lame man healed:

> . . . *and that He may send Jesus Christ, who was preached to you before.*
> (Acts 3:20)

Believe me, friend, this man Simon Peter is in on something now. He realizes that Jesus Christ has to come again in order to establish the Kingdom, although he thought at one time that Jesus would establish the Kingdom when He was here on earth.

Prophetic Divisions

It is helpful to know that prophecy can be divided not only into fulfilled and unfulfilled, that which is passed into history and that which is predicted in the future, but also it divides into Old Testament prophecy and New Testament prophecy. Here's an example.

THE OLD TESTAMENT AND THE CHURCH

Some prophecy applies to Israel, and some applies to the church. There's a sharp division right here, so much so that I'd like to call your attention to something that will deliver you from making mistakes there. In the Old Testament no prophet gave any prediction concerning the church. When you get to the Book of Daniel I hope you will not make the mistake of thinking that Daniel is talking about the church, because he is not. That was not his theme at all. A great many people wonder why there is that hiatus, that silent period between the sixty-ninth and seventieth week of Daniel. Well, I'll tell you why. Because between the sixty-ninth and seventieth week of Daniel, the church is being called out of this earth. Daniel was not writing about the church, friend. It's a very reasonable explanation when you begin to look at it.

You'll find that God revealed things to the prophets back in the Old Testament, but not one of them ever predicted the birth of the church, that is, the body of believers who came into existence on the Day of Pentecost. Not one prophet knew of it because it was not the theme of Old Testament prophecy. But it *is* the theme of New Testament prophecy.

THE CROSS AND THE CROWN

Here is another division. Back in the Old Testament you will find that the prophets always put the first coming of Christ and the second coming of Christ together. They never made a division between the two. You must have the New Testament to know about the first coming of Christ. Then you are able to go back and make that division in the Old Testament. But in the New Testament you definitely have the two comings of Christ. You have His first coming as the suffering Savior and His second coming as the Sovereign. The first coming the Cross; the second coming is the Crown.

Let me repeat that you'll find them both back in the Old Testament, but the prophets never made that division—it was something they desired to look into. In the little Book of Malachi, the last book in the Old Testament, we find that even up to that period, the prophet did not divide the first and second comings of Christ for us:

> "Behold, I send My messenger,
> And he will prepare the way before Me.
> And the Lord, whom you seek,
> Will suddenly come to His temple,
> Even the Messenger of the covenant,
> In whom you delight.
> Behold, He is coming," says the LORD of hosts.
> But who can endure the day of His coming?
> And who can stand when He appears?
> For He is like a refiner's fire
> And like launderers' soap.
> (Malachi 3:1-2)

The first part of this passage is quoted in the New Testament by Mark as referring to Christ's first coming:

> As it is written in the Prophets:
> "Behold, I send My messenger before Your face,
> Who will prepare Your way before You."
> (Mark 1:2)

Then, before he even finishes his sermon, the New Testament writer ends the quotation. Why? Because the first part applies to Christ's first coming, and the rest of it applies to His second coming.

You see, in the Old Testament we can point out several places where Isaiah did not make the distinction, but in the New Testament we have that division made for us so we'll not make the mistake of thinking the Book of Daniel has an interval between the first and second comings of Christ. It does not, my beloved, for that is not the theme of any of the Old Testament prophets.

Now let's turn our attention to the Gospel of Luke, where the Lord Jesus Christ makes the division for us:

> So He came to Nazareth, where He had been brought up. And as His custom was, He went into the synagogue on the Sabbath day, and stood up to read. And He was handed the book of the prophet Isaiah. And when He had opened the book, He found the place where it was written:
>
> "The Spirit of the LORD is upon Me,
> Because He has anointed Me
> To preach the gospel to the poor;
> He has sent Me to heal the brokenhearted,
> To proclaim liberty to the captives
> And recovery of sight to the blind,
> To set at liberty those who are oppressed;
> To proclaim the acceptable year of the LORD."
>
> Then He closed the book, and gave it back to the attendant and sat down. And the eyes of all who were in the synagogue were fixed on Him. And He began to say to them, "Today this Scripture is fulfilled in your hearing."
> (Luke 4:16-21)

We are told that He turned to Isaiah 61 and quoted:

> The Spirit of the Lord GOD is upon Me,
> Because the LORD has anointed Me
> To preach good tidings to the poor;
> He has sent Me to heal the brokenhearted,
> To proclaim liberty to the captives,
> And the opening of the prison to those who are bound.

That's verse 1, and that's where He was quoting. I read on, "To proclaim the acceptable year of the LORD. ..." Well, that's where He closed the book, and He sat down and said, "This has been fulfilled." But He hadn't finished the sentence, because in Isaiah 61:2 we see that the sentence continues, "and the day of vengeance of our God." Why did Jesus omit that? Because it wasn't being fulfilled at that time. You see, Isaiah had put the first and second comings of Christ right together, and our Lord separated them. That's what He did in the synagogue that day.

Jesus read only the part which He was fulfilling. Well, won't the rest be fulfilled? Yes, when He comes again. You see, the first and second comings of Christ are a subject of the Old Testament, but they are put together. When you come to the New Testament, you find both the first and second comings, but by that time the first coming is history. It's no longer prophecy.

All during the first coming of Christ, from His birth to His death, His resurrection and His ascension, the Gospel writers made it clear that all was done in fulfillment of what the prophets had written, but a great deal of prophecy mentioned in the Old Testament has not yet been fulfilled. It concerns His second coming to this earth. It looks to a day that's in the future when He will come again and establish His Kingdom on this earth. The interesting thing is that His coming again is repeated over and over again in the New Testament. I have been told that it averages one verse in every twenty-one verses, although I have never myself checked to see if this is accurate.

However, suppose you got a letter from, say, your uncle in Iowa. He writes to you, "Well, the weather is so bad back here, I think I'm going to come out and visit you where it's nice and warm." And suppose he wrote about one hundred lines, and every twenty-one lines he would repeat, "I'm coming out to see you." Well, when you had finished the letter, you would start getting the guest room ready, wouldn't you? You would say, "My uncle is sure coming to see me because in a letter of a hundred lines, he said four times that he is coming!" Likewise, friend, when you read the New Testament you certainly find out that Jesus is coming back again because it's repeated again and again.

Then we have another confirmation. Did you know that when Christ came the first time, there were at least 330 prophecies in the Old Testament concerning it? All of these were literally fulfilled when He was here among us, and they are so quoted in the New Testament. Now, friend, that is a remarkable thing! That in and of itself ought to alert any intelligent-minded person to say, "This Book goes back thousands of years and gives prophecies concerning the coming of a certain person and keeps pyramiding them up until there are 330, and all of them were fulfilled accurately and literally. There must be something supernatural to a book like that." I don't care what anyone says to the contrary, it is not humanly or scientifically possible to turn out a book like that!

I'm told that by mathematical law, when you prophesy something, you have only a fifty-fifty chance of its being right. Now suppose the weatherman says that on New Year's Day, the day of the Rose Parade in Pasadena, it's going to rain. Well, he stands a fifty-fifty chance of being right, because it's either going to rain or it's not going to rain—we all know that.

Now suppose he also says that it's going to start raining in the morning, and if he's right, believe me, friend, there are going to be a lot of folks getting wet in Pasadena. Wait just a minute though. He might be right, but he now stands only a 25-percent chance because he has put in another uncertain element, and every one he adds reduces his chance by one half. If he had a fifty-fifty chance before, now he has a 25-percent chance.

Then suppose he says it won't quit raining until late afternoon. That will ruin the football game, so if he says that, oh my, it'll be bad, and if he's accurate it will be worse. But he will surely qualify as a pretty good weatherman dispite the fact that he has only a $12\frac{1}{2}$-percent chance of being right.

Do you see that when you add 330 of those, you've pretty much eliminated any human being's ability? Humans might guess right sometimes, but they can't guess right all the time. The weatherman may guess right sometimes, but even with his mathematical and scientific gadgets, he misses it a great deal.

I sort of feel a kinship to the person who posted this sign on the bulletin board in the General Motors plant at Detroit a number of years ago. It's a statement which has always interested me:

> According to the theory of aerodynamics and as may readily be demonstrated through wind tunnel experiments, the bumblebee is unable to fly. This is because the size, the weight, and the shape of his body in relation to the total wingspread makes flying impossible. But the bumblebee, being ignorant of these scientific truths, goes ahead and flies anyway. And he makes a little honey every day.

I am a little amused when I hear people say today that the Bible is an unscientific book. Well, for an unscientific book, it sure has hit the nail on the head as far as prophecy is concerned. The skeptic is going to have a lot of trouble, explaining those 330 fulfilled prophecies if he disbelieves the Word of God.

The Bible's greatest proof is the abundance of prophecies concerning the first coming of our Lord Jesus, a specific person, all of which have been literally fulfilled. The prophet Micah told the place of His birth— that He would be born in Bethlehem, and He *was* born in Bethlehem. The same is true of the events surrounding His death. Seven hundred years before He was born, the Old Testament prophesied where and how these things would happen! It's a marvelous thing! In fact, it's the most amazing thing imaginable to see Christ's first coming so literally fulfilled. I think the normal, natural conclusion would be that His second coming will be just as literally fulfilled. And beloved, He *is* coming again some day. That's one of the great themes of prophecy.

Two other great themes of prophecy are the nation Israel and the Gentile nations. We won't discuss them here, though they make excellent studies.

The Prophets and Priests

Now I want to turn our attention to the subject of the prophet himself. These men whom God raised up to relay His message of future things were a special group, but they actually were men of like passions as we are. The Scripture says:

Elijah was a man with a nature like ours.
(James 5:17)

He was not any different, friend. But God raised up such men, and in matters other than their prophetic office and the writing of Scripture, they erred. Moses made a terrible mistake by killing an Egyptian who was beating one of the Hebrew slaves. He shouldn't have done it. However, when Moses wrote the Pentateuch—that is, the first five books of the Old Testament—he didn't make any mistakes at all.

Back in the old days when the pulpit was standing true to the Word of God, there traveled over America a man by the name of Robert Ingersoll giving his famous lecture, "The Mistakes of Moses." The interesting thing is that after a few years, there was a certain preacher who apparently had a real sense of humor. He would follow along Ingersoll's trail, and after Ingersoll had given his lecture, the next night this man would come to town and give his lecture titled "The Mistakes of Bob Ingersoll."

You see, friend, the folks today who say Moses made mistakes neglect to tell us in what area they are talking about. He made mistakes, but not in writing the Pentateuch. On the wilderness journey he made the mistake of losing his temper and striking that rock more than he should have, but he did not make a mistake when he recorded it because he was writing by the guidance of the Holy Spirit. The prophets, therefore, were men of like passions as we are.

This is how prophets came to be: In the period following the leadership of Joshua, after the nation of Israel entered the Promised Land, the priesthood failed. But after the failure of the priesthood,

God raised up judges, and many of the judges also belonged to the priesthood. Then, after the judges had failed and the priesthood had failed, God raised up the kings, and along with the kings God raised up prophets to be the mouthpiece for God to the kings. Many times, by the way, a prophet was a member of the priesthood. That was true of quite a few of them—the last prophet in particular, John the Baptist.

Over the years the kings became exceedingly corrupt, and God's prophets delivered God's message of rebuke and warning to them as well as to the people. Therefore, in the Word of God these prophets who spoke out were not only foretellers but they were forthtellers; that is, they spoke for God. In fact, that's the great difference you have in the Word of God between the priest and the prophet.

THE PRIEST SPEAKS TO GOD

You see, the priest and the prophet are on a two-way street: One is going one direction and the other is going the opposite direction. The priest is one who goes to God for man; the prophet is one who comes from God to man. In other words, the priest has no business issuing a message at Christmastime or at the first of the year. He is not to come from God with a message to man. That's the business of the prophet.

The priest is to represent a man before God—that's his business. In fact, that's the way the Scripture puts it in Hebrews:

> *For every high priest taken from among men is appointed for men in things pertaining to God, that he may offer both gifts and sacrifices for sins. He can have compassion on those who are ignorant and going astray, since he himself is also subject to weakness.*
> (Hebrews 5:1-2)

This is the definition of a priest. He is taken from among men, and he is to go on behalf of men to God.

THE PROPHET SPEAKS FOR GOD

Now the prophet goes in the opposite direction, and here is God's definition:

> *So the LORD said to Moses: "See, I have made you as God to Pharaoh, and Aaron your brother shall be your prophet."*
> (Exodus 7:1)

In other words, God said to Moses, "You are going to be as God to Pharaoh. And the one who will speak for you will be Aaron, and he is going to be your prophet." This tells us that the prophet is to speak for God.

In the earlier chapters of Exodus, we get a little more light on this subject of the prophet. When God called Moses to go to Pharaoh to obtain the release of the people of Israel,

> *Moses said to God, "Who am I that I should go to Pharaoh, and that I should bring the children of Israel out of Egypt?"*
> (Exodus 3:11)

Now here is a fellow who, forty years before this, had taken things into his own hands and had murdered an Egyptian who was beating a Hebrew slave. And when it was known, he had to leave the country. But after forty years of training in the backside of the desert, poor old Moses doesn't want to go to Egypt and deliver his people—because he realizes he cannot do it. And that is exactly what God wanted to teach him. And, beloved, that is what God wants to teach you and me.

Our difficulty today is that we have too many people in the church who think they *can* do it. My, I hear from a great many people who tell me they want to serve God, and it's amazing how many gifted individuals we have in this country today—that is, according to their letters. The pastors, the singers, and the missionaries—they all are outstanding, according to their letters. Well, they are the very folks, friend, you don't want to use, because if anyone thinks he is able to be used of God, he is wrong. But if you feel you cannot be used of God, you are the very person God is looking for. Remember, it took Him forty years to get Moses to that position.

Now Moses said he could not do what God asked of him. And God said to him:

> So [Aaron] *shall be your spokesman to the people. And he himself shall be as a mouth for you, and you shall be to him as God.*
> (Exodus 4:16)

There is the picture, you see. The prophet was God's mouthpiece.

Now let's see what the New Testament tells us about the prophet:

> *For prophecy never came by the will of man, but holy men of God spoke as they were moved by the Holy Spirit.*
> (2 Peter 1:21)

When you read this statement about holy men, you may get the impression that I was wrong a moment ago when I said that they were men of like passions. And of course it wasn't I, but James who said it, and it would seem that James and Peter are in contradiction, for James says the prophets are men of like passions as we are, and Peter says they are holy men.

What does Peter mean by holy? Well, holiness here has no reference to innate character. *Holy* actually means "that which is set aside for God." For example, in the tabernacle there were vessels which were used there, pots and pans, and they were called holy. Why were they called holy? Was it because they were unusual and were made of a little better quality material than the others? No, they were exactly like the others, no different from the pots and pans used in the homes. Well, then, how were they holy? They were holy because they were set aside solely for the use of God. And anything that is set aside for the use of God is holy, my friend. And that is what holiness means primarily.

Now I must agree that if anything is going to be set aside for the use of God, it ought to have a character different from that which is ordinary, but I'm trying now to get at the meaning of the word. And I do believe that God pays some attention to the innate character of an individual. In fact, I know He does, especially of those who are His own. In fact, God exercises a great deal of intelligence in this particular matter. For instance, suppose you were in danger of dying out on the desert from lack of water, and you walked and walked and walked, and finally you came to a spring there in the hot desert. Lovely, cold water was bubbling up. And you saw two cups there. One was a gold cup, highly ornamented. Oh, it was a lovely thing and must have been very expensive, but it was dirty. Then you looked at the other which was an old, white, crock cup, even broken on the side. Oh, but it was clean, shining there in the desert air. Which one would you drink out of?

Well, give God credit for having as much sense as you have. He will take the clean one also. That which is dedicated to His use is called holy, my friend. And the men whom He chose were holy in the sense that they were set aside for this particular service of being prophets of God. That was their business.

We are told that the holy men of God "spoke as they were moved by the Holy Spirit." You will remember that we dealt with this in the chapter on inspiration. The word here for *moved* is a nautical term. Its actual meaning is the picture of a sailing vessel. The sails have been run up, and the wind gets into those sails and bellies them out and pushes that little ship forward. It is carried along by the wind, you see.

Likewise these holy men, these men set aside for the use of God, were carried along by the Holy Spirit as they served God. And that is the reason we believe that whatever they wrote was inspired. I mean by this that the Word of God is without any error at all and that God is able to communicate to you and me today exactly what He wants communicated by having used these men because, as they wrote Scripture, they were carried along by the Holy Spirit.

This does not mean that God in some way or other infringed or impinged upon their personalities. He did not. These men, as they wrote, fully expressed their personalities. If one normally used certain clichés, he used them here. And if another had a peculiar way of writing, which each of them did, then he would use that. In other words, the wonder of the Word of God is not that God picked up these men like you would pick up a series of colored ball-point pens today, writing with this one and putting it down to write with another. God didn't pick up Isaiah and write with him and then use Jeremiah, then Ezekiel, then Daniel. That wasn't it at all. God was able to take these holy men who were absolutely committed to Him for His use, and God was able to use each man's personality. The Spirit of God was able to use them in such a way that He gets through to you and me today the exact thing that He wants to say.

And if God were to say it again today, my friend, He would say it just like Isaiah wrote it. He would say it just like Daniel wrote it. Why? Because that's the way God wanted to say it, and He never changes.

Three Offices of Christ

Now the very interesting thing is that the Lord Jesus Christ holds three offices. He is Prophet. He is Priest. He is King.

His office as *Prophet* was first mentioned by Moses, who said:

> *The LORD your God will raise up for you a Prophet like me from your midst.*
> (Deuteronomy 18:15)

Moses was a unique prophet, by the way. When Miriam, and even Aaron, spoke against Moses, feeling that they also were able to speak with a prophet's authority, God gave Miriam a good dose of leprosy to let her know that Moses was the one He had chosen as His prophet. He was "My servant Moses." While it's true that God will speak through others—and has and will—Moses was different. He was unique. God had given him a special message, and He talked to him face-to-face. And the Lord Jesus Christ is a prophet like Moses whom God raised up.

When Christ came to this earth, He came as a Prophet. He came forth from God with a message to mankind; in fact, He *was* that Message: "He who has seen Me has seen the Father" (John 14:9). All that the Father told Him to do, He did. As He said, He came to do the Father's will. And He was the revelation of God:

> **No one has seen God at any time. The only begotten Son, who is in the bosom of the Father, He has declared [exegeted] Him.**
> (John 1:18)

Christ has led God out into the open. He's brought Him out where men could see Him, for He is the revelation of God to man. He is a Prophet.

But He went to the Cross. Actually He went to the Cross as a Prophet. That was God's message to man, God's love story to man. "God so loved . . . that He gave His only begotten Son," and that's the message that He came to bring to this earth, the message of redemption and release, if you please.

He went back to heaven a *Priest*. If Jesus Christ were on this earth now He would not be a priest. The writer of the Epistle to the Hebrews was very careful to make this clear. He says He would not be a priest because the priests in that day belonged to the tribe of Levi. And according to the Mosaic system, that's the way it should be. But our Lord Jesus Christ is a "priest forever according to the order of Melchizedek" (Hebrews 5:6), yonder in the heavens. When He rose from the dead and went back to heaven, He became our Great High Priest. And that is His ministry today. He's the Great High Priest, ministering to His own here upon this earth.

He is as busy today, friend, as He ever was when He walked over those Judean hills and along the Sea of Galilee, down the streets of Jerusalem and by the side of the Jordan River.

He's the Great High Priest who has entered the Holy of Holies for those who are His own, and we come to God through Him. He is the only way to God. He is making intercession for us, and He is

able to save to the uttermost those who come to God through Him, since He always lives to make intercession for them. (Hebrews 7:25)

Not only is the Lord Jesus Christ a Priest today; He is coming someday as the *King*. That is the message which will go forth again. Elijah will give the message the next time, and the message is the same as the message of John the Baptist: "Repent, for the kingdom of heaven is at hand." The Kingdom will be at hand because the King will be coming. And the next time He will come in power and great glory to execute judgment on all unrighteousness and to put down all iniquity and to establish His Kingdom.

He is a Prophet. He is a Priest. He is coming as the King of kings and Lord of lords.

So, you see, He's the great theme and subject of the Word of God, whether it be prophetic or any other way, and He is a Prophet Himself. My, how important that is! That is something that needs to be examined, and He needs to be exalted today. He is King of kings; He is Lord of lords; He is the Great High Priest today entered into the heavens. But He is God's Prophet. He came to speak for God. He came to reveal God. And yonder on the cross you have Him revealing redemption for mankind.

You see, we are looking at the most glorious Person in the world. When you look at prophecy you look at Him. You have to look at Him, for He is the subject of prophecy, He's the spirit of prophecy. The Man of the ages, the Man of eternity, the Man of all times, the Man not just of this year, but the Man of the past and the present and the future, and that's the Man Christ Jesus, the Son of Man who someday will come in the glory clouds of heaven. He is the Prophet, God's Prophet, and He is the subject of prophecy, if you please.

The Prophetic Office

Now I want you to notice that the prophetic office actually begins in the Old Testament with Samuel, and it extends to John the Baptist. For instance, we find in the Book of Acts Simon Peter's statement concerning Samuel:

> *Yes, and all the prophets, from Samuel and those who follow,*
> *as many as have spoken, have also foretold these days.*
> (Acts 3:24)

When Peter was preaching his second sermon, he referred to Samuel and all the prophets that followed him. So Peter was referring to the prophetic office itself, although there were prophets before Samuel. Moses, as we have seen, was an earlier prophet. But actually the *office* of prophet begins with Samuel and concludes with John the Baptist.

Will you notice this very carefully, for it is important. I'm going to say something that may sound a little strange, but don't dismiss it until you check it with the Word of God. John the Baptist is not a New Testament character. He's an Old Testament prophet. That's what he is! He is the one who brings down the curtain on Old Testament prophecy. It was Jesus Himself who said:

> *But what did you go out to see? A prophet? Yes, I say to you,*
> *and more than a prophet.*
> (Matthew 11:9)

John was an outstanding prophet, our Lord was saying.

You see, all the prophets had spoken of the coming of Christ, and that's what Peter said in his second sermon. Beginning with Samuel, they all told of these days. And then John the Baptist came. He was the forerunner of the Messiah, and he said, "I'm not the one you think I am. I'm just a voice crying in the wilderness," and his message was, "Repent, for the kingdom of heaven is at hand."

Now John the Baptist never preached about the church, friend. No, he didn't. It wasn't his office; he was the last of the Old Testament prophets. And his office was very, very important. As our Lord said, there was none greater:

"Did you go out to hear a prophet?"

"Yes."

"Well, he was a prophet all right, but he's greater than a prophet. He's outstanding. He's unique," Jesus said.

> **Assuredly, I say to you, among those born of women there has not risen one greater than John the Baptist.**
> (Matthew 11:11)

Now the great question arises, how could the people back in those days know whether the prophet who was speaking to them was accurate or not? After all, it's all right for Micah to come along and say Jesus is going to be born in Bethlehem, but that wouldn't happen for about seven hundred years. Today we can look back at the historical record and see that it was fulfilled. We can understand that Micah was an accurate prophet, but how did the people in his day know?

Well, the interesting thing is that every prophet who prophesied in Israel had to give a local prophecy—that is, he had to predict something having to do with the immediate future and immediate circumstances. This is the reason that in all of the prophetic books you find so much that is local, so much that is practically contemporary. It was something that would take place shortly and did take place shortly, by the way.

It was true of Isaiah. You will recall that Isaiah prophesied the virgin birth, and he looked down the ages seven hundred years into the future as he spoke also of a suffering Savior. How did people in his day know that he was accurate? Well, he had to prophesy something locally, and it had to be fulfilled. So when there were 185,000 Assyrians camped outside Jerusalem (Isaiah 37:36), all of them with bows and arrows, and some of them trigger-happy, Isaiah made a prophecy that they would not enter the city of Jerusalem and that not even one arrow would be shot over the wall (Isaiah 37:33). Well, if some half-drunk Assyrian soldier had pulled an arrow out of his quiver, put it in the bow, and just looked out into the darkness and let the arrow fly, and if that arrow had fallen inside Jerusalem, Isaiah would have been declared a false prophet. But it turned out exactly as Isaiah had predicted!

You see, they had a way of testing a false prophet. According to the Mosaic Law this is what they were told to do:

> *But the prophet who presumes to speak a word in My name, which I have not commanded him to speak, or who speaks in the name of other gods, that prophet shall die. And if you say in your heart, "How shall we know the word which the LORD has not spoken?"—when a prophet speaks in the name of the LORD, if the thing does not happen or come to pass, that is the thing which the LORD has not spoken; the prophet has spoken it presumptuously; you shall not be afraid of him.*
> (Deuteronomy 18:20-22)

If a prophet wanted to make a prophecy and he said, "This is of the Lord," they would put it down on the bulletin board and say, "All right, we'll just wait and see if it happens as you said it." When things failed to happen as the false prophet predicted, God said, "That prophet shall die."

Now let's look at another prophet. More than a century after Isaiah, suppose Jeremiah had made the statement that the Babylonian army would not capture the city of Jerusalem and would not even shoot an arrow into the city—well, Jeremiah would have been a false prophet if he had said that. But the interesting thing is, Jeremiah did not say that. Jeremiah, on the contrary, said, "Nebuchadnezzar will take Jerusalem, and he will destroy this city." And history bears out the accuracy of that prophecy.

This was the test, you see, that was made. And many a prophet lost his life by prophesying falsely. It wasn't healthy in Israel to be a prophet unless you really were God's prophet.

Now Daniel was a prophet in a heathen court, a gentile court. Would the Mosaic Law apply to him? Yes, it did. Although the Gentiles didn't apply it, the Jews did. You will remember that Daniel is the one who interpreted Nebuchadnezzar's dream, and it did come to pass exactly as he said it would. In fact, his prophecies were so accurate that even when he was an old man, the queen mother told Belshazzar, the reigning king of Babylon, "You call for Daniel. He can tell you what these things mean." Even in a pagan culture they knew that Daniel was God's prophet.

So, you see, the prophets were pretty well vouched for in the day in which they prophesied. And in our day we have an airtight way of testing the Old Testament prophets because, as we said, one of the greatest proofs that the Bible is the Word of God is this matter of fulfilled prophecy.

The Anchor Book of Prophecy

The Book of Daniel is the anchor book of prophecy. It is a book that has been seriously questioned and rejected by the critics, and we'll say a word about that in a moment. But Sir Isaac Newton made this statement: "To reject Daniel is to reject the Christian religion." And I do not know how better to put it than that.

In the Olivet Discourse, our Lord quoted from the Book of Daniel, and in Matthew 24:15 He called him "Daniel the prophet," saying,

When you see the "abomination of desolation," spoken of by Daniel the prophet. . . .

Paul speaks of "the man of sin." And if you are going to know anything at all about the "man of sin," you will have to turn back to the Book of Daniel for amplification and clarification of this term.

Daniel has borne the brunt of the attack on the Bible by the critics. Some time ago someone wrote a book titled *Daniel in the Critics' Den.* And by the way, Daniel has suffered more in the critics' den than he ever did in the lions' den. The lions never touched him, but the critics have been ruthless, especially the extreme higher critics who insist that the Book of Daniel was written at the time of Antiochus Epiphanes and the Maccabees, about 170-166 B.C. Well, you see, that makes quite a difference because many of us believe the dating of Daniel begins in 606 B.C. and concludes in 536 B.C. So to move him way up to 170 B.C. is quite a move, it's over four hundred years, and four hundred years is bound to make a difference in the life of any of us. And so we find that the extreme higher critic has attempted to discredit Daniel by this method.

Why do they do that? Well, they have to do it to get rid of the supernatural. You see, the Book of Daniel is one of those remarkable books of the Bible in which a man predicted the future in such detail and outlined it so clearly that it almost takes your breath away—so much so that when the unbelieving critic comes along, he has to say, "Well, it cannot be prophecy. This manuscript had to be written after it was history."

Daniel mentions the four great world empires in chapters 2 and 7. These great world empires are the *only* great world empires that there have been, friend, from that day to this. And you and I are living at the time of the fourth great world empire. It has fallen apart, but Daniel says it will be put back together again.

And isn't it interesting that even if they do want to move the writing of the Book of Daniel to 170 B.C., there still would be a whole lot which has happened since then that the critics would have difficulty explaining because Daniel had outlined it so clearly. The thing is, we believe it was written by the Daniel who is mentioned back yonder in the court of Nebuchadnezzar, beginning at about 606 B.C.

Actually, most of the Book of Daniel has been fulfilled, although I think the most important part is yet in the future. Now when you have a book that outlines four great world empires, and three of them have already come and gone—and the fact of the matter is, we're way up into the fourth empire—you have a pretty good reason to believe the rest of it will be fulfilled exactly as it is written.

And the same thing would be true with the seventy weeks of Daniel. Since sixty-nine weeks have been fulfilled right to the letter, I consider those are pretty good odds. I know practically nothing about racing and betting, but I know enough to realize that when you can get odds of sixty-nine to one, you really have something! And here is a book that I am betting on, because the odds are sixty-nine to one. And with odds like that, you can't lose, my friend.

That makes the Book of Daniel a remarkable book, and conservative scholarship has always accepted the early dating of Daniel because there has been a good, sound, scholarly basis for it. The historical character of the man Daniel and the prophetic character of the Book of Daniel have given a real basis for it. Let me give you several reasons why we know that the Book of Daniel goes back to the early dating.

The Septuagint is a translation of the Old Testament from Hebrew into the Greek language. It was produced approximately one hundred years before Antiochus Epiphanes lived, and it contains the Book of Daniel! So obviously, the translators back there had the Book of Daniel long before the days of Antiochus Epiphanes.

Josephus records an incident involving a high priest by the name of Jaddua. Alexander the Great was making his attack upon Jerusalem, and the high priest went out to meet him and to have an interview with him. The priest showed Alexander the Book of Daniel and pointed out to him where Alexander was mentioned there. And Alexander the Great—who had a reputation for destroying every great city that he captured and building a new one—did not remove one stone from another when he came to Jerusalem but actually went to the temple and worshiped the living and true God!

Why? Because Alexander the Great had been shown the Book of Daniel where he was so clearly identified that it made that kind of impact on him. And Jerusalem is one of the few cities that Alexander the Great did not destroy. Do you know what the date was? 332 B.C.! What happens to the critics' viewpoint that the Book of Daniel was written in 170 B.C.? Evidently they must be wrong about that date.

And then may I say to you that the final evidence I have—and as far as I am concerned I don't need any better evidence than this: The Lord Jesus Christ called him "Daniel the prophet." I've already given you that quotation. And you can be sure of one thing, since our Lord put His seal of approval on Daniel the prophet, I personally will take His word over and against all the critics! And by the way, they have very shaky evidence for the position which they take. They are hard-put to get rid of the supernatural, but they continue to try. They will not accept it.

Prophecy in Today's World

There is today a great controversy concerning prophecy that has nothing to do with believing or not believing the Bible, because the controversy is among those who believe the Bible to be the Word of God, and it's a matter of interpretation. But the interesting thing is that you and I have moved into a cycle today where people in all walks of life are beginning to pay attention to prophecy, and they are turning to it. Even Charles Hodge, in his great *Systematic Theology*, mentioned the fact that though he gave very little space to prophecy, he predicted a day would come when men would spend more time in the study of this subject.

Well, this century has seen two world wars and many lesser conflicts along with the Cold War. We've seen the Great Depression and several recessions. The atomic bomb followed by nuclear arms have brought fear to the hearts of mankind everywhere. No man knows what a day will bring forth.

My friend, today no one dares to say that the world is improving. No one is daring to say today that we're going to have utopia tomorrow. There are too many gangsters and terrorists about who have a nuclear bomb in their hip pocket. We're living in a day when the human family is looking into the future with fear. But there is one thing which is quite sure today: The child of God has a more sure word of prophecy.

Prophecy, especially in the Books of Daniel and Revelation, is not something merely to excite your imagination or to arouse or satisfy your curiosity or, somehow or other, to tickle your intellect. The purpose of prophecy is to improve your life, and it will, you see, if you and I have the right viewpoint of it. Daniel was a real man of God. He walked with God, and he was separated unto God. He was a man of prayer, and that's what prophecy does for you.

And, friend, if it doesn't do that for you, you must not be studying prophecy. You may be studying some of these harebrained schemes of certain preachers you hear today, but you're not studying the Word of God because the Word of God and the prophetic Scriptures will reach right in where we are. You see, prophecy is something that wears shoe leather, and it can walk through the streets today, and if it doesn't, beloved, it's not *Bible* prophecy.

NOTES

Chapter 3

1. Arthur Budvarson, *The Book of Mormon: True or False* (Concord, CA.: Pacific Publishing Co., 1959).

Chapter 4

1. Heribert Nilsson, *Synthetic Artbildung*, Vols. 1-2 (Lund, Sweden: Velaq Cuk Gleerup, 1953), 1212.

2. Bernard Ramm, *Christian View of Science and Scriptures* (Grand Rapids: Eerdman's Publishing Co., 1954).

3. Ibid.

Chapter 5

1. Keith L. Brooks, *The Spirit of Truth and the Spirit of Error* (Chicago: Moody Press, 1985).

2. Dr. D. Martyn Lloyd-Jones, "The Christian Message to the World," preached on November 6, 1955, printed in *The Westminster Record.*